EP-E-366

SOCIOLOGY OF PAKISTAN

FAZLUR RASHID KHAN, (M. A. (Dac.))
M. A. (Ann Arbor, Michigan.)
Senior Lecturer in Sociology
University of Dacca

SHIRIN PUBLICATIONS
DACCA-1

Published by
S. Eusufzi, B. A.
Shirin Publications
28, Kotwali Road
Dacca-1

First Edition November, 1966

Price : Rs. 9·00

Printed by
M. M. Ali
Zeenat Printing Works
19, Ramakanta Nadi Lane
Dacca-1

Dedicated to
My most respected teacher
Professor A. K. Nazmul Karim

ACKNOWLEDGMENTS

I owe my greatest debt to six prominent sociologists namely Prof. A. K. Nazmul Karim, Prof. P. Bessaignet, Prof. Afsaruddin, Prof. John E. owen, Prof. H. Langerhans and prof. Theodore Pirkar who taught and worked in the Department of Sociology, Dacca University. Prof. A.K. Nazmul Karim and Prof. Afsaruddin are presently teaching, conducting valuable researches on different sociological subjects and working hard for the further development of this Department and the improvement of the teaching methods in Sociology. Much of my researches and studies on sociological problems in Pakistan are due to the strong and proper foundations laid by these scholars of profound knowledge and vast experience. Their endeavour to spread the spirit of independent research among the students of sociology encouraged me very much to write this book.

It is my pleasant duty to thankfully acknowledge the help and assistance of Mr. Ahmaduzzaman Chowdhury and Mr. Syed Ali Naqi who immensely helped me in the process of writing the introduction of this book.

I would be failing in my duty if I do not express my gratefulness to my brother, Mr. Harunar Rashid Khan for his ever diligent and skilful work in writing the manuscript of my book.

I am deeply indebted to Mr. S. Eusufzi, the proprietor of Messrs Shirin Publications for publishing my book with utmost care and sincerity.

I am also greatful to my wife Suraiya Begum for her occasional help in seeing the proofs of my book.

I also thank the staff of Messrs Zeenat Printing Works, Dacca who printed the book with special care.

November 1, 1966

FAZLUR RASHID KHAN
Dept. of Sociology,
Dacca University.

CONTENTS

CONTENTS

CONTENTS

INTRODUCTION

Man, the Homo Sapien, is a creature on earth whose study has been the most absorbing from time immemorial. The term Homo Sapien (Man, the wise) is what has been intriguing our comprehension about his nature and his variegated works and activities. The problem before us is, therefore, how we can analyse and understand his 'doings' on earth. Any visitor from a different part of the world, not familiar with our ways of life is most likely to take a 'dispassionate' view, albeit an objective view of our doings. But again, what that objective view is likely to be is equally our concern. It lies in the attempt at extricating various interwoven and interconnected spheres of life so that an approach can be made for a better understanding of human life and society.

The manifestations of any sphere of human activity is usually sought out in what is so termed as its origin. This, nonetheless, forms only an aspect of the whole study which may even tend to bypass any superimposed conception of human society. In so far as sectoral or segmental studies are concerned, this has over the years, been the dominant trend. Apart from general social philosophy this sectoral study has been found to be most revealing and makes itself conspicuous by its spatial and timely illumination.

Sociology is concerned with the scientific and objective study of society. Human beings, wherever he might be,—if they are bound enlocked in relationships, provide ground for study. Sociologists, in particular, have thought it fit to undertake studies of such human relationships in as much as these contribute to the institutional expression and an understanding of his basic behavioural patterns, since these relationships have shown social characteristics, i.e., interactional ; these indeed form subject matters for analytical discussion.

Therefore analytical albeit, scientific study of social relations is Sociology proper. We may look at a man as an individual, —secluded or alienated or as a member of a social group. The kinds of propellants in such participation require investigation. Sociology does the job.

The application of Sociology in the study of any problem of political, social, economic or religious nature is an imperative necessity because Sociology will investigate or analyse the problem in relation to its social back-ground within a social structure. Sociology has a wide scope for its application in different socio-economic fields in Pakistan. Before we go into detail about the application of Sociology in Pakistan we may be interested in inquiring about the time and condition when Sociology first began here. Though in Pakistan as in Europe there is a long traditional reflection upon Society. Sociology, the systematic study of society, actually began during the British rule. Its introduction in India and Pakistan came in connection with the economic and commercial growth. And lately its importance and use have grown rapidly because of the different social and economic revolution in this subcontinent. After partition Pakistan has undergone many changes in its socio-economic structure mostly because of the industrialization and urbanization. These changes have created many problems. In order to examine the real causes of these socio-economic problems sociological study and research which will take into consideration the effects and relations of all socio-economic and religio-cultural institutions and organizations, have to be conducted. Sociological research and sociological treatment of social problems are mostly necessary in every country, especially in the country like Pakistan which is going through a very crucial transitional period.

The sociological approach may reveal the real nature and the cause in the analysis of any social problem and this ultimately may suggest the way to solve such problems. Under the conditions of rapid social change and specialized social relationships only accurate knowledge can serve as a basis for social policy and for individual adjustment. The role of sociology is therefore, very important in Pakistan. Sociological researches have got priority in every sector of social life.

The importance and necessity of Sociology is much more felt in the developing country like Pakistan because no planning for social development is possible without the sociological knowledge of the social structure. It is perhaps due to this that the Universities in Pakistan are gradually establishing a separate department of Sociology.

The analysis of the social problems, arising out of the industrial growth in Pakistan can be done only by a thorough sociological investigation of the structure and functions of the society.

The necessity of modernizing the rural life in Pakistan raises many vital economic and social problems which can be thoroughly examined, analysed and understood with the help of sociological study and research. Another important research area is the study of the pattern of behaviour, closely related to the system of values and beliefs held by the community. Within each village community and inherent in the pattern of social organization is the pattern of authority, embodying the process of decision making and the role of leadership.

Since Pakistan is predominantly inhabited by the Muslims the sociologists should give proper attention to the analysis of the structure, institutions, culture, values etc., of the Muslim society.

Although we have a wealth of materials there has been very little sociological study of the Muslim society in Pakistan. In writing this book the author has tried to give emphasis on this point. Rapid changes are taking place in the Pakistani Muslim social structure due to the partition in 1947, and the impact of western culture, industrialization, urbanization, commercial development and the Second World War. It is time that we should make an effort to study Pakistani society and culture.

This book deals at length with the battery of sociological concepts and their implications in Pakistani society and culture. The specific areas include sociology and its development and the problems of methodology to study sociology in Pakistan, social stratification and mobility, social institutions population problems, culture, family and marriage pattern, crime and delinquency, urbanization and industrialization, social change and social problems, social groups, influence of geography on social life, village life and the description of the life of the Chakma tribe of Chittagong Hill Tracts in East Pakistan.

The writer will feel extremely happy and consider his labour justified if the book is proved to be helpful to the students and the public alike.

CHAPTER 1

SOCIOLOGY, ITS DEVELOPMENT AND PAKISTANI SOCIETY

Sociology in the scientific sense, is not only one of the youngest social sciences but almost entirely a Product of Industrial Revolution. Sociology is the scientific and objective study of the society. Society is nothing but the network of relationship, found among the human beings. No other social science takes society as its central concept. Cultural anthropology studies man in terms of the whole scheme of his activities and his products. History studies the records of man. Psychology studies man as a behaving individual. Social psychology is a branch of psychology, concerned with the ways in which the individual reacts to his social conditions. Political science deals with the political behaviour and activities of man. Thus we see that these social sciences leave room for a more comprehensive science and there is a science which studies society as a whole. That science is known as sociology. According to MacIver, "Sociology alone studies social relationships themselves and society itself."

Ginsberg defines "Sociology as the study of human interactions and interrelations, their conditions and consequences." The word relationship is a key word. Sociology is not concerned primarily with man as a biological being nor with his history, nor with his accomplishments. It is concerned with man's behaviour in relation to other man i.e., with human interaction. According to Gillin & Gillin, "Sociology, in its broadest sense, may be said to be the study of interaction arising from the association of the living beings."

Giddings defines it "An attempt to account for the origin, growth, structure and activities of society by the operation of Physical, Vital and Psychical causes working together in a process of evolution". So to understand more precisely the definition of sociology, we must have

a comprehensive idea of what is meant by society. By society generally
we mean companionship and association. It now in its widest
sense, means every kind and degree of relationship, entered into by men
with one another. It means the whole system of social relationships.
Society is a system of usages and procedures of authority and mutual
aid, of many groupings and divisions, of controls of human behaviour
and of liberties. This ever changing, complex system is called society.
It is the web of social relationships and is always changing. But
not every relationship of man with man is social. Willing and conscious activity is essential for the formation of a society.

DEVELOPMENT OF SOCIOLOGY

The history of social life with its problems is as old as society
itself. When man at the dawn of civilization was first confronted
with the difficulties and complexities of life in the company of his
fellow men, he could not but apply his attention to find a solution to
them. If man is by nature a philosopher he must as naturally be a
sociologist when the perplexities of social life become the object of
his deliberations.

Thus the ancient social thinkers were the prophets, saints, teachers
and men of wisdom who thought about social life and explained
how to lead a good and orderly life . The modes of ancient social
thought which have been preserved in contemporary societies, were
not concerned with detached scientific analysis of social phenomena
which is the characteristic of modern science.

The systematic study of society did not come into existence in the
West until the Greek philosopher, for the first time, approached the
study of society as an endeavour to create an ideal society. In Plato's
Republic (427-347 B.C.) and in Aristotle's Ethics and Politics
(384-322 B.C.) we find the first major attempts to deal methodi-
cally with law, state and society. Their social thought however,
did not distinguish between social and political institutions. Among the
Romans, Marcus Tullius, Cicero, transmitted to Rome, the treasures of
Greek learning in philosophy, politics, law and sociology. There
were also scholars in this field in the middle ages such as St. Thomas
Aquinas, St. Augustine and Dante. The first major break with
traditional social philosophy was made by the social contract theories

of Hobbes, Locke and Rousseau during the 17th and 18th centuries. Though these theories were political in nature, it made a distinction between society and its government which helped in the development of sociology.

In the East the most famous work on the study of society was the laws of Manu which dealt with the rites, laws and social customs. The most authentic production on the subject is undoubtedly the "Arthasastra" of Chanakya or Kautilya (321-297 B.C.). It is a treaties on practical and theoretical economics, politics, sociology and the law of that period.

Abul Fazal's "Ain-i-Akbari" gives a wonderful description of Akbar's empire (1556-1605) in all its social aspects. In the middle age, Ibn-i-Khaldun, the distinguished social thinker in Islam founded the modern science of sociology in his monumental work "Muqaddamah". In this famous book he studied the causes of the rise, decay and fall of the states and empires. He also explained the influence of geography on social life.

Sociology as a science emerged only about hundred years ago. The name sociology is of modern origin. It is derived from the latin word 'Societas' (society) and the Greek 'Logos' (science). A conscious and deliberate approach to the establishment of a new science by the study of changes in Socio-economic condition of the Post-Industrial Revolution was made by Saint Simon. This new science was named as sociology by his desciple August Comte (1798-1857). In his "Positive Philosophy" he defined sociology as the science of social phenomena which are subject to natural laws. The discovery of these laws is the object of investigation. Comte was the first thinker of the modern world to say clearly the fact that all the aspects of social life are bound in a unity and he was the first to show that this unity has an evolutionary character. Herbert Spencer (1820-1905) another pioneer of sociology was from England. He was the father of evolutionary School of Sociology. The writers like Karl Marx, Charles Darwin and Freud exerted great influence on the current sociological thought. Emile Durkheim of France (1858-1917) and Max Weber (1864-1920) of Germany, L.H. Morgan (1818-81) and E. B. Taylor (1832-1917) are also important sociologists of modern times. Among the later sociologists the names of F. H. Giddings, R. M. MacIver and Ginsberg should be mentioned.

The scope or subject matter of sociology varies as its definitions differ from writer to writer. The province of sociology similarly varies from one group of sociologists to another as the social concepts have differently been understood since the days of its founder August Comte. With his idea of the filiation of sciences on which he based his conception of the hierarchy of sciences, Comte understood sociology as the final science to apply the results of the previous sciences and occupy the domains of all other sciences. He thus gave sociology an all-inclusive character which has been repudiated by sociologists themselves, apart from other social scientists. His conception that social phenomena are indivisible and to be studied as a whole by a single science,—sociology, appears however, tenable since sociology focused its attention on social relationship as a whole. Although social phenomena have been compartmentalised into Economics, Political science, History and other social sciences for purposes of study, they are in reality one. Sociology is very comprehensive to include all the aspects of the various social sciences .

Sociology studies man as social being, not in relation to property or state but man in relation to his fellows. Its field is the whole life of man in society. It studies the particular ways and usages that express social relationships and beyond that it unfolds the nature of society, the greater social life that is the matrix of the particular associations, such as family, state, trade union and church etc. Sociology traces the history of human civilization and tries to discover the law of its development. It deals with the fundamental and general aspect of society as a whole . Before we attempt to find out the scope of sociology in Pakistan, a clear and precise meaning of sociology in the context of our social system is necessary. The study of sociology is a recent phenomenon. Although the sociological treatment of social problems is as old as the human thought, men have always lived in the society with various problems. It is doubtful if a society free from problems ever existed or will ever exist. Man consequently has always been faced with problems of all kinds.

Many scholars of our country have accepted the view that sociology in Pakistan is rather social and cultural anthropology.

The essence of this conception clearly owes to the fact that the people living in this part of the world are still living in a primitive level. Objectively speaking the social life of our country specially in some areas obviously coincides with the social life of many non-literate societies. Pakistan, at present, is undergoing a rapid cultural transformation. The complicated conflicts and tensions as well as failures and successes in this transformation of our cultural life need to be correctly analysed and properly understood.

These rapid changes have occured and are still taking place in our social structures as a consequence of such events as world war, emergence of independent Pakistan, influx of refugees, population growth and increase of industrialisation and urbanisation etc. As a result of these changes the age-old traditions of Pakistan are being challenged.

For the proper realization of the problem we should take into account the whole situation in the context of the changing social institutions. Before dealing with the scope of sociology in Pakistan it is essential to understand our customs, traditions and institutions. The historical records and facts available on our country will give us comprehensive view of the character of the social structure of Pakistan.

Pakistani sociology though still in its infancy has made a promising beginning in spite of many current problems. University and College students of sociology are compelled to use American and British texts since these are the only ones available. The students tend to discuss topics such as industrialization, urbanization, stratification, status, social control, family patterns and social change in terms of American data derived from American texts, overlooking the fact that the data and the resulting generalizations are not applicable to their own society.[1]

Pakistan is predominantly inhabited by the Muslims. We require a social theory of Muslim society. There has been very little sociological research on Muslim societies in other parts of the world. Hardly we have any sociological theory of Muslim society inspite of

---

1. I.H. Zuberi, "Translation and Adaptation of Text Books in Social Science." Round Table Conference on the teaching of social sciences in south Asia (Delhi ; UNESCO, 1954) P. P. 82-87.

the fact that there is a wide scope for field studies in our country to construct the social history for the Muslims in Pakistan. This is not all, there are many other problems for our sociologists to deal with. Pakistan has got many social problems i. e., crime and delinquency, prostitution, beggary, unemployment, housing, sanitation and health and growth of population where sociological study and analysis are essential to find out the causes of such problems and to measure the impact of these problems on our society. With the introduction of modern technological devices new values are emerging in the society. These new values are coming in direct clash with the old traditional values of our society. Because of this clash the old values are already in a state of transition and an epoch is in formation. This area of our life needs a sociological treatment. This will help our social planners to formulate programme and policy to solve some of the problems, arising out of the conflict of new and old values. The phenomena of industrialization and urbanization in Pakistan should be properly discussed to understand their impacts on our social life. Like other societies Pakistan is to function through different social, economic, political, religious and recreational institutions.

Sociology should study the origin, development and nature of these institutions in relation to the social structure of Pakistan. In Pakistan general people think sociology, a discipline which is basically connected with the reformation and reconstruction of the society. This indicates the presence of confusion in the minds of the public about the discipline of sociology and its subject matter. We have to admit the fact that we are also in a fix to answer the question as to what is the practical application of sociology ?

Most of us have felt the difficulty of establishing easy communication with our society, but very few of us have tried to analyse it.

What August Comte and Durkheim developed in France or what Westermark and Hobhouse evolved in England may not be exactly applicable in Pakistani society. The generalisation derived by Thomas may not be applicable to the conditions of Pakistan. But the contribution of Comte, Durkheim, Westermark, Hobhouse and Thomas have immense value for the development of sociology in Pakistan.

Bibliography

Afsaruddin, Md. *Sociology and Social Research in Pakistan.* The Pakistan Sociology Association, (East Pakistan Unit.) Dacca 1963.

Thomas, W. D. & Znanicki. *The Polish Peasant in America.* New York, Dover Publications, Vol. II. 1963.

MacIver, R.M. *Society.* Macmillan & co, London 1962.

Gillin & Gillin. *Cultural Sociology.* New York 1954.

Gisbert, P. *Fundamentals of Sociology*, Orient Longmans Ltd. Calcutta 1959.

Ginsberg, M. *Sociology.* Oxford University Press, London 1934.

Koening, S. *Man and Society.* New York, Barnes and Noble 1957.

Ogburn and Nimkoff. *Sociology.* H. M. Company, The Riverside Press, Cambridge 1940.

Cuber, F. *Sociology—A Synopsis of Principles.* New York, D. Appleton Company, 1947.

Bottomore, T. B. *Sociology.* George Allen and Unwin Ltd. London 1963.

CHAPTER 2

PROBLEMS OF METHODOLOGY IN THE STUDY OF PAKISTANI SOCIETY AND CULTURE

METHODOLOGY IN SOCIOLOGY

The term method comes from the Greek meta (with, after) and hodos (way). It is a way of doing something with brevity and thoroughness. A method is sometimes confused with a technique, but they are different. The method of a study applies to the whole process or procedure that is to be followed in the study, while the technique consists in the means used or the mode in which the whole method or a stage of it is to be followed. There is no one single method for the study of sociological problems. With the development of the science   of sociology, many methods have evolved to deal with the multitudes of social problems, faced by both developed and underdeveloped countries in the   world. Different structures and natures of the society with different level of development have become the root cause of the variation in the nature of the problem from society to society.

CLASSIFICATION OF METHODOLOGY

The general methods for handling sociological problems can be divided into the following :

1. Historical Method

This method studies various social institutions, organizations and problems through a historical approach by studying their origin, development and change. August Comte, Herbert Spencer, L.T. Hobhouse, Westermark, Max Weber and C.W. Mills applied historical method in their sociological studies.

2. The Comparative Method

The basic aim of this method is to test the hypothesis by systematic comparison between similar units of society to find out the causal connections. Durkheim, in his "Rules of Sociological Method" discussed the significance of this method and applied it to his famous study on "Suicide". He tried to show the social causes of suicide by relating the rates of suicide in different social groups to characteristics of the groups. As regards the applicability of this method, it is more effective in small-scale studies. Hobhouse, Wheeler and Ginsberg are some of the notable scholars who made systematic comparative study of some major institutions in primitive societies.

3. The Functional Method

The functional approach in sociology is nothing but the reaction against historical and comparative approaches. In recent methodological theory, the concept of function has come to take a prominent place. It originated in the writings of Malinowski and Radcliffe Brown. "It was Durkheim who first gave a rigorous formulation of the concept of social function in the Division of labour in society and in the Rules of sociological method. He defined the function of a social institution as a correspondence between it and the needs of social organism. He also distinguishes between the normal and pathological functioning of institutions". In the functional approach we find an attempt to establish relationships of single variables. It seeks to show the order in which different activities performed in a group depend on each other. It operates with the concept of an equilibrium, i.e., with the interlocking system of activities in a group at a given time. In spite of many criticisms levelled against it, structural-functional analysis represents one of the major line of methodological development in sociology.

4. The Statistical Method

This method is largely used in the U.S.A. and other technologically developed countries in Europe and Asia. Burgess in Gurvitch and Moore's Research Methods in sociology, says that there are two basic methods of research,—"statistical and case study around which exists questions that evolve almost every consideration of sociological method". This is mainly an American approach to sociology. The American society and its technological devices have developed to such an extent that they can easily utilize this method well.

In addition to the statistical method, Gurvitch distinguishes between Micro-Sociology or the studies of small segments of social systems and Macro-Sociology or the studies of large scale social entities.

5. Formal Method

George Simmel is the originator of this approach. It is concerned with the forms of social interaction in minor and fleeting relationship between individuals as distinguished from the historical content. Von Wiese developed the method on the basis of relational concepts such as social distance. G. C. Homans used the method in studying small groups more in psychological terms. The formal approach remained largely German approach to sociology. It helps to formulate limited scientific generalizations.

To apply the methods, discussed above, the sociologists or social scientists have to divide a method into the following six stages :

1. Formulation of problems

At this stage the researcher should be conscious about the problem he is going to study. He will definitely have in mind a tentative objective of the study. In the process of investigation it may be found that the formulated problem needs modification and the objective has to be changed. But in case of any radical change of the problem we may have to begin the whole procedure anew.

2. Observation

Observation implies the application of our mind and its cognitive power to the phenomena which we are studying. It may be done directly or indirectly through history, records, accounts and other ways. The schedule, questionnaire, interview and other techniques, used by social scientists belong to this stage of the scientific method.

The observation may be spontaneous or controlled. The former is conducted when the phenomena are spontaneously happening as when a sociologist is witnessing a riot. Controlled observation (experiment) is obtained when the phenomenon takes place at the will of the observer or in circumstances devised by him. It can very rarely be used in social sciences.

3. Classification

Once the facts we observed and data collected, we should classify them in accordance with relevant norm. As for example if we wish to study the occupation and income of the people of a country we have to classify the occupation and income of the people of that country.

4. Hypothesis

Hypothesis is a tentative conclusion at which we arrive when the previous stages of the scientific method have been covered. After having rejected some factors which are irrelevant and inconsistent, we may find out a high degree of correlation between two or more events. But from this correlation it is difficult to jump to the conclusion that one event depends upon the other, because correlation does not necessarily mean causality or dependence. Yet a considerable degree of correlation, found between certain events and a study of their nature and mutual interaction may lead us to formulate a hypothesis.

5. Verification

The hypothesis that we have formulated in the previous stage by induction or the careful observation of many cases, is assumed to be valid for all cases where similar conditions prevail. It is this universality which gives to a proposition the quality of law.

6. Prediction

Prediction is the aptitude of a law or principle to be fulfilled wherever those conditions prevail for which it has been formulated.

It was thought by some of the scholars that sociology or any other social sciences could not be a real science because its predictions might not come true owing to the fact that socitey is too vast and human motivations are too complex. There is no denying the fact that the prediction of the physical science has a degree of necessity far higher than that of social sciences. Yet these may also attain a large measure of necessity in the fulfilment of their predictions owing to certain uniform tendencies of human nature which only admit of few exceptions. Hence predictions in the social sciences is possible, though not with the same degree of accuracy as in the physical sciences.

PROBLEMS OF METHODOLOGY FOR THE STUDY OF PAKISTANI SOCIETY AND CULTURE :

The areas that became Pakistan at the 1947 partition of India were the poorest regions of the entire subcontinent, educationally and culturally as well as economically. Social research in both Pakistan and India has also suffered from the British tradition that regarded universities as centres of literacy and humanistic learning for the training of civil servants.[1]

Pakistani sociology though still in its infancy, has made a promising beginning in spite of many current problems. One such problem is the development and application of different methods for the study of Pakistani society and culture.The study of society with scientific attitude involves the real understanding of the various aspects of the culture of the people who are the subjects of sociological investigation. Sociology of a particular country, unlike physical sciences, should take into consideration the local peculiarities, customs and traditions for the proper analysis of the society. It is therefore, natural that in the first stages of the development of sociological studies in Pakistan, the researchers are to be very careful to apply the methods, mostly developed by the American and European sociologists to suit the conditions, prevailing in those advanced countries. Unless and until we are in a position to develop our own methodology for the study of Pakistani society, we have to depend on various methods developed by the American and European sociologists and social scientists.

Pakistan belongs to one of the old civilization areas. As a result customs, traditions and various institutions have survived in our society from very ancient times. The understanding of the social structure and system of Pakistan is impossible without proper appreciation of those cutsoms, traditions and institutions, however fragmentary and antiquated they may be.[2] For the study of Pakistani society, one single method will not do. The method or methods to be applied, will vary from problem to problem, depending on the nature of the prob-

---

1. John E. Own "University Life in Pakistan," Teachers College Record, 61 (December 1957), P.P. 151-157.

2. A. N. N. Karim—"The methodology for a Sociology of East Pakistan" in Pierre Bessaignet (ed.) Social Research in East Pakistan, Asiatic Society of Pakistan, 1960, P. 2.

lems. There may be areas in social life where statistical method or survey method should be followed because of the recent growth of the problems for which no literature and written documents are available. When a survey method is followed for the study of a problem, the statistical technique is inevitable to analyse the collected data. As for example if a researcher wants to study the socio-economic backgrounds of the students in the Universities and Colleges in East Pakistan, he has a little choice but to apply the survey method with questionnaire technique to study the problem scientifically. This is simply because of the lack of any scientific and systematic literature on the problem. Moreover he is to use different statistical techniques for the final analysis of the available data.

There are other areas and problems in our social and cultural life where the historical and analytical methods will be most appropriate and helpful to have a correct picture of the problem. As for example if a researcher wants to study the social implication of the land tenure system during the British rule in India, it will be wise for him to follow the historical and analytical methods because of the availability of literatures and documents ont he problem. The researcher will deeply study every piece of available material and try to analyse the problem with an objective and scientific mind. In this case the application of survey method with questionnaire and statistical techniques will be of little value. There are other problems where we can apply more than one method combined together.

It is true that to develop the sociological theory and social history of Pakistan we have to depend on historical method to a great extent because the literary tradition of Pakistan is very rich. This will help us to develop our heritage which will give us greater understanding of the minds of the people of the country. It will help us to get an idea of the whole social mechanism which will be very much helpful to apply empirical methods in certain areas of life. From the above discussion it can be said that the study of Pakistani society and culture will demand the application of both historical and empirical methods. It will not be very wise to stick to one particular method even if there are difficulties and handicaps in the application of some of the empirical methods. The empirical method sometimes can not give us very correct result because of the high rate of illiteracy and non-

cooperation of the people of the country. Noncooperation originates
because of suspicion of the people about the purpose of the study.
This can be to a great extent, avoided by rapport building. The success
of rapport building depends on the quality of interviewers, working
in the field.[3]

---

3. M. Habibullah, "Some Problems of Socio-economic Research in Rural
Setting" in Afsaruddin (ed.) Sociology and Social Research in Pakistan, Dacca.
1963. P. 41.

Bibliography

Afsaruddin, M. (ed.) *Sociology and Social Research in Pakistan*. Dacca.
Pakistan Sociological Association (East Pakistan Unit). 1963.

Bessaignet, P. (ed.) *Social Research in East Pakistan*. Dacca, Asiatic
Society of Pakistan, 1960.

Bottomore, T.B. *Sociology*, (A Guide to Problems & Literature).
George Allen & Unwin Ltd. London 1963.

Durkheim, E. *The Rules of Sociological Method*. (English Translation)
Glencoe, the Free Press, 1938.

Gittler, J. B. (ed.) *Review of Sociology*. New York, John Wiley & Sons,
Inc. 1957.

Karim, A.K.N. *Changing Society in India and Pakistan*. Dacca 1956.

Odum, H.W. *American Sociology*. Longmans, Green & Co. New York
1951.

Owen, J. (ed.) *Sociology in East Pakistan*. Dacca, Asiatic Society
of Pakistan. 1962.

Weber, M. *The Methodology of Social Sciences*. (English Translation)
1949.

CHAPTER 3

SOCIAL STRATIFICATION AND MOBILITY IN EAST PAKISTAN

Social Stratification defined : The division of society into classes or strata which form a hierarchy of prestige and power, is an almost universal feature of social structure which has throughout history, attracted the attention of philosophers and social theorists.

Social stratification is the division of society into groups or categories linked with each other by the relationships of superiority and subordination. It is these relationships which determine the position that the group and the individuals therein will occupy in the society, while at the same time they will largely decide whether groups in question are social classes, castes, ranks or ethnical groups.

In most societies people classify one another into categories and ranks from higher to lower. The process of defining and ranking such categories is called social stratification. Briefly speaking social stratification refers to social gradation, ranking, classification and hierarchy. According to Sorokin social stratification means the differentiation of a given population into a hierarchically superimposed classes which is manifested in the existence of upper and lower social layers. Social stratification can be called the placement of the people of a given society in the hierarchical order. The people is placed in order of status and prestige in the society. Sociologists have commonly distinguished four main types of social stratification i.e., slavery, estate, caste and social class. We are mainly concerned with the phenomena of caste and social class in East Pakistan.

First of all we shall deal with the caste system among the Hindus of East Pakistan. The caste system among the Hindus is unique. This is not to say that the system is wholly incomparable with other types of stratification and no elements of caste are to be found elsewhere. In the first place, the system possesses the common characteristic of being evidently connected with economic differentiation. This is apparent whether we consider the effective caste groups (jatis) or the four traditional 'varnas' of Brahmins, Khatriyas, Vaisyas and Sudras. The varnas, as Senart observed in a classical study, originally resembled feudal estates in certain respects. They were like estates both in character and to a great extent in the hierarchical ordering of the groups (priests, warriors, nobles, traders and serfs) and also is the fact that they were not totally closed groups ; individual could move from one 'varna' to another and intermarriage was possible.

The 'jatis' which developed later and which continued to grow in number through the extending division of labour, the incorporation of tribes and to a lesser extent the operation of factors such as religious innovation are the basic units of the traditional caste system.

On the other hand elements of caste can be observed in other societies where more or less strict segregation of particular groups occurs, for instance segregation of those engaged in unclean occupation or of those belonging to a particular ethnic group. But such individual features do not constitute a caste system.

The sociological problem of caste is, therefore, to account for the existence and persistence of this unique type of social stratification. An explanation may be sought in two ways,—either in terms of historical events or in terms of some other factors which are present in East Pakistani Hindu society. Any historical explanation is bound to be speculative in the present state of knowledge and its value would consist chiefly in historical research. One of the most plausible accounts so far offered seems to be given by J. H. Hutton who suggests that the original Aryan invaders of India with their distinct ranks introduced the principle of social stratification into a society, already divided into exclusive tribal groups by taboos connected with food and that they took over and consolidated these taboos as a means of maintaining social distance between themselves and the subject population. In this manner the principle of stratified exclusive groups was reinforced and provided with a powerful sanction in the shape of a religious and magical doctrine of pollution through food and later through contact.

The second way of explaining caste in terms of some other specific feature of Indian society involves a brief consideration of the relationship between 'jati' and 'varna'.   Here is the role of magical and religious ideas of the varna system as expounded in the ancient religious literature. M. N. Srinivas observes that the notion 'Karma' which teaches a Hindu that he is born in a particular Sub-caste because he deserved to be born there and 'Dharma' the code of duties (or rules of the caste) have contributed very greatly to the strengthening of the idea of hierarchy which is inherent in the caste system.

Hindu tradition relates that the major divisions were established about 600 B.C.   The ancient laws of Manu gave the four chief castes as follows :   (1) The Brahmins or priests who were "assigned the duties of reading the Vedas (the sacred books), of teaching of sacrificing, of assisting others to sacrifice, of giving Alms if they be rich and if poor of receiving gifts." This group of people came from the mouth of the God. Therefore, they are sacred.   (2) The military chieftains or overlords called the Khatriya, whose duties were "to defend the people, to give alms, to sacrifice, to read the Vedas, to shun the allurements of sensual gratification."   (3) The agriculturists, herdsmen and traders are called the Vaisya and (4) the servile class of menials and industrial workers or Sudra, whose duty it was to serve the above mentioned classes without depreciating their worth.

Actually, the laws of Manu mention 50 castes besides these major varnas. Outside these four orders and outside the pale of Hinduism, is a varied mass of outcastes the lowest of whom,—the Chandalas are regarded as the dust of the earth, about on a par with such 'unclean' animals as dogs and donkeys.

SOCIAL CLASS

A social class system differs radically from those systems which we have so far considered.   Social classes are defacto (Not legally or religiously defined and sanctioned) groups ; they are relatively open. Their basis is indisputably economic ; but they are more than economic groups.   They are characteristic groups of the industrial societies which have developed since the 17th Century. Considerable

2—

difficulties arise when the attempt is made to specify the number of social classes or to define their membership precisely.

However, most sociologists would probably agree in recognizing the existence of an upper class (comprising the owner of the major part of the economic resources of a society), a working class (chiefly the industrial wage-earners), and a middle class or middle classes (a more amorphous group often treated as a residual category, but including most white coller workers and most members of the liberal professions).

Now we are to look at the stratification in the social system of Islam. According to the Islamic injunction all men are equal. But from the standpoint of social classes and social stratification, the development of Islam in India in general and East Pakistan in particular has been peculiar. Popular Islam in India in many respects copied the essentials of Hindu beliefs, ideas and social institutions and adjusted them to the Islamic system in a very strange way.

It will be interesting here to note that in an attempt to conform itself to the requirements of the Indian social structure, Islam in India patterned its social classes roughly in imitation of the four main Hindu caste divisions. The Indian Muslims used to divide themselves usually into (1) Syed, (2) Moghal, (3) Sheikh and (4) Pathan ; the Hindu counterpart being: (1) Brahmin, (2) Khatriya, (3) Vaisya and (4) Sudra.

Although such pattern of the Islamic social organization was found in India, the "fanciful" fourfold division of the Muslim society does not correspond strictly to the Hindu caste structure. It is also true that the members of the major four groups were recruited from the Muslim society and they also at times "freely" intermarried and therefore the fourfold system never became rigid like Hindu caste system. As E.A.H. Blunt points out, "A Muslim may marry any woman outside the prohibited degrees." The Hindu caste system is entirely incompatible with the tenets of Islam.

In East Pakistan, among the Muslim lower classes, there are different grades or classes who maintain a hierarchical relationship on the basis of their occupations and professions which are often hereditary. The lower classes get the name and titles according to their occupations.

Now the structure in the traditional East Pakistani villages according to Prof. Nazmul Karim, consists of the following :

(1) The Chaudhuris who claim to have once been the feudal chiefs of the village.
(2) The Khandakers who claim to have belonged to the priestly class.
(3) The Muharirs who claim to have once belonged to the writer class.
(4) Bhuyans whose forefathers were wealthy peasant proprietors.
(5) Agriculturists, owning their own cultivable land and cultivating it themselves or through 'Bargaders'.
(6) Landless agricultural labourers who cultivate other's land.
(7) Wage earners of other kinds.
(8) Wood cutters.

Besides there are many professional groups like Teachers, Hakims and Peers who enjoy a better status in the village. In the lowest class of inferior status are groups like Barbers, Washermen, Potters, Shoe makers, Carpenters, Boatmen, Weavers etc., who in the past were functionally subservient to the Husbandry class.

But the social stratification in the urban areas differ greatly with that of the rural East Pakistani society. There, the social classes are working as economic unit. There, the position in the society is based not on birth but on the mode of production or owning the means of production and the types of jobs. There are the following classes of peoples:

(1) The class of capitalists and industrialists who own and run industries and business enterprises based on private investment.
(2) Economic structure apart from capitalist class, has other interdependent economic units such as the managerial or administrative class, the technicians, the non-technicians and the menials which are off-shoots of the capitalist structure.
(3) The high ranking officials and their subordinate class III and class IV workers also represent differentiation in the administrative and economic structure of the society.
(4) The specialised professional classes include many groups of people such as Lawyers, Doctors, Engineers, Professors, Teachers etc.
(5) Hereditary professional classes as detached from the village

community in the wake of industrialization and urbanization are also numerous. Dyers, Weavers, Butchers, Hajams, Cooks etc., are few of them. In this connection it is important to remember that though such classes are lower in status their services are utilized by the groups belonging to the upper stratum of the society.

It is important to note here that status in the urban society is based primarily on the control of means of production ; not on the ownership of cultivable land or birth. It depends on the nature of job and professions. Those who are employed in higher jobs are placed in the upper stratum of the hierarchy of urban society.

SOCIAL MOBILITY

By social mobility we mean movement within the social structure. In the ordinary sense of the term mobility refers to any movement or migration of people in time, in physical space or in a social framework. But social mobility is not a movement for social reform. It does not mean mass movement. One's class-status is originally determined by the class-status of his parents. When one achieves a different type of education from that of his parents or moves into a different occupational stratum or adopts a different style of life, he has been socially mobile. Movement within the social structure may occur for a whole category of people.

SOCIAL MOBILITY AS A PROCESS

Social mobility brings about a change in the status of an individual, a group, or a class. It is in other words, a process. The term mobility is also used to indicate the spatial movement or migration of a population, but we shall restrict our discussion to social mobility or movement within a social structure.

TYPES OF MOBILITY

Social mobility may be defined as any shifting of position within the structure. Social mobility is classified into horizontal and vertical. Horizontal mobility means movement back and forth on the same social level from one similar social group or situation to another. It is a theoretical assumption that people of the same social class have access to one another because they share the same status. But in practice, there are sub-classes within the same class and therefore people of the same social class do not always have access to one another. Horizontal social mobility is the permanent movement of an individual from one set to another in the same social order. In case of horizontal mobility the persons, involved in the movement, more or less, know each other. As a result the transition is often smooth. Vertical mobility is more significant than horizontal mobility.

It is defined as the movement of people from one social order to another, from one class to another. The factors and conditions of vertical mobility are numerous and complex. Vertical mobility can be either upward or downward. One might shift to a higher status or he might shift to a lower status. In any of these cases the situation is very significant for the individual, involved in the change.

In our discussion on the social stratification, we have distinguished between two types of social structure,—rigid and flexible or closed and open on the basis of the kind of criteria of status and function, the degree of association between various strata and the degree of vertical mobility between them. The structure with the caste system has little or limited association between the members of the different castes and sects. The limited degree of social interaction between them is also formally prescribed. The relationship between them is like the relationship between the master and slave, between the professional and client, between the rich and the poor and between the local and foreigner. Consequently in the Hindu caste system in East Pakistan there is little scope for social mobility.

In the Hindu caste system the son of a Brahmin will be equally honoured by all the Hindus whatever may be his economic position. The son of a Sudra or Vaisya will be given lower status whatever high or low his economic position may be.

But in the Muslim society in East Pakistan we find the freedom of association between the members of all strata and there is the scope for vertical mobility. In the Muslim social structure the status of the people is theoretically determined by their achievements.

Although every society from time to time, provided some of the social avenues for mobility whereby the members of lower strata have risen up in the social scale. Social mobility is the characteristic of modern societies. It provides necessary avenues for individual development in which education and occupational training are important.

The social mobility is always from the lower level to the higher level and vice versa. As for example the tenant class of East Pakistan has assumed higher status in the society when the right of ownership of land is given to them by the Land Acquisition Act of 1951 and the Zamindar class had to go down in the status scale when the Zamindary system was abolished by the same act of 1951.

Now we shall consider the extent of social mobility in relation to the system of stratification in East Pakistan.

Social mobility is much more visible in the urban Community in East Pakistan. The classification of the urban community on the basis of profession, signifies the vertical stratification. But as the urban pupulation is heterogenous and exposed to a different way of life under the impact of modern technology, it welcomes changes, goes on creating new outlook, new thought and new belief. The urban people are very mobile and always try to improve their social and economic condition. This causes both horizontal and vertical mobility among them. As the urban society is divided into upper, middle and lower class, there is always competition between the different classes of people to occupy a dignified position in the community. In the urban community they always try to capture the higher position in the society. This is the peculiar characteristic of East Pakistani society.

Due to the abolition of the Zamindary system in East Pakistan there is a vacuum of the upper class people in the rural East Pakistani society. This has made the tenant of East Pakistan as the real owners of land. As a result, the lower class cultivators have raised their social position in the hierarchical order of the system of social stratification of East Pakistan.

Bibliography
Gaudefroy, D. *Muslim Institutions*, London 1954.
Lundberg. *Sociology*, New York 1958.
MacIver and Page. *Society*, London 1957.

Nazmul Karim, A.K. *Changing Society in India and Pakistan*, Dacca 1961.

Ogburn and Nimkoff. *Sociology*, Boston 1950.

Afsar Uddin Md. *Sociology and Social Research in Pakistan*, Dacca 1963.

Desai, A.R. *Social Background of Indian Nationalism*. Popular Book Depot, Bombay 1959.

Davis, K. *The Population of India and Pakistan*. Princeton University Press, 1951.

Hunter, W.W. *Annals of Bengal*, London 1868.

Ginsberg, M. *The Study of Society*, London 1939.

CHAPTER 4
INSTITUTIONS IN PAKISTAN

Institutions are so vital a subject for the understanding of society that the chief concern of sociology is with an analysis of their nature and function. They constituted the essential elements in the study of society. Society is the clustering of people in interaction with each other and by its products creates the condition for the survival and perpetuation of the group. Out of the interactions, strivings and aspirations of group life grow social institutions,—those relatively permanent, organized and structuralized systems of behaviour, attitudes, purposes, material objects, symbols and ideals which give direction to much of life.[1]

INSTITUTION, DEFINED

The term institution, like other sociological terms which are also found in popular usage, has been given different meanings. Even in sociology there is no unanimity as to the exact definition of this term, although the concrete forms of institution are readily recognized. According to Sumner and Keller, who contributed perhaps the clearest and most satisfactory explanation of the term, an institution is a vital interest or activity which is surrounded by a cluster of mores and folkways. For example, the fact that social life is lived by two sexes and that their relationships to each other, to their offspring, and to society as a whole need to be regulated, give rise to a set of practices which, when they become crystalized, are recognizable as an institution.[2]

CHARACTERISTICS OF INSTITUTION

Sumner, in his Folkways conceived on the "institution, as consisting not only of a concept, idea or interest, but of a structure as well." By structure he meant an apparatus or a group of functionaries. Through

---

1. John L. Gillin and John P. Gillin, Cultural Sociology, The Mackmillan Co., New York, 1954, P. 313.
2. Sumner, W. G. Folkways, Ginn and Co. Boston, 1906. PP. 53, 54.

this apparatus the idea takes a concrete form and is put to work to serve the needs of society. We may summarize the significant general features of social institutions as follows:

(1) An institution is an organization of conceptual and behaviour patterns and is manifested through social activity and its material products. Thus it may be regarded as a cluster of social usages and as composed of customs, folkways, mores and trait complexes organized, consciously or unconsciously, into a functioning unit. In short the institution functions as a unit in the cultural system viewed as a whole.

(2) A relative degree of permanence is the characteristic of all institutions. In our society monogamous marriage and private property have been widely accepted for a long time.

(3) A third feature of an institution is one or more fairly well defined objectives. The Objectives are not necessarily the same thing as the functions of the institution. The social function of an institution may be unknown to everyone and may be recognized often only after experience shows that it actually performs a function different from its intended objective.

(4) Cultural objects of utilitarian value which are used to accomplish the purpose of the institution are usually involved,— buildings, tools, machinery, furniture and the like. Their forms and usages become institutionalized.

(5) Symbols are the characteristic feature of institutions. They may be either material or nonmaterial in form.

(6) An institution has a fairly definite oral or written tradition which contains a formulation of the purposes, attitudes and behaviour of the individuals participating.

(7) Authority : Those who act in or for a social institution are invested by society with the authority necessary to effect its purpose.

(8) The personnel : Operative social institutions function by means of a specialized personnel,—teachers, officers, leader, mollah, priest, etc. On the other hand merely regulative institutions (betrothal, the family etc.) have no such agents.

FORMS OF INSTITUTION

Institution can be grouped according to the basic social needs they serve. In the economic and industrial fields property, contract, inheritance, exchange, money and credit, interest, joint stock companies and labour unions are outstanding. In the political field conspicuous are law, legislatures, courts, police, army, administrative bureaus, municipal corporations and political parties. In the domestic field one comes on such institutions as betrothal, courtship, marriage, divorce and the family. In the religious fields we have priesthood, creeds, theologies, public worship, mosque, temple, prayer, fasting, pilgrimage etc. In the educational and scientific fields there occur schools, colleges, universities, libraries, museums, scientific institutes, research bureaus etc.

Generally social, economic, political, religious, educational and recreational institutions are found in Pakistan.

1. SOCIAL INSTITUTION

Social institution in Pakistan may be divided into three categories, namely family, marriage and divorce.

Family : The institution of family has been great at all stages of human culture. In an agricultural society it is functionally more important. It has special economic significance for the peasant in Pakistan because every one of his family helps him in the processes of agricultural production. The family is the nursery of human nature, a procreative, child-bearing and status giving group. The family in Pakistan is mostly monogamous ; while a small fraction of its old Muslim generation practises polygamy. In all societies, the family has been charged with responsibilities for performing certain necessary functions, essentially for the well being of the society. The most important of social functions usually performed by the family may be listed as follows :

(1) The reproduction of species. (2) The sustenance, care, and rearing of the offsprings especially during infancy and the years of complete dependency. (3) The education and training of the young. (4) Recreation. (5) Protection of members from enemies and dangers and from psychological isolations and (6) The care of the aged and other incapable members and relatives.

In Pakistan the males are considered to be superior to the females. The conception of male domination has given birth to the patriarchal type family in the urban and rural areas of Pakistan. All matters, concerning the family are decided by the head of the family who is usually the father. Sometimes, he consults various family problems with his wife and grown-up children.

This type of family system has got great influence on the personality development of the children. They are taught to obey the orders of their superior.

The joint or extended family is a predominant form of family in Pakistan. In this type of family the husband and wife live with their children, married sons and their wives and children, unmarried daughters and other relatives. It has got immense impact on our social life. Because of many members and therefore many minds, ideas, whims and wishes there are occasional conflicts in the family. The joint domestic arrangement also becomes a problem when all the aged members of the family are not the earning members. On the other hand, the joint family system in our country provides security for the members of the family by taking care, showing sympathy, giving protection in danger and by financial support. In case of death of a man, his children and wife are usually supported by other family members.

The institution of family is one of the important and significant agencies of social control. It helps in the process of our socialization by giving emphasis to the practice of our cultural and social values.

Marriage : Marriage is the central feature of all human societies. It is commonly called the mating relationship between a man and a woman. It may elaborately be described as an arrangement of admitting men and women in their intimate personal relationship as husband and wife with a set of rights and duties towards one another to serve the primary purpose of begetting and rearing children and establishing a home. Marriage, therefore, is not merely a conjugal or sexual relationship between the opposite sexes. It is a means to an end, such as co-existence of husband and wife and other members of the family.

Exogamy has been described as the custom of prohibiting a man to marry a woman of his own caste or clan as against endogamy under which it is binding for a man to marry within his own tribe or clan or caste. Among the Hindus marriage, which is conducted by the regulation of caste system, is predominantly endogamous. Among the Muslims of Pakistan as elsewhere, marriage is a civil ceremony which is sacred but not sacrament. It is invariably preceded by "Nikha' (betro-thal) solemnized by a 'Kazi' or the marriage registrar. The common custom, practised in this regard is the consideration of 'Hasab' and 'Nasab' which necessarily makes the marriage, endogamous i.e., marriage in the same 'Khandan' (line).

A Muslim belonging to a particular class, language or colour and trade or profession may marry a Muslim of any other social grade or professional group. Some of the Muslims, however, are as much endo-gamous as the Hindus. Prof. A.F.A. Hussain through his case study in the discussion of the social conditions and cultural patterns of East Pakistani villagers has found that the Muslim weavers called the 'Jolhas' are endogamous because of not marrying their sons and daughters outside their caste-like group. Monogamy is the most widely practised form of marriage in our country. Polygamy is rarely practised by the Muslims. The institution of polygamous marriage, which is disappear-ing fast affects our social and private life by bringing conflict and unhappiness in the family. Like all other countries marriage regulates the sexual life of the people of our country.

Divorce : The Islamic Law of divorce, connected with the institu-tion of marriage permits divorce among the Muslims. Divorce is the lawful practice of cutting the marriage bond between a husband and a wife. It is lawful because it is sanctioned by our religion. But it does not mean that divorce should be effective without any conditions.

It has to follow certain principles. Its methods are, of course, com-plex and confusing for the general people. According to Islamic injun-ctions divorce should take place strictly in accordance with the "sunnah" which prescribes the revocation of divorce enabling thereby the husband to reclaim his wife without remarriage and a new 'mohar". If however, divorce is pronounced by the husband, he is given a chance of revoking his decision during the period of three months following the date of his pronouncement. This period is called the "Iddat". Divorce has got various impacts on our society. Firstly it disturbs the normal functioning in the family life and in many cases acts dangerously for the children in the family. The children of a family where the father or the mother is divorced have a greater chance to deviate from the normal ways of life and to indulge in antisocial activities. This does a positive harm to their personality development.

2. ECONOMIC INSTITUTION

Economic activities occupy a prominent place in all societies. They have to do with the production, accumulation, distribution and consumption of wealth. Economic institutions are those groups of traits and complexes which are organized around some objective or set of objectives in this field.

The economic institutions are a part of the culture complex of a people. They bear the marks of every other aspects of social life. They, in turn, affect the nature, structure, and function of every other institutions,—the family, religion, morals, education etc. A remarkable discrepancy exists in the economic patterns of different societies and it may be worth while to inquire what factors bear upon them.

(i) Natural resources and environment exercise a limiting influence upon them.

(ii) The degree of technological advancement of the culture affects the economic activities.

(iii) The dominating interests of the culture, reflected particularly in religious, political and social organization, influence the form of economic activities.

The economic institutions of Pakistan can be classified into the following :

Property : The nature of property in any society is determined by the pattern of ownership. From the standpoint of ownership, property can be collectively owned or privately owned. In a collectively owned pattern each and every member enjoys equal fruits and advantages from their property. In Pakistan property is predominantly privately owned. The system of private property with all its peculiarities are found in our country where an individual owns a definite amount of property whatever may be the method of obtaining it. Because of the prevalence of the private property system which implies the inequality in the possession of wealth, one class will have greater opportunity to exploit the other, economically, politically and morally.

Bank : It is an economic institution which is essential for the development and progress of our country. Through this institution the national and international business, trade and commerce are controlled. By extending loan to the people for the industrial and agricultural development in Pakistan, it is indirectly helping in the changes in the social structure of Pakistan which is heading towards industrialization and mechanization of agriculture.

Insurance : It is another thriving economic institution in Pakistan. It has got tremendous impact on our social life. It gives the people an opportunity to save for the future which is very uncertain in our country because of the lack of any social security system. It saves the society from disorganization by preventing disorganization and break-down of family where the earning member dies. It also helps to gain economic prosperity by encouraging savings and capital formation.

Co-operatives : The establishment of some co-operative societies in Pakistan may be looked upon as an economic institution of recent growth. It came into existence out of the attempt of consumers to eliminate the middleman's profit in the purchase of commodities. The sellers are also trying through co-operatives, to eliminate the middleman's role in the sale of goods. The main purpose of the co-operatives in Pakistan is to save the consumers and growers from the exploitation of the middlemen and to ensure a fair price for the commodities.

Trade Unions : Unions of labourers have developed in Pakistan out of the wage system and the clash of interests between the employers and the employees, engaged in the productive process. One of the important purposes of this institution is to fight for the welfare of the employees. In addition there are other economic institutions such as state regulation, the holding company and large scale factory production etc.

3. POLITICAL INSTITUTION

Political institutions are those which deal with the state and the government. The word "state" as here used, refers to the most political organization of the country. Nation is best described as "Psycho-social "concept. The people have a common descent, language, mores, customs and often religion. Normally they live within their country under their state; but sometimes nationals may live outside the country and nationals of other countries within its confines . The sovereign power of a state is limited by its constitution which may be changed by the people but is binding while it exists.

In the United Nations is demonstrated a new concept of the political institution, i.e. the U.N. represents the force of decisions, reached by conference and vote of representatives of its member nations. Modern political institutions developed out of the critical conditions arising from the efforts of a powerful group within a society to obtain advantages by the control of private property or by war and conquest. The main purpose of the political institution is to regulate the relationships within a society in which customs, traditions are no longer adequate to do so. They work as important agencies of social control by regulating the activities of the people. The concept of political institution in Pakistan is mainly demonstrated in Basic Democracies and different political parties.

Basic Democracies : There are very few successful democracies. Those that seem firmly established have developed their tradition of social and political justice over a period of many generations. It is truism, but none the less vital to say that democracy depends on the insistence by public opinion that the holders of power conform to the spirit of the constitution. The system of democracy inevitably takes time to grow and must be rooted deep in the consciousness of the people.

In 1959 a scheme of local self Government popularly known as Basic Democracies was established. It was claimed that Basic Democracies would form the basic structure on which the super-structure of the representative institutions will ultimately grow and flourish. But there are divergent views about its utility and worth.

The institution of Basic Democracies is a pyramidal plan, enabling the people to elect directly to local councils, the men they know. These, in turn, will elect the upper tiers of the hierarchy. Broadly speaking the five-tier local Government scheme launched by the Martial Law regime particularly by President Ayub Khan represents a system which begins at the bottom and after building a base, goes to construct the upper tiers.

Now we will try to analyse the significance and philosophy behind the new political order in Pakistan. Although the purpose and significance of the new political order have not been stated clearly and objectively the assumption is that the development of democracy needs an evolutionary process.

The development of the concept of democracy had a long history

whose final chapter is yet to be written. In consequence, it is not sus-
ceptible to a cut and dried definition. The expert is conscious of this ;
but not the average man.   Caught in the fast moving world around
him, he has little time, even if he had the inclination to ponder over
this. He is quite willing to accept the identification of democracy with
a well-known form of Government or with mechanism of its election
and recall.

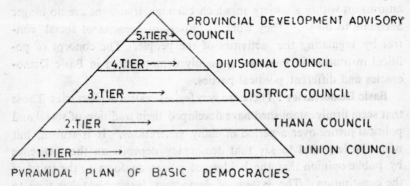

PYRAMIDAL PLAN OF BASIC DEMOCRACIES

To limit democracy merely to a particular form of Government
or a system of its election is to take too narrow a view of the concept
which has, over the centuries, come to be based upon the recognition
of the equality of man enjoying the inalienable right to happiness as
a member of society.   It is a whole way of social life seeking to work
for the welfare of the community through conscious group effort.
It embodies both the ideals of human endeavour and the means of
their achievement.   And the life of any one community being essentially the creation of its particular environment may not be the same
as that of another.   As a result there can be no single method of
bringing about an organization that would effectively look after the
well being of all the differing social groups the world over. The
methods must vary from time to time.

Some aspects of the Basic Democracies have been outlined as
briefly explained below.

The underlying idea of all democracy is that the ultimate right to
govern is vested in the people themselves who are the real sovereign.

Note : In 1962 constitution of Pakistan the Provincial Development Advisory
    Council has been done away with.

Now we shall try to explain the mechanism of the whole structure of the Basic Democracies.

Union Council : The Basic Democracies propose the establishment of Union Councils ordinarily covering a group of Villages with a total population of 10,000 to 15,000. A group of 1,000 to 1,500 will be represented by one member, elected on the basis of adult franchise. The council will elect its own chairman from amongst its members.

Under Basic Democracies it proposed to constitute Town or Union committees in the Urban areas. Like Union Council they too, will be composed of directly elected members.

Thana Council : The next tier in Basic Democracies is the Tehsil Council for West Pakistan and Thana Council for East Pakistan. This body will consist of the Chairman of the Union Councils, Town and Union Committees.

District Council : The third tier will be formed by the District Council. In Basic Democracies, it is next in importance to the Union Council. It will consist of nominated official and non-official elected members.

Divisional Council : The next tier in Basic Democracies is the Divisional Council. It will be presided over by the Divisional Commissioner and its functions will include the Co-ordination of the activities of Local Councils, Municipal Bodies and Cantonment Boards. At least a quarter of the membership of this body will be composed of chairmen of the Union Councils and Town and Union Committees which, under the new system, are the basis and the most important unit in the entire structure.

Provincial Development Advisory Council : Law and Order are the essential features of an organized society, but they are by no means the ultimate aim of endeavour. In a free society that distinction must necessarily belong to the welfare of the people. Basic Democracies propose the establishment of high powered Development Advisory Councils for the two Provinces of Pakistan.

Experience in other countries seems to indicate that unless local bodies are properly staffed, even given a substantial degree of political consciousness, a high level of efficiency cannot be attained. Pakistan has to face twofold problems of an absence of the right type of political institution and a limited supply of good administrators at a period

3—

in our history when we have to make the maximum use of all the resources available to us.

Purely from an administrative point of view, rather than the Socio-
Political point of view, the new arrangement will lead to a substantial
measure of genuine decentralization. Problems relating to local
areas will be disposed of at these levels. This should result in greater
efficiency.

The introduction of Basic Democracies is not an end in itself. To
quote President Ayub Khan, "It is a means to an end. The task
of reconstruction will indeed begin when the system of Basic
Democracies starts working. What we have been able to achieve in
the last year is, in fact, the beginning of the real task which we have
to accomplish".

Political Parties in Pakistan : Political parties are often founded
upon the shared recollection of powerful emotion. It is for this
reason that the significance of the period from 1919 to 1947 is
essential to an understanding of the political parties in Pakistan.
The Khilafat Movement was the symbol of the unity of the Muslim
world and of the political independence of the adherents of Islam.
Secondly by a process of reaction, the movement strengthened the
tendency towards opposition to anything Occidental. The third
product of the Khilafat Movement in the minds of the Muslim
politicians lies in the field of Political Organization and tactics.

The system of political parties in Pakistan bears little resemblance
to that of most other democratic countries. Pakistan has neither a two
party system, in which the political struggle is waged between fairly
stable groups ; one of which is in power and the other in opposition
nor a multi-party system, in which clear differences of programme
or ideology separate a variety of opponents.

In Pakistan politics is the business of a large number of leading
persons who with their political dependents form loose agreements to
achieve power and to maintain it. Consequently rigid adherence to a
policy or a measure is likely to make a politician less available for
office. Those who lack fixed ideas but can control legislators, money-
influence, have tended to prosper in political life.

The Muslim League was the oldest political party in this region.
But the establishment of the All Pakistan Muslim League in 1948 was,

therefore, no more than a mere separation from its parent body,—
the All India Muslim League. The chart mentioned below will give
us an idea about the number of political parties in Pakistan which was
formed after independence :

1. Muslim League.
2. Krishak Sramik Party.
3. Awami League.
4. National Awami Party.
5 Pakistan National Congress.
6. Nizam-e-Islam.
7. Jamaat-e-Islami
8. Republican Party.
9. Scheduled Caste Federation.
10. United Progressive Party.
11. Ganatantri Dal.
12. Socialist Party.
13. Jinnah Muslim League.
14. Azad Pakistan Party.

Apart from these parties there were few others namely :

1. Sind Awami Jama'at.
2. Sind Hari Committee.
3. Sind Jinnah Awami Muslim League.
4. Sind Dastoor Party.

The electorate of Pakistan is predominantly rural and overwhel-
mingly illiterate. It is there that political parties usually function. A
politician in Pakistan does not need to pay much attention to the
opinion of the ordinary voter. He pays attention to the party. A
politician must also consider the men who control blocks of votes in
local areas. We find that the Zamindars, Pirs, Mirs, Makhdoms,
Khans and Nawabs retain vast political influence in Pakistan.

The second major party to emerge in Pakistan since partition was
the "Krishak Sramik Party".

The Krishak Sramik Party was the revival of an old organisation,
founded by Mr. A. K. Fazlul Haq in 1927, which till early forties had
functioned under different names in undivided Bengal. Under the
label of Krishak Praja Party, it was the most popular aspirant to political power in the Province in 1936, against which were arrayed in a

single camp most of the prominent leaders of Muslim Bengal, including Khawaja Nazimuddin, Mr. Suhrawardy and the Nawab of Dacca. As its chequered history bears out, the Party's only source of strength was its leadership. The legendary figure of Mr. Haq needed neither an organisation nor a programme to lead a party to electoral victory. The change in name from Krishak Praja (peasants) to Krishak Sramik (peasants and workers) was in keeping with the changing economy of the Province which was now being given an industrial reorientation. Emphasis on the improvement of the peasants' lot and rapid industrialization was however not spelled out into a specific programme of reconstruction and reform.

Awami League : Discord and dissatisfaction within the Muslim League became evident soon after its Governments were installed in all the Provinces. This conflict within the party created a condition which culminated in the formation of new political parties. The Pir of Manki Sharif, an influential worker of the Muslim League withdrew from the League to form a rival organisation of his own, known as the Awami League. In East Pakistan the younger elements in the Muslim League reacted sharply and organised a party of their own, also known as the Awami Muslim League. If we look objectively to the emergence of the Awami League we will find that East Pakistan was seething with discontent when the Awami League successfully exploited the issue. Many educated and illiterate people, students, teachers, lawyers, and doctors were attracted by the call of the Awami League. Thousands of people participated in the language disturbances, quite a few courted arrest and suffered imprisonment. The extent of the party's large following among the people, however, remained a matter of guess until the election of April, 1954. The manifesto of the party was announced on November 16, 1953. But the party never clearly declared its ideological affiliation. Abolition of landlordism without compensation, nationalisation of jute and tea industries were the main economic planks in its platform ; expansion of education and health facilities were the principal objectives of its social policy.

Republican Party : The circumstances under which the Republican Party came into existence were different from those responsible for the growth of the Awami League and the Krishak Sramik Party, though the underlying cause of its origin was the same i.e., the wide spread demoralisation in the Muslim League. Dr. Khan Sahib was the founder of the Republican Party.

The Republican Party, it proclaimed, was wedded to the democratic form of government and was opposed to all other concepts of government. It stood for territorial nationalism based on "a community of equals bound by common ties of patriotism and love for their homeland" ; it pledged to the protection and enlargement of personal freedom through the repeal of all legislation repugnant to the normal exercise of Civil Liberties ; and dedicated to the creation of a welfare state in which the bulk of the wealth produced would not be funneled into a few private pockets but returned to the people in the shape of lower prices, higher wages and adequate services and amenities for their welfare. As a sociologist what we find is that, the practical application of these theoretical programmes was, however, a different story. The party thus functioned within the four walls of the Parliament. What comes to our mind is that the Republicans were serious about competing for the allegiance of the people in East Pakistan, by subscribing to so radical a policy. It is doubtful that even in its soil of birth it could have had more than a limited sectional and class appeal, particularly to the landowning interests which dominated its composition.

National Awami Party : The National Awami Party was a product of forces very different from those that had gone into the making of other political organisations. The party did not emerge out of dissensions within the Muslim League nor was its leadership entirely drawn from that source. Khan Abdul Ghaffar Khan, Mr. Abdus Samad Achakzai, Prince Abdul Karim and Maulana Bhashani and Mr. G.M. Syed, all these personalities formed themselves into the National Awami Party at the Convention of Democratic Workers held in Dacca in July 1957. Their approach to problems of provincial reorganisation, redistribution of powers between the Federal and the Provincial authorities determined the nature of the constitution and the structure of the organisation as well as its aims and objects. The pattern, adopted was more or less the same as followed by other political parties.

The party claims to represent the interest of the workers and peasants in Pakistan. Its programmes include the abolition of the zamindary system without compensation, nationalisation of jute and cotton trade, betterment of the lot of the peasants and workers and the redistribution of wealth in the country.

Nizam-e-Islam : The Nizam-e-Islam was originally a component of the United Front and as such a party to the 21-Point Programme. The preamble of the Programme might have been incorporated on its insistence. As its very name suggested, the Party was opposed to secularism in any form. It stood for the establishment of a religious polity based on the teachings of the Quran and the Sunnah without giving any concrete expression to Islamic principles to guide the formulation of state policies. What we find about this party is that in the Islamic society there would be no room for exploitation of one class by another nor any justification for the existence of poverty and unemployment. One more thing we will have to admit about the means through which a harmonious social era was to be ushered in, the party was scrupulously non-committal.

Jamaat-e-Islami : The Jamaat-e-Islami was an organisation. In the language of its manifesto, it was not a "Religious" or "Political" party in the ordinary sense of the word, but a movement which stood for an ideology embracing every walk of human life,—personal or social, public or individual, political or cultural, economic or moral, educational or judicial, internal or international. The party was not a post-partition growth. In the initial years, the Jamaat concentrated its energies on social services and intellectual activities ; and only after the ground had been prepared it took part in politics. After going deep into the investigation about the working of this party, we find that the party had a programme not only for the election purposes, but also for its day-to-day operations. Adult education centres, reading rooms, libraries and dispensaries for the distribution of free medical aid were established all over the country as a means to build up its popularity among the masses. These activities required funds, which the party was able to mobilise through voluntary contributions from its members, donations from the well-wishers, zakat from the well-to-do and from the sale of hides and skins, collected from the general populace on the occasion of the Eid-al-Adha (the feast of sacrifice).

Now we will try to explain its election manifesto which was a document in which its social, economic and political ideas were presented in a concise and readable form for the information of the general public. The party was not opposed to modern techniques and methods of production, which it considered essential to the progress of the economy and urged their application in agriculture and industry. It attached the highest importance to the sanctity of private property, no matter how big were the properties in individual possession. All that it was concerned with was how the properties were acquired.

Political parties, in a real sense, stand for a lot of other things, besides their labels and representatives, to be able to perform their true function in a democratic state. All that we need for an ideal political party is organisation, membership, adherents, funds and leadership,— all form the part of ideal mechanism of a political party. In an era of universal suffrage, the existence of mass parties is inconceivable without a network of branches, spread all over the country. It is through these branches alone that a party can recruit its members, maintain contact with the electorate and popularise its programme. While all parties in Pakistan had accepted this basic element in their organisation, few had grasped its real significance.

No party was in a position to raise funds to conduct its routine activities and its election campaigns which were the items of heavy expenditure. A single seat in the Provincial and National Assemblies costs a heavy amount. The party had to rely on donations from businessmen, industrialists and landlords. The organisations were consequently unable to exercise control on their parliamentary representatives who frequently changed their sides. Apart from the economic pressure on the parties and the electorate, another factor which undermined the value of elections as barometers of public opinion was the interference exerted by other different organizations.

Schooled in the old traditions of politics, the leaders of political parties in Pakistan in general could not fully discard the elements of conservatism, which were responsible for the slow progress and reform. Many leaders of different political parties lent their services to classes which were opposed to social change in Pakistan.

But the kind of governments will be determined by the nature of political parties on which ultimately rests the responsibility of running the affairs of the state. A decade is too brief a span in the history of a nation to judge the success or failure of a form of government. But in the case of a new state like Pakistan, the first ten years formed a crucial period of democratic experiment for more than one reason. The politicians were not unfamiliar with the principles and practices of democracy. Many of them had theoretical grounding in the working of parliamentary institutions abroad and a few of them had practical experience of their working at home. Their supreme test will lie in the political education of the electorate, interpretation of their hopes and aspirations, and above all, in developing a sense of accountability to the people whose consent is important for thier sustenance and survival.

4. EDUCATIONAL INSTITUTION

The educational institutions in Pakistan can be classified into the following :

Primary School : In the beginning of the 19th century the Indo-Pakistan subcontinent had a network of indigenous schools. There is considerable evidence to support the conclusion that most of the villages had a school, although in many cases formal building did not exist ; and many of them were mere domestic centres of instruction where a father taught his own children along with a few others, or a teacher was engaged to teach the children of one or a few families.

During the 19th century, primary education in this region could not develop as much as might be desired. The indigenous elementary schools in the rural areas gradually disappeared as a result of the neglect to which they were subjected. The rural areas were neglected and the major emphasis was placed on cities, district headquarters and subdivisional towns. Pakistan possessed grave problems in the field of primary education since independence. The responsibility for the provision and maintenance of primary schools at the time of independence was vested on the local bodies of the provinces of Pakistan. The local bodies never worked well and was, in fact, a hindrance in the way of the expansion of primary education.

The curriculum, in force in primary schools at the time of emergence of Pakistan was dominated by the three R's. Very little attention seems to have been paid to the needs and interests of the child and to his environments, in framing curriculum. The entire system of primary education was bookish and theoretical which made maximum demands on the pupil's use of his energy. These conditions had naturally made the primary school very unattractive to the children and accelerated the rate of drop out.

The number of primary schools in East Pakistan gradually decreased from 29,633 in 1947-48 to 26,000 in 1954-55 and slowly increased thereafter, reaching 27,562 in 1963-64. The decrease during the 17-year period under consideration was mainly due to the policy of consolidation, improvement, abolition of weak and ineffective primary schools and the amalgamation of inefficient girls' primary schools with those of boys' institutions in neighbourhood, thus encouraging Co-education at the primary level.

Secondary School : Secondary education in Pakistan is structurally organized in three stages. The first stage comprising class IV to VIII covers the age range of 10 to 14 years and is known as the middle or junior secondary stage ; the second stage composed of classes IX and X, covers the age of 15 to 16 years and leads to Secondary School Certificate Examination ; the third stage, known as higher secondary or Intermediate stage consists of classes XI and XII, covering the age of 17 and 18 years and leads to the Higher Secondary School Certificate Examination. The syllabi, for these three stages of education are practically identical in both wings of the country. Historically, the system of secondary education in East Pakistan formed a part of the general system of education which Pakistan inherited at independence in 1947. As a matter of fact, secondary education was the foundation on which the rest of the education system was built on Western line. The zilla schools, established in the third decade of the last century following new educational policy of the court of directors of East India Company, were the forerunners of other educational institutions that grew up later within this system. The core of this new policy in education was formulated by Macaulay. The important gain during the Post-Independence period was the substantial improvement in the ratio of the number of students of the secondary stage to that of the primary stage. As for example in 1947-48 the total enrolment at the secondary stage was less than one-tenth of that at the primary stage, but in 1963-64, this ratio rose to one fifth.

During the same period the ratio of enrolment at the higher secondary stages rose from 1 : 6 to I : 9

Meanwhile, in West Pakistan, a considerable improvement has, so far, taken place in the field of secondary education. One could list the tremendous increase in the number of students at the secondary level, which in fact expanded from 15 lakhs (1,500,000) in 1958-59 to nearly 25 lakhs (2,500,000) in 1964-65 . One could show the steady increase in trained teachers at this level whose number now stands at nearly 70,000. In Pakistan there is an awareness of the fact that secondary education is of utmost practical importance to the country, because it is at this stage that a talent acquires the education and training through which he can contribute to the economic and social life in Pakistan.

College : The education system was developed throughout the Indo-Pakistan sub-continent in a manner which caused the emergence of a class of educated elites, and a class of partially educated and non-literate class. The function and organization of these classes have been and is different and dissimilar. In accordance with the facts of history the educated elite was organized by the ruling Englishmen for the purpose of winning loyalty from these influential native group, while partially literate and non-literate were organized as a set of mass functionaries whose main purpose was to provide work force for the elite group and the ruling British. Before the emergence of education commission, all the colleges of Pakistan were under the respective universities, but now XI and XII classes are (formerly intermediate class) taken under the Board. And the degree section remained under Universities. In intermediate colleges generally Humanities, Science and Commerce groups are taught and final examination, at the end of two years called H.S.C, is held.

In the degree colleges a student can generally read either Arts, Science or Commerce, leading to the degree of B.A., B. Sc. and B. Com., after two years, and after three years in the honours course. But very few colleges have honours courses. In B.A. courses, a student has to take up the following subjects : (a) English, (b) national language (Bengali or Urdu) and any three out of many elective subjects.

Technical Educational Institution : There has never been a stronger conviction than today that in the expansion and improvement of education in general and technical education in particular, lies the future progress of the world. An underdeveloped country like Pakistan can only make use of its resources if technically trained and experienced people are available to utilize and harness the known and unknown resources within the country. Although Pakistan is mainly an agricultural country yet there is a potentiality to become an industrial country as well. Even in agriculture, mechanization is sinequanon and there is such increasing use of earth moving-machinery, tractors and harvestors, that technical know-how is very important for increasing the production capacity in the agricultural sector. For the effective execution of Engineering Projects, a team of technically trained people at three different levels is generally required. This team consists of the engineer, the technician and the skilled worker.

University and College of Engineering Education : The University or collegiate programme of Engineering Education will be taken up to comprise all those courses in different fields of engineering which, at the minimum, attain a standard equivalent to that of a first degree course of a University. The basic qualification for admission is Higher Secondary School Certificate i. e., 12 years of schooling with Physics, Chemistry and Mathematics. The duration of Engineering degree course is four years after the Higher secondary school certificate. The course is mainly theoretical and the basic sciences of Engineering are taught to a high standard. Some post-graduate courses have now been started in civil, electrical and mechanical engineering at the University of Engineering and Technology, Lahore and Dacca.

University : The basic qualification for admission into the university is Higher Secondary School Certificate viz., 12 years of schooling in arts as well as in science subjects. University offers three years honours course in respective subjects. He who passes honours examination is entitled to admit himself in M. A, (final) class. But those who pass the B.A.examination, they can admit themselves in M. A. (preliminary) class. After passing the M.A. (preliminary) examination they become M.A. (final) students. The education and training in the university help the students in their future life.

Medical College : Medical education in Pakistan, as anywhere else revolves round the basic health requirements of the country.

However, it may be briefly stated that our requirements are based on the following existing data in relation to our population:

	Number of Persons
Doctor...I	7,000
Nurses...I	30,000
Health Visitors ...I	1,10,000
Qualified Midwives...I	49,000
Qualified Dentist ...I	3,00,000
Hospital beds ...I	3,000

The above figures show a serious inadequacy of our health personnel and facilities in the country. In order to make up this deficiency, medical education has been planned in such a way so as to aim at the removal of these discrepancies at all levels and grades. At the present moment there are a dozen medical colleges in Pakistan. These are turning out approximately 1000 graduates each year. In the third Five-year plan more institutes for post-graduate training and research have been planned. It is anticipated that their expansion will take a practical form during the third Five-year plan period. This procedure will enhance the number of doctors from 13,000 in 1964-'65 to 20,000 in 1969-'70. A scheme for setting up a school of Tropical Medicine in Dacca is under way and will be soon implemented. The purpose of establishing Post-graduate Medical Institutions is to train qualified doctors and in carrying out research in the numerous medical and public health problems which we are faced with.

5. RELIGIOUS INSTITUTIONS

The religious institutions vary in various societies. In the complex literate societies religion produces elaborate theories or theologies to explain man's place in the Universe. It sets up systems of ethics with elaborate rules and conduct.

The religious institutions in Pakistan may be divided into the following categories:

Muharram : On the 10th day in the month of Muharram, Imam Hossain, the grand son of our prophet Muhammad, died in the field of Karbala in an encounter with Yezid-bin Moabia. To commemorate the tragedy in the battle field of Karbala the Shia sect of the Muslims observes this day in a particular manner which signifies their extreme devotion to the descendants of our Prophet. On that day the symbol of the tomb of Hossain, generally called the 'Tajiah' is made. They take out a procession with the 'Tajiah' and beat their breasts and cry aloud 'O', son of Ali or 'Hossain' 'Hossain'. After that the 'Tajiah' is either thrown into water or preserved with honour. The institution of Muharram has united the Shia sect of the Muslims all over the world.

Milad-Un-Nabi : Milad is a significant institution of the Muslims. This has become an occasion for rejoicing because our Prophet was born on the 12th day of the month of Rabi-ul-Awal. On the 11th and 12th of this month the adult Muslims are supposed to keep fast. The Quran is read by them, especially by the Mullahs. Bakeries and sweets are distributed among friends and relatives. The poor are given food and money by the rich. Religious meetings are arranged. This institution has got immense influence on the Muslim Community. The teachings and the life of the Prophet are remembered on this day.

Shab-i-Barat and Shab-i-Qadar : It is believed that on the day of Shab-i-barat 'Allah' determines the courses of the lives of his creations for the coming year and at the same time the spirit of the dead comes out of the grave to see their relatives. It is observed on the 14th of Arabic month of 'Saban'. The Muslims say their prayers and read the Quran. Both the fear of punishment and promise of reward govern the behaviour and the activities of the Muslims. Shab-i-Qadar is observed on the 27th night of the month of Ramzan when our Prophet received the Quran from God. A Muslim can acquire virtues at this night by offering prayer and giving food to the religious minded people and the poor. There are many feasts, arranged at this night by the people who can afford it.

I'dul-Fitre : It is observed on the first day of the month of 'Shawal'. After one month of fasting in the month of 'Ramzan' this day is observed with great rejoicings. People take their bath early in the morning, put on generally, new clothes and take breakfast by sweets. After some time the male and the children go to the I'd-gah or field or mosque to say I'd prayer. 'Fitre', a fixed amount of money per head should be paid to the poor. It is sanctioned by Islam. There is exchange of greetings and food among the friends and relatives. This is one of the important festive occasions for the Muslims. It upholds the spirit of charity, unity and recreation for the Muslim Community

I'dul-Azha : It is observed on the 10th day of the month of Zilhajj. Like that of I'dul-Fitre, people rise early in the morning, take their bath, take improved breakfast with sweets and put on new clothes. They go to the field or mosque to say I'd prayer. Cows and goats are generally sacrificed in the name of 'Allah' by the rich who can maintain his family smoothly with his earnings and also have some surplus income. The amount of money which is derived by selling the skins of the sacrificed animals are distributed among the poor. Feast is one of the elements of this institution. It teaches the people the spirit of sacrifice and devotion to God.

Namaz : It means the saying of prayer to 'Allah.' Every adult Muslim is to say prayer five times a day. It is compulsory for them except when they are ill. This is called "Faraz" (compulsory) namaz. There are also extra prayers, called 'Nafal' namaz. It is believed that if one can say 'Nafal' prayer he will acquire more virtues. Before starting the prayer one is to perform 'Azu' (ablution) i.e., to be cleaned by washing hands, feet, mouth, ear, nose, neck etc. It is good to say 'namaz' in the 'jamat' or the gathering in the mosque

Roza : It means fasting. The adult Muslims are to keep fast throughout the whole month of Ramzan. It is compulsory for all excepting when they are seriously ill and too old.

The women are not supposed to keep fast if they are in their menstrual period; but they are to keep it afterwards. It is prohibited to eat or drink anything from dawn to dusk. Fasting starts with the taking of 'Sehri' (special meal, taken in the late hours of night). Immediately after the sun set, they are allowed to eat or drink which is generally known as 'Ifter' in which some new items of food are added. It gives the opportunity to realize the pangs of hunger.

Hajj : It is observed in the month of Zilhajj. It is compulsory for every rich adult Muslims. To perform the Hajj (pilgrimage) one is to go to the 'Kabah' in Mecca. Islam says that the 'Kabah' is the

House of Allah and therefore it is most sacred to perform prayer in the 'Kabah'. The popular belief is that if anybody says prayer, sitting inside the 'Kabah' and asks for forgiveness and blessings for self and others, living or dead, it is sure to be fulfilled.

After performing the 'Hajj' one is to sacrifice generally 'goats' or 'dumba' or camels to the name of 'Allah' and His Prophet Muhammad.

Zakat : Every rich person is ordered by Islam to pay 2½% of his surplus yearly income to the poor and it is known as the institution of Zakat. It is compulsory ; the violation of which is a great sin.

The Zakat can be paid both in cash and kind. Zakat can also be used to the establishment of religious institutions like mosque, jumma ghar (house for congregational prayer on Friday).

Peer and Dargah (shrine) : The peers are supposed to be sent by Allah to conduct His creations to the right path as directed by Him and His Prophet. The popular belief is that whenever the followers of Islam are seen to be deviated from the directed path of Islam the peers come to re-direct them. They are thought to have divine power. Their living places are supposed to be sacred and holy and after their death these places are known as Dargah (shrine). The orthodox Muslims visit these 'Dargahs' off and on, and say fateha (holy verses) to the departed soul of the peer. They think it a holy duty to make presentation either in cash or in kind to these 'Dargahs'.

Social Significance : Islam is a modern and simple religion. It is simple in the sense that like that of Hinduism, it does not have so many religious institutions and ceremonies. Above all almost all the festivals are observed more with devotion than pomp and grandeur. During the Muharram many disturbing incidents are found to take place, specially in the urban areas where maximum programmes are chalked out to perform it. People from the rural areas flock to the urban areas in large number; and make the normal functioning of life difficult, at least for some period. Some festivals are blessings for the poor. Festivals like I'dul-Fitre, I'dul-Azha are of great rejoicing and therefore welcomed by all. But the poor accept these a bit differently. During these festivals the rich pay Fitre, Zakat etc., to the poor. Islam, at least in theory, speaks of equality and probably these sanctions, though not remarkable, bear the testimony to the fact. By this help the poor section of the community are, to some extent, benefited.

Islam advocates regularity and patience and probably with that end in view 'Namaz' and 'Roza' were made compulsory. By performing 'namaz' one can maintain more or less regularity in his daily life and mental peace. 'Azu' without which Namaz can not be performed, is a remarkable step to cleanliness. Roza teaches patience. Some pioneers of modern medical science advocate that the keeping of fast at regular intervals is good for health.

The offering of prayers in 'Dargah' and making of presentation to it, is supposed to be a sacred duty. Both the sexes are allowed to do so. Very often, it is found that by false promise and bluff the 'Khadems' (who are in charge of Dargahs) exploit the ignorent people both morally and economically.

If we observe all the religious institutions we will see that class distinction is not advocated; but in practice we can come across with distinction. The Muslim festivals, at least in theory denounces this sort of distinction. But it is interesting to note that, while observing these festivals class distinction is found. One important aspect of the 'give the poor' policy should not be overlooked. The paying of 'Zakat', Fitre to the individual person indirectly encourages the rise of dependants and parasites in our society. The money, from the Fitre and Zakat can be utilized for the development and welfare of the poor community in Pakistan. The institution of 'Hajj' increases the interaction among the Muslims of the world. It has got economic impact on our society.

6. RECREATIONAL INSTITUTION

The main purpose of this institution is to give recreation and pleasure to the people. For the normal functioning of the society recreational institutions are essential.

A society, without adequate recreational facilities will develop various social problems. Cinema or Motion Pictures, Theatre, Club, Jatra (village opera), Jari are some of the important recreational institutions in Pakistan. From the motion pictures we can know much about different societies. This institution gives us both pleasure and knowledge. Theatre, 'Jatra, Jari etc., are organized for the mass of

---

---

the people who enjoy different aspects of it. Jatra and Jari are common sources of recreation of our rural people. The club is popular in the urban areas. Various types of facilities i.e., games, swimming, dance, songs, music, dinner etc., are the main sources of recreation for the club members in our country.

Bibliography

Afsaruddin, Md. *Sociology and Social Research in Pakistan*, Dacca, 1963.

Alport, F.H. *Institutional Behavior*. University of North Carolina Press, Chapel Hill, 1933.

American Sociological Review, October 1937.

Bessaignet, P. *Social Research in East Pakistan*. Asiatic Society, Dacca. 1960.

Burgess, E.W. and Cottrell, L. S. Jr. *Predicting Success or Failure in Marriages*, Prentice Hall, New York 1939.

Cooley, C.H. *Human Nature and the Social Order*. Charles Scribner's Sons, New York 1922.

Hussain, A.F.A. *Human and social impact of Technological change in Pakistan*. Oxford university Press, Dacca 1956.

Karim, A. *Social History of Muslims in Bengal*. Asiatic Society of Pakistan, Dacca 1959.

Karim, A.K.N. *Changing Society in India and Pakistan*. Ideal Publication, Dacca 1956.

Mallick, A.R. *British Policy and the Muslims in Bengal*. Asiatic Society of Pakistan,

Rahim, M.A. *Social and Cultural History of Bengal*, Vol.I. Karachi. 1963.

Chowdhury, G.W. *Democracy in Pakistan*. Dacca Social Science Research Committee, University of Dacca. Green Book House, 1963.

Levy, R. *The Social Structure of Islam*. Cambridge University Press, 1957.

Spate, O.H.K. *India and Pakistan*. London Methuen and Co. Ltd., 1954.

A Handbook of Basic Democracies. Dacca, Government of East Pakistan, Basic Democracies and Local Government Department, 1964.

Gopal, R. *Indian Muslims : A Political History*. Bombay, Asia Publishing House, 1959.

4—

CHAPTER 5
POPULATION OF PAKISTAN

Pakistan stands sixth in size of population among the countries of the world, surpassed only by China, India, U.S.S.R., U.S.A. and Indonesia. This may be, to some ethnocentrically patriotic Pakistanis, a privilege, but it also means a great challenge which must be encountered to raise the standard of living, as a great part of the entire population in Pakistan is close to the famine level. Pakistan falls under the category "Under-developed and densely populated Countries". Ninety-four million people or so in Pakistan need not constitute a problem, if serious efforts are made to provide all with a fair share of irreducible minimum requirements of a decent human existence.

Indo-Pakistan sub-continent had its first census taking in 1871 and since then it had been repeated every ten years. Although these censuses obtained a large volume of data, the extent of demographic analysis to which they were put was meagre. The census data were also not studied, to any extent, in academic circles. It was in 1941 that, with the development of modern statistical science in the country, statisticians began to take an interest in demographic research and stimulate it. Interest which earlier had been confined largely to the study of death rates and life tables, began to extend to the consideration of problems of differential fertility and of population projection.

Growth of Population : According to an estimated calculation, the territory which now comprises Pakistan had 70 million people in 1941 and perhaps 79 million in 1950.

Table : 1. ESTIMATED POPULATION OF SOME COUNTRIES, 1939-41.[1]

Countries	Year	Area (thousand sq. mile)	Population Million	Density per sq. mile.
Japan	1940	1,47·5	73,114	496
Germany	1939	2,26·3	79,530	352
Pakistan	1941	3,61·0	70,135	194
France	1939	2,12·7	41,200	194
Turkey	1940	2,96·1	17,620	59
Mexico	1940	7,60·2	19,654	26
Chile	1940	2,86·5	5,024	18

Pakistan's density of population in 1941 was 194 (Table-1). France in 1939 had exactly the same number of people living per sq. mile.

The population of East Pakistan grew from 33·3 million in 1921 to 35·6 million, in 1931 and perhaps 42·0 million (this figure is believed to have been artificially inflated to the extent of about 3 per cent) in 1941, the increase being by 7 per cent in the 1921-31 period and about 15 to 18 per cent in the 1931-41 period. The population of West Pakistan increased from 21·1 million in 1921 to 23·6 million in 1931 ; about 28·3 million in 1941 and 33·7 million in 1951, the decennial increase being by 11,20 and 19 per cent, respectively.

The rate of growth of the population of Pakistan from 1901 to 1961 (Table—2) was far from uniform. East Pakistan presents a much more uneven picture than West Pakistan. There was practically no increase of population in East Pakistan from 1941 to 1951. West Pakistan's population has been increasing at a higher rate than that of East Pakistan at each of the last six censuses. At this rate it is likely that West Pakistan's total population will catch up with East Pakistan's population in a few more decades.

1. Davis, Kingsley. *The Population of India and Pakistan*, Princeton University Press ; New Jersey 1951.

Table : 2. GROWTH OF POPULATION IN PAKISTAN FROM 1901 to 1961[1]

Year	Pakistan (In Millions)	E. Pakistan (In Millions)	W. Pakistan (In Millions)
1901	45·5	28·9	16·6
1911	50·9	31·6	19·4
1921	54·4	33·3	21·1
1931	59·2	35·6	23·6
1941	70·3	42·0	28·3
1951[2]	75·8	42·1	33·7
1961[2]	93·7	50·8	42·9

It is significant that in first thirty years from 1901 to 1931 (Table-2) Pakistan's population increased by 13·7 million or by 30 per cent; in the second thirty years the increase has been nearly three times that in the first. In the period from 1931 to 1961, 34·6 million souls were added, which means an increase of 58·5 per cent. East Pakistan grew from 28·9 millions in 1901 to 42·1 million in 1951 adding 13·2 million in 50 years but, in just 10 years from 1951, she has added 8·7 million to her population. West Pakistan nearly trebled her population since 1901, growing from 16·6 million to 42·9 million. Her growth has been more rapid than East Pakistan. In the last ten years 9·2 million have been added to her population.

The total area of Pakistan is 3,65,529 sq. miles of which 3,10,403 sq. miles are in West Pakistan and 55,126 sq. miles in East Pakistan. The two wings of Pakistan,—East and West are separated from each other by more than one thousand miles of Indian territory. West Pakistan with 84·9 per cent of the total area has 45·8 per cent of the population. On the other hand, East Pakistan with only 15·1 per cent of the area has 54·2 per cent of the population (figure 2). During the decade between 1951 to 1961, Pakistan's total Population increased by 23·9%, to which West Pakistan contributed 12·1 per cent and East Pakistan 11·8 per cent (Table 3).

1. Pakistan Census Bulletin—Vol. 2 1961.
2. Including Non-Pakistanis.

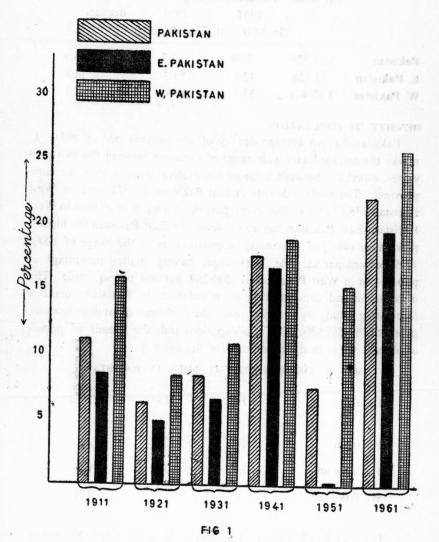

GROWTH of POPULATION
(Percentage of Increase)
1911—1961

PAKISTAN

E. PAKISTAN

W. PAKISTAN

FIG 1

Table : 3. PERCENTAGE OF INCREASE IN THE POPULATION OF PAKISTAN, 1951-'61.

Locality	Area in Sq. Miles	Total[1] Population 1951 (In Millions)	Total[1] Population 1961 (In Millions)	Percentage of in-crease during the decade.
Pakistan	3,65,529	75·8	93·7	23·9
E. Pakistan	55,126	42·1	50·8	11·8
W. Pakistan	3,10,403	33·7	42·9	12·1

DENSITY OF POPULATION

Pakistan has an average density of 256 persons per sq. mile. I marks the extraordinary wide range of variation between the two pro-vinces, especially between large administrative areas within the same province. The average density in East Pakistan is 922 and in West Pakistan 138 (Table 4). For every person on a sq. mile of land in West Pakistan, East Pakistan has about seven. In East Pakistan the highest percentage (48·7) of provincial population is in the range of 1000-1199 persons per sq. mile. The range, having highest percentage of population in West Pakistan is 200-299 persons per sq. mile. The distribution and concentration of population in Pakistan make a fascinating study by bringing out the problems of land utilization, prospects of diversification of occupations and the trends of popul-ation movement in different zones of the country.

Table : 4. DENSITY PER SQ. MILE IN PAKISTAN

Locality	1941	1951	1961
Pakistan	192	207	256
E. Pakistan	762	762	922
W. Pakistan	91	109	138

1. Including Non-Pakistanis. According to the census of 1961, Pakistan has 1,11,369 Non-Pakistanis.

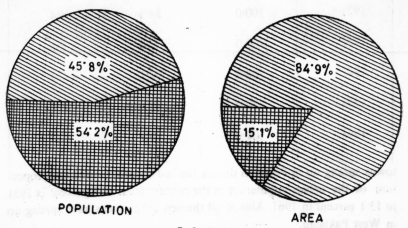

AREA AND POPULATION
1961

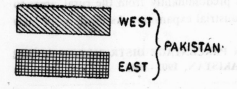

WEST
PAKISTAN
EAST

45·8%

54·2%

POPULATION

84·9%

15·1%

AREA

FIG 2

RURAL AND URBAN DISTRIBUTION

A glance at the Table-5 is sufficient to prove that ever since 1921, there has been acceleration in the trend towards urbanization. This acceleration in the shift of population from rural to urban areas has gained tremendous momentum since the partition. The process of industrial growth has involved radical shifts in the use of manpower and natural resources ; it has entailed drastic alterations in the occupational structures, as well as, in the type and location of major economic activities. The social effects of industrialization has also been diverse. These changes have, in turn, tended to accentuate local inequalities in the scope of social and economic development and thus to give impetus to large-scale movements in the country. The direction of these movements has been predominantly from the rural areas to the urban centres of rapid industrial expansion. As many as lll new

Table : 5. RURAL AND URBAN PERCENTAGE DISTRIBUTION OF THE POPULATION OF PAKISTAN, 1901 - 1961.

Year	Total	Rural	Urban
1901	100·0	94·9	5·1
1911	100·0	95·9	4·1
1921	100·0	94·6	5·4
1931	100·0	93·5	6·5
1941	100·0	92·1	7·9
1951	100·0	89·6	10·4
1961	100·0	86·9	13·1

towns sprang up in Pakistan during the last decade, raising the proportion of the urban population in the country from 10·4 percent in 1951 to 13·1 percent in 1961. Almost all the new urban areas have sprung up in West Pakistan.

Table : 6. RURAL AND URBAN DISTRIBUTION IN PAKISTAN, 1951-61.

Locality	RURAL			URBAN		
	P.C. of Population 1951	P.C. of Population 1961	P.C. De-crease	P.C. of Population 1951	P.C. of Population 1961	P.C. Increase
Pakistan	89·6	86·9	2·7	10·4	13·1	2·7
E. Pakistan	95·6	94·8	·8	4·4	5·2	·8
W. Pakistan	82·2	77·5	4·7	17·8	22·5	4·7

West Pakistan has a proportion of urban population of 22·5 percent while East Pakistan has 5·2 percent (Table-6).

RELIGION

Pakistan is predominantly a Muslim country. There are more than 82·5 million Muslims in Pakistan or 88·8 percent of the total population, and they are far more numerous than any other country of the world. The Muslim population shows quite a rapid growth. There are 45, 90,417 caste Hindus and 54,11,057 scheduled castes in Pakistan. A big fall in Hindu population in 1951 may be attributed to the interchange of population which took place soon after the emergence of Pakistan. Most of the Hindus are settled in East Pakistan.

Table : 7. PERCENTAGE DISTRIBUTION BY RELIGION IN PAKISTAN, 1961.

Religion	Pakistan	West Pakistan	East Pakistan
Muslims	88·8	97·2	80·4
Caste Hindus	4·5	0·4	8·7
Scheduled caste	5·45	1·0	9·8
Christians	0·8	1·3	0·3
Budhists	0·4	0·06	0·7
Others	0·05	0·04	0·1

Christianity has grown faster than all other religions in Pakistan. Ever since 1901 they have increased about 23 times and in the last decade alone the christians have increased by 35·8 percent in Pakistan. The Chiristians form 0·8% of the total population of Pakistan (Table-7). Most of the christians are settled in West Pakistan. During the last population decade (1951-1961), the Buddhists have grown by 17·7% and they form 0·4% of the total population.

AGE AND SEX

An examination of the age structure of the population of Pakistan reveals that during the period, 1951-61, there has been a remarkable rise in both the provinces in the percentage of children below working age, a corresponding fall in the percentage of the working age population between 10-59, and a substantial increase in the proportion of the age group of 60 years and above. Now, the child population in Pakistan is unusually large and the children who are below 10 years of age, form 35·14% of the total population. It is 36·97% in East Pakistan and 32·78% in West Pakistan. They reflect not only the large proportion of inactive or dependent population but also indicate the ever-increasing rate of population growth. According to the 1961 census, in the young age-group of 10-24, there are 25·27% males as against 25·22% females. In the same age group in East Pakistan, females (24·54%) outnumber the males (24·12%), while in West Pakistan, in the same age group the males (26·68%), are more than the females (26·14%) (Table-9).

Table : 8. POPULATION OF PAKISTAN BY SEX[1], 1961.

Locality	Both Sex	Males	Females
Pakistan	9,37,20,613	4,93,08,645	4,44,11,968
E. Pakistan	5,08,40,235	2,63,48,843	2,44,91,392
W. Pakistan	4,28,80,378	2,29,59,802	1,99,20,576

1. Excluding non-Pakistanis.

Table : 9. PERCENTAGE OF MALES AND FEMALES BY AGE IN PAKISTAN 1961.

	Age and Sex	Pakistan	East Pakistan	West Pakistan
BOTH SEX	0-9	35·14	36·97	32·78
	10-24	25·25	24·32	26·44
	25-59	33·65	33·49	33·85
	60 & above	5·96	5·22	6·93
	Total both Sexs.[1]	100·00	100·00	100·00
MALE	0-9	34·10	35·86	31·92
	10-24	25·27	24·12	26·68
	25-59	34·26	34·47	34·02
	60 & above	6·37	5·55	7·38
	Total Males	100·00	100·00	100·00
FEMALE	0-9	36·29	38·16	33·78
	10-24	25·22	24·54	26·14
	25-59	32·97	32·45	33·67
	60 & above	5·52	4·85	6·41
	Total females	100·00	100·00	100·00

1. Excluding non-Pakistanis

Table : 10. PERCENTAGE OF MARITAL STATUS ON THE BASIS OF AGE AND SEX IN PAKISTAN, 1961.

Age Group And Sex[1]		Total	Single	Married	Widowed or Divorced.
BOTH SEX	10-14	100	88·20	11·53	0·27
	15-24	100	42·59	55·93	1·48
	25-34	100	8·97	86·95	4·08
	35-44	100	2·50	86·95	10·55
	45-59	100	1·67	75·97	22·36
	60 & above	100	1·15	56·59	42·26
Both sex total		100	26·14	64·05	9·81
MALE	10-14	100	96·76	3·18	0·06
	15-24	100	68·47	30·56	0·97
	25-34	100	15.58	81·43	2·99
	35-44	100	4·35	90·83	4·82
	45-59	100	2·37	88·92	8·71
	60 & above	100	1·60	77·67	20·73
Male total		100	35·34	59·78	4·88
FEMALE	10-14	100	77·45	22·02	0·53
	15-24	100	15·57	82·32	2·11
	25-34	100	1·99	92·75	5·26
	35-44	100	1·16	82·41	16·43
	45-59	100	0·81	59·33	39·86
	60 & above	100	0·59	29·57	69·84
Female Total		100	15·45	69·12	15·43

1. All persons under 10 are treated as single.

MARITAL STATUS

At the time of the 1961 census in Pakistan there were 58559,502 persons 10 years of age and above. Of this total 26.14% were single (Table 10), 64·05% were married and 9·81% were divorced or widowed. The females on the average are married at a younger age than the males. In 1961, while the married females far exceeded the single females in the age group 15-24, a corresponding excess of the married over the single males did not occur until the 25-34 age group. This obviously illustrates the general tendency among the men towards the high age at marriage. The proportion, married reached its maximum for the females in the 25-34 age group with 92·75% married, and for men ten years older, with 90·83% married, in the age group 35-44. The percentage, married decreased steadily for subsequent age groups as the rise in mortality at older ages brought about an increase in the percentage, widowed. Since the married women tend to outlive their husbands and because the widowed males more frequently remarry than the widowed females, the rate of decrease in the proportion, married was much more rapid for the females than the males.

PROBLEMS

In the present demographic situation of Pakistan, the unevenness in the growth of population, both on the national and local basis, is the most disturbing factor. The two provinces of Pakistan separately, present different pictures. While West Pakistan is thinly populated and more ahead in the field of industrialization, East Pakistan's population is already very dense and she is also lagging behind in technological advancement. The population problems of Pakistan are greatly arising from East Pakistan.

Nowhere the situation is more difficult than the Eastern Zone of Pakistan, where the population pressure is a deadweight on all efforts at socio-economic development.

Geographical diversity nullifies greatly, all homogenity and uniformity in the efforts to tackle the population problem in Pakistan on a national basis. It is for this reason that the possibility of relieving East Pakistan, even to some extent, of its staggering total population through the migration of people from this zone to West Pakistan, has so far not been taken into account very seriously.

The real problem which East Pakistan is facing, is the massive number of the existing population, and so even a modest rate of increase constitutes the problem, because it nullifies all efforts to improve the admittedly very low standard of living of the East Pakistani people. All programmes to increase the production of food and other commodities and services to give a better per capita share to the existing population are either deferred or frustrated as the increasing population overstrains the capacity of education, public health, sanitation, and rural development. Thus in the present circumstances, efforts in raising the standard of living in East Pakistan and the increasing growth of population are incompatible.

Another important problem which is common for both East and West Pakistan, is the effect of urbanization and industrialization on social organization and on the health and well-being of population. The quality of the people is related to the quantity, and it cannot be improved in the context of our available resources, without controlling the quantity.

The demographic situation in any region is largely the product of its peculiar social characteristics, affecting, in their turn, births, deaths and migration. The population problem of Pakistan would be very different if the social institutions of early marriage, universality of marriage and the joint family and other institutions and attitudes, resulting in a high birth rate and a sex ratio in favour of males did not exist. But as these institutions with a socio-religious tradition and cultural sanction behind them exist, the demographic problem has become what it is today.

Early and universal marriage are the dominant features of the Pakistani Social Scene. Here the girls attain puberty between the ages of twelve and fifteen and though often physically and emotionally immature they are physiologically ready to bear children. Particularly in the rural areas the girls marry as soon as they reach puberty, and begin bearing children early with no adequate spacing between child-births—all this resulting in exhaustion and premature death. Early marriages, ill-adviced pregnancies and deliveries, and high maternal and infant mortality—all seem to go together.

The second factor is the universality of the marriage. Every one in East Pakistan, sooner or later, gets married. It is a religious duty. As an individual's economic security is not usually a pre-requisite to marriage and as there is no individual choice, by and large, in obtaining a partner, there is no economic or emotional deterrent to marriage.

The social ban on widow remarriage, among the Hindu population of East Pakistan is reactionary feature of our society. The demographic situation in Pakistan is, to a considerable extent, the product of its social institutions for one undesirable social institution leads to another, and so on in an endless chain. The practice of "social sterilizing" the widows among the Hindus results in a considerable disparity in age between the husbands and wives. Since most widowers remarry, and since they do not marry the widows they have to seek wives among the young girls. This unequal age combination itself leads to an increasing number of widows, for the old husband soon passes away, leaving behind his young wife ; a widow, and of course, she cannot marry. This disproportionate sex ratio and the resulting deficiency of the women keep up the custom of early marriage and consequently the growth of population.

Among all demographic factors, the rate of fertility is the most important. The high,—almost stationary birth rate and the comparatively faster rate of fall in death rate in Pakistan envisage the pupulation, growing at an increasing rate.

The factors leading to high rate of population growth in Pakistan may be enumerated as follows:

1. Early marriages.
2. Low mortality rates.
3. Improved economic conditions and higher level of living, leading to more children (urban phenomenon).
4. Promotion of widow remarriages and withdrawal of social ban on widow remarriage.
5. Relaxation of existing religious and cultural taboos, restricting sexual intimacy.
6. Absence of family planning as an intensified and vigorous system.

FACTORS, AFFECTING FERTILITY AND MORTALITY IN PAKISTAN

The reproductive behavior of the people is commonly believed to be a natural biological reaction between a male and a female. But from the sociological point of view the significance of the problem lies in the fact that human beings are tied up to a culture in the society where their reproductive behavior is always controlled by different factors in society. Let us discuss the important factors favouring the high fertility in Pakistan.

ECONOMIC FACTOR

One of the important factors for high fertility in Pakistan is the economic factor. Thronton in his work on population has pointed out that "misery breeds population". A vast majority of the poverty stricken people in Pakistan tend to have large families. The poorer an individual or a group the larger the size of the family. Poverty of the people has been generally associated with the absence of prudential considerations and a consequent attitude of irresponsibility could not feel the burden of the rapid growth of population as a very serious problem if it would have been an economically developed and industrialized country.

This has made the population growth a serious problem. Large-scale industrialization of Pakistan may give some solutions to the problem of population growth by changing the social structure and pattern of life. These changes in social setting of the people will no doubt reduce their fertility and bring down the population growth as has happended in highly industrialized countries like U.S.A., U.K., France etc.

An overwhelming proportion of the population (about 90%) is dependent on agriculture for their livelihood. Since agricultural methods tend to be, some what, static and inefficient, industrialization is considered a vital measure for relieving the population pressure on the land, for increasing the total national income and to raise the standard of living. The presence of many untaped natural resources with the surplus man power is considered a favourable condition for industrialization in Pakistan. But industrialization will not take its proper shape until the limiting factors such as shortage of capital, deficiencies in skilled and semi-skilled labourers and technical hands, shortage of entrepreneurs, lack of marketing facilities both in and outside the country, presence of crude techniques of production, old type production relations and cultural and social resistance to new innovation in the economic institutions are removed by the joint endeavour of the government and the capitalist class of the country. So long the process of industrialization is not given the top priority in Pakistan, no amount of propaganda will be able to exert any significant influence on the fertility of the people of the country because any super-imposed idea on the society will not give any good result unless the structure and mechanism of that society create a strong base for accepting the idea.

EDUCATIONAL FACTOR

The illiteracy of the vast majority of the people in Pakistan is the important cause of high fertility because of their ingnorance about the population growth and consequent effect of the pressure of our population on the economic, social and political life of the country. They do not have any idea of the control of fertility. We do not have reliable statistical data on fertility on the basis of education. But observation of fertility in relation to the education of husband and wife has generally shown that higher the grade of education, the fewer the number of children.

RELIGIOUS FACTOR

The illiteracy of the people has given religious orthodoxy, conservatism, prejudice and fatalistic attitude towards life. It is true that the people in our country, specially in rural and semi-urban areas traditionally believe that what God has planned and fixed for them must happen. This faith in fatalism is the contribution of the religion of the people. Due to fatalism every type of misfortune and calamity is thought to be sent by God as punishment to the sinners. That is why, when a misfortune comes for which scientific, objective and rational explanation might be found, the people would consider it the just punishment, coming direct from God and therefore, it is impossible to find any remedy of it.

In many cases, the people are seen to be aware of the fact that the growth of population is at the root of the deterioration in the economic conditions in the country. But as births are in the hands of God, the decline in economic conditions is certainly due to the will of God and the homosapiens by their own efforts cannot improve their condition. We can see the people, being aware of the problem of population

5—

growth and population pressure in every sphere of the society, are not in favour of birth control which is, according to them, goes against the religious faith and the fatalistic attitude towards whole life.

Thus inspite of poverty, distress, hardship caused by reckless breeding, the people of Pakistan do not effectively respond to the propaganda of family planning to which our present Govt. is giving more and more attention. The widow remarriage and the practice of polygamy, permitted by the religion of Islam give impetus to the high fertility among the Muslims. On the contrary, the Hindu religion tabooed these two institutions of the widow remarriage and the polygamy which reduce the fertility a bit among the Hindus.

In addition to the factors, discussed above there are other factors like universal and early marriage, lack of recreational facilities, aspiration for a son, low status enjoyed by a childless woman and high child mortality rate, responsible for high fertility in Pakistan.

FACTORS AFFECTING MORTALITY

The chief causes of the high death rate in our country are the various epidemic diseases, poverty and the consequent malnutritions and insanitary houses and inadequacy of medical aid. Cholera, small pox, malaria, tuberculosis and other diseases take away a large mumber of people every year. Most of the deaths are among the infants. It was estimated in pre-partition India that infant mortality ranged between 170 and 180 per 1,000 births. A person in Pakistan lives, on the average, 32 years as compared to 60 or more in various western countries. Female mortality is also high in Pakistan. This is due to particular social conditions under which the females receive much less care and, sometimes, live in insanitary seclusion under the purdah system. Moreover, the mortality rate of women in child birth is high due to ignorance, the custom of their early marriage, early pregnancy and the lack of medical facilities.

INTERNAL AND EXTERNAL MIGRATION IN PAKISTAN

The first problem which one faces in the study of the internal and external migration of Pakistan, is the non-availability of relevant data. The volumes of population census of Pakistan fail to give us any information whatsoever, concerning the out-migration and internal migration ; and in the section of in-migration the only available data are about the population exchange which took place after the partition of Indo-Pakistan sub-continent. In the 1951 census of Pakistan a separate enumeration of the Muhajirs was made. It is therefore, a difficult task to give an empirical base to this part of the study.

As most of the available evidence points to Asia as the original home of man ; so it is legitimate to believe that, for most of the period man has lived in this world and Indo-Pakistan sub-continent has witnessed the habitation of mankind. The excavations of Mainamati in East Pakistan and Harappa, Mohenjodaro, and Taxila in West Pakistan, clearly indicate that in the territory which is now known as Pakistan, there have flourished civilizations much before than any of the recorded civilization of history.

In this section, we limit ourself to the partition of the Sub-continent into India and Pakistan and deal with the Internal and External Migration in Pakistan, under three heads e.g. (a) Refugees, (b) Emigrants, (c) Internal Migration.

REFUGEES

There have been many forced movements in the history of mankind, but they were mostly due to war or tyranny. They were caused by a number of factors;—either they tried to escape the religious and political persecution or it was the memory of persecution and extermination and the fear of their recurrence which drove them away from homes. Even forced transfer and exchange of ethnic groups are recorded in history. There are countries where a mass of humanity has been deported for forced labour or even exterminated. At times, war has resulted in exchange of population as a repatriation movement. But in the case of refugees from India to Pakistan and from Pakistan to India which was the outcome the of exchange of population after the partition of the sub-continent, it was a different movement.

A refugee is defined as a person who would not like to migrate from his homeland ; but for reasons beyond his control,—political, religious or economic, that might have rendered his life unbearable. Pakistani Muhajirs are defined as "Persons who moved into

Pakistan as a result of partition and for fear of disturbances, connected therewith."[1]

The partition of Bengal and the formation of East Pakistan caused the emigration of about 3 million Hindus, only partly compensated by an immigration of fewer than one million Moslems."[2] The 1943 Bengal famine and the loss of 2 million people after partition, account for the fact that during 1941-51 the population of East Pakistan grew by only 0.1 million. In West Pakistan, the immigration of the Muslims was greater than the out-migration of the Hindus. "There was an immigration of about 6 million Moslems and an emigration of about 4 million Hindus and members of other religious communities."[3] The increase of population in West Pakistan by 19 percent during the decade of 1941-51, is partly due to the population exchange which followed the partition. Though the exchage of population after the partition did not affect the over-all population growth of Pakistan but on the regional basis, it wrecked the economy of newly established Pakistan and resulted in great social disorder.

Separate enumeration was made for the "Muhajirs" in the 1951 census of Pakistan and a similar but separate enumeration of displaced persons was also made in the 1951 census of India. The number of 'Muhajirs', counted in East Pakistan was 699,000. The number of displaced persons from East Pakistan, counted in India was 2,549,000. The number of Muhajirs, counted in West Pakistan was 6,528,000. The number of displaced persons from West Pakistan, counted in India was 4,700,000. Though these figures are of considerable value, they do not constitute an exact balance of movements between the partition and the date of the Indian and Pakistani censuses of 1951, because there were variations of the extent to which the childern of the refugees were included in the count, and because it was not ascertained from which part of Pakistan the additional 47,000 displaced persons in India had come.[4]

1. Yusuf, Muhammad. "Population of Pakistan and its characteristics" Proceedings of world population conference, 1954, Rome, 31, August-10, September 1954 (United Nations Publication) PP.67-104.

2. & 3. United Nations., The Population of Asia and the Far East, 1950-1980 ; New York, Department of Economic and Social Affairs 1959. P. 12-13.

4. Ibid P. 52.

The recent communal disturbances in India and Pakistan which took place in the first quarter of 1964, have again impelled migration of the Muslims from India to Pakistan and of Hindus from Pakistan to India. "Exchange of Population" is still continuing. This uprooted a mass of humanity, which constitutes a major problem. The refugees are frightened, frustrated, dislocated and confused, with no idea of the future. They have lost all they had and have been cut off from their own family members without knowledge of what had happened to them. The Government of Pakistan is facing the same problem which it had to face just after the partition i.e., the rehabilitation of the refugees and thus to create an order out of the social disorder.

EMIGRANTS

The partition had changed the definition of movement between certain areas of India and Pakistan. What had been internal migration became external (i.e., international) migration. Emigration and Immigration between Pakistan and India have been dealt with under the caption 'Refugee'.

The density, poverty and peculiarity of social organization are the conditions, discouraging immigration from the foreign countries other than India. There is little prospect that Pakistan will become an area of net in-migration, but there is every likelihood that it will continue to be an area of net out-migration.

Attempts in the enumeration of the emigrants were indeed made by the Government of Pakistan, but a complete census of Pakistanis who have emigrated to other lands, temporarily or otherwise, has never been possible.

The British rule came to an end in this sub-continent on the 14th August, 1947 ; but the link between Great Britain and the part of the globe now known as Pakistan, has not been severed and in fact due to that association Great Britain is the Principal country to receive the immigrants from Pakistan. Those who have attended the occasional Pakistani gatherings in Britain (at one gathering in London in 1960 over 7,000 Pakistanis attended) and are familiar with the number of new passports, issued to Pakistani nationals in this country by the Pakistan High Commission in London, are inclined to believe that there cannot be fewer than 100,000 Pakistanis in the British Isles.

The number of passports, issued by the Pakistan High Commission in this country runs into six figures (upto the middle of 1960) which does not include the passports, issued in Pakistan for those, travelling to the U.K. Many Pakistanis in Britain are, in fact, without passports."[1]

Apart from Great Britain no estimate is available about Pakistanis, living in foreign countries.

INTERNAL MIGRATION

Internal migration in Pakistan consists mainly of the movements from rural areas to urban centres of rapid industrial and commercial expansion. A number of urban areas has been gaining in population far beyond what might have been expected from natural increase alone, whereas not a few rural areas have been losing population more or less consistently. A brief comparison of the rate of growth within the two provinces indicates large-scale population movements and greater development opportunities in West Pakistan and a rather immobile population with little room to shift the pressure in East Pakistan (Table 6).

The scope of the possibility of internal migration as a method of relieving the population pressure in East Pakistan is much wide. We know that the two wings of Pakistan show a contrasting picture in density of population. While the Western wing is very scantily populated the Eastern wing has the credit of carrying the weight of 922 persons per square mile. But before materializing the project of inter-wing migration from East Pakistan to West Pakistan, the deserts of Sind and Baluchistan will have to be reclaimed. Two small batches of the East Pakistani farmers have been settled around the Ghulam Mohammad Barrage in Sind. But in order to relieve East Pakistan of her population pressure, to some extent, such inter-wing group migrations should be frequently undertaken and should be carried out in a systematic way i.e., to relieve those parts of East Pakistan where the density of population is relatively high and to settle them at places in West Pakistan where they can adjust themselves geographically and temperamentally.

There are several factors which discourage the inter-wing migration from East Pakistan to West Pakistan. The primary factor is the

---

1. Hunter, Kathleen. History of Pakistanis in Britain ; London. Page Bros. (Norwich) Ltd., Page 2.

physical feature, that the two wings of Pakistan are separated by a big gap of more than one thousand miles of a foreign territory. The poor mass of the East Pakistani agriculturists cannot affortd to spend a considerable amount of money for trying their lucks in the Western wing. Besides this consideration, several other factors of social, economic and religious nature, characteristic of Pakistani economy, can be cited to explain the traditional immobility of the Pakistani population and the slender volume of internal migration. The principle of 'stay-at-home' of the Pakistani population is also a regular feature.

The economic reason of this immobility is simple. As the majority of the people are wedded to an agricultural life, and since land is a chief source of sustenance, the average East Pakistani peasant cannot possibly leave the farm on which he was born and where he works. It is not that agriculture in Pakistan is in such a paying position that it renders the emigration to urban areas or to West Pakistan unattractive. In Pakistan agriculture is not just an occupation, but a way of life to an overwhelming majority of population. There is an incredibly large rural indebtedness that chains the peasants to their mortgaged homesteads.

Certain social factors also contribute to the essential home-living character of the Pakistani people. Caste, language and the diversities of regional and communal mores render severance from home, village or town, uncomfortable. In these circumstances, the internal migration offers no substantial relief from the population pressure. And the partition of the country which has already forced upon both Pakistan and India communal migrations, renders the prospects of further internal migration dim, unless the government plans a systematic transfer of population.

POPULATION GROWTH AND POLICY IN PAKISTAN

Human arithmetic is basic and simple : births minus deaths equal the growth or decline of world population. But the implications of population trends are infinitely complex, interwoven as they are in the tangled affairs and the aspirations of the human race. Modern man lives with an unprecedented anxiety,—rapid population growth which springs from his own ingenuity in deferring death.[1] Death rates have

---

1. Population Bulletin, Pop. Reference B. Vol. XVIII No. 3 May 1962, INC.

72   SOCIOLOGY OF PAKISTAN

declined in Pakistan, while birth rates remain traditionally high. Over-large population, which are already straining the economy and available resources of Pakistan will double in about 28 years.

Pakistan has had only a brief career as an independent country. Her people have, no doubt, a long history. After independence tremendous changes have occurred in the size and composition of the population in Pakistan. Therefore, past demographic trends cannot definitely be cited as being representative of present day conditions in Pakistan. Moreover vital statistics, available in this country are of poor quality. With all these limitations and inadequacies past demographic trends are still essential in understanding the population growth problem in post-independence period.

PRE-PARTITION POPULATION

The population census of undivided India does not date back very far as the year of the first census was 1871. In 1871 the population of India was officially put at 203.4 million. The 1871 census, however, did not cover all the areas of the country and was believed to have under-enumerated the total population by about 52 million. In view of this, and by a backward projection of 1881 census data, the estimate for 1871 was later revised upwards to 255 million.[2] By 1941, the population increased further to 388.9 million indicating an increase of 52% in 70 years. During this 70-year period, the population grew by fits and starts, —period of rapid increase alternating with periods of very slow increase.

The extremely sporadic nature of the population increase is shown below:

Percentage increase of Population from 1881 to 1941[3]

Year	Percentage of increase
1881	0·9
1891	9·4
1901	1·0
1911	6·1
1921	0·9
1931	10·6
1941	15·0

According to the table, it is only since 1921 that the period of oscillation has stopped and population has increased steadily. The increase

2. Davis, K. The Population of India and Pakistan. Princeton University Press, 1951. PP. 24-27.
3. Ibid. P. 28

of 9·7% from 1921 to 1931 and 4·4% from 1931 to 1941 was recorded in
the censuses. Thus the accelerated population growth in the subcontinent started only about 45 years back. This rapid increase of population
since 1921 has been accounted for by a quick drop in death rates. Since
1921 the death rate has gradually declined from about 40 per 1000
to, by 1945 about 22 per 1000. Thus in 24 years as much as 18
points had been knocked off the death rate, while Europe took more
than a century to show a 20-point death rate decline.[4] In undivided
India the death rate fell quickly because of the modern medical services
available to the people ; but the fertility rate declined only slightly
from an average of about 39 in the quinquennium, 1911-15 to about
38 in 1941-45. It is true that in the large cities, the birth rate was
slightly lower than in the villages, but there was no positive evidence
that a general decline in the birth rate had been initiated in the general
areas. It is interesting to mention here that the Muslims generally
constituted the larger proportion of the urban population in the
smaller cities. They also registered a faster rate of increase in literacy
than did the Hindus. Despite this the Muslim population had a higher
fertility rate than any other religious communities in the subcontinent.
From 45·5 million or 19·97% of the total population in 1901, the
Pakistanis increased to 93·7 million or 24·28 per cent in 1961,
doubling itself in 60 years. After partition the population census reports of 1951 and 1961 show a steady increase of population in Pakistan.

The following figures of the increase of population in each successive
decade from 1901 to 1961 show the rapid rate of growth of population
in Pakistan :

Growth of population, 1901-1961[5] (Pop. in million).

Year		East Pakistan		West Pakistan		Pakistan
1901	:	28·9	:	16·6	:	45·5
1911	:	31·6	:	19·3	:	50·9
1921	:	33·3	:	21·1	:	54·4
1931	:	35·6	:	23·6	:	59·2
1941	:	42·0	:	28·3	:	70·3
1951	:	42·1	:	33·7	:	75·8
1961	:	50·8	:	42·9	:	93·7

4. Lewis, A. W. The Theory of Economic Growth. George Allen & Unwin
Ltd., London, 1956. P. 315.
5. Davis, K., The Population of India and Pakistan. Princeton University
Press, 1951 and Pakistan Censuses of 1951, 1961.

The unexpected population increase of 23·8% in 10 years,—from 1951 to 1961 may seriously threaten all the development programmes in Pakistan. This growth of population by 2·4% per year has created an alarming situation in Pakistan. If this situation continues for some years the economy of the country is sure to break down and Malthus' positive check of population is sure to play its role in Pakistan. This has become a great concern of the Govt., of Pakistan. The Govt., as its population policy, has chosen the family planning as a measure to check the rapid growth of population. Different voluntary organizations with the full support of the Govt., of Pakistan are contributing much for the propagation of family planning among the cross section of the population of Pakistan.

The economic progress in Pakistan has been slow. During the First Five-Year Plan of 1955-1960, it became evident that per capita income was increasing slowly. The rate of population growth was almost unknown during the 1950's although a commonly used figure was the official estimate of 1·4 per cent per annum. This figure was not well-based nor seriously regarded although the correct figure was not known. In 1959, well before the 1961 census gave some basis for estimating the rates of growth. Said Hasan, Deputy chairman of Pakistan's Planning Commission remarked as follows : "When the First Five-Year Plan was being framed I urged....that the rate of population growth should not be shown as higher than 1·4% .....We are, however, all convinced that population is growing faster than that."[6]

During the mid-1950's intellectuals, including the economists in the Planning Commission were interested in and concerned about the impact of the population growth on the economic development. In the principal cities a small but articulate planned parenthood group was increasingly active. Moreover, there was the example of India which had first shown concern about the population growth in the early 1950's, and had developed an active programme to reduce the rates of growth by the middle of that decade.

Although the First special meeting on Family Planning was called by the Director General of Health Services of Pakistan in February, 1958 and Rs. 500,000 were sanctioned for family planning it is difficult

---

6. First Five-Year Plan of Pakistan (1955-'60) Govt., of Pakistan.

to fix the time when Pakistan adopted its policy to reduce the rate of population growth.[7]

The New Govt., which assumed power in October, 1958, took a more vigorous stand on population and in 1959, additional funds for family planning were sanctioned. The Director General of Health Services was given the responsibility of implementing the new family planning policy. In 1960 he described the policy as follows:

The Government of Pakistan has recognised the challenge of increasing population pressures in the country and the evil effects of uncontrolled child birth on maternal and child health, domestic prosperity and national economic development. The Govt., has, therefore, taken a bold and clear decision in favour of family planning and has accordingly provided a substantial sum of Rs. 30·5 million for expenditure towards this purpose during the second Five-Year Plan (1960-1965) of Pakistan. A family planning scheme would be operative throughout the country. This grand plan has been given effect from 1965. The aim of the scheme is to encourage the parents to practise birth control entirely on a voluntary basis with a view to:

(a) Spacing of children at suitable intervals to ensure the maternal and child health ;

(b) Helping the parents to limit the number of children so as to ensure good and healthy upbringing within the family's means and thus ensure domestic prosperity ;

(c) Controlling the population growth in relation to available and potential resources of Pakistan.

Overgrowth and overpopulation beyond the limit of national resources place increasing strain on the national economy.

Food shortages, unemployment, illiteracy and ill health confront a nation with serious situations. Pakistan, once a food surplus area, is now a food deficit area, partly because the population has grown so rapidly. Constant improvements in health facilities and gigantic health measures such as malaria eradication and T.B. control, now under way will sharply cut down the death rates in Pakistan.

If the birth rate is allowed to remain high an undue increase in population and consequent dependency load will be inevitable and the national progress will indeed be hampered. Inspite of tremendous

7. Haque, M. S. "Family Planning in Pakistan."

achievements in the economic field during the last 13 years of national existence, the average per capita income in Pakistan is as low as 14 annas a day. Such an unfavourable situation, which cannot but cause serious deterioration in the health and welfare of the people and negate all developmental efforts, cannot be viewed lightly. Here lies the philosophy behind Pakistan Government's resolve to undertake the policy of population control through an organized Family Planning Campaign.

"A Family Planning Scheme to be operated throughout the entire country has now been prepared with the following objectives : (1) To improve the Health of mother, children and family ; (2) To check the rate of population growth through voluntary participation of the people; (3) To improve the socio-economic condition of the people and thereby of the nation ; (4) To provide wholesome information to the people on the necessity and feasibility of family planning ; (5) To reduce the number of marital pregnancies terminating in abortions; (6) To make people family-minded and to help them understand the real value of family life, its responsibilities and obligations ; (7) To provide training in techniques and information on the purpose and philosophy of family planning to the medical and nursing personnels of the country to enable them to render service to the people in their respective areas, (8) To orient and educate the social welfare and village-Aid workers and the Basic Democrats to the ideology of family planning so that they might, in turn, create wholesome awareness amongst the masses, they serve and whenever possible render services in this connection".[8]

Pakistan has taken up a vigorous family planning programme. The Second Five Year Plan allocates 30·5 million rupees for the purpose of family planning. The family planning budget is 7·6% of the total health budget of Rs. 400 million. The family planning programme today aims at the training of the medical and paramedical personnel in family planning, adding family planning services to the existing medical centres, planning for a National Research Institute of Family planning, undertaking limited clinical studies of some of the new methods of contraception, small-scale experimentation with mobile and visual vans in the areas where there are no medical centres and some limited use of the mass media

8. Sharif, M. "Outlook for Govt., action in Family Planning" in Research in Family Planning, ed. by G. V. Kaiser.

of communication such as radio, films and slides in cinemas, posters and newspaper articles. Although family planning is a new service with the Health Directorate, grade levels are modest. No special incentives have been incorporated into the programme to attract the people. Similarly, clinics where the family planning services have been added to the existing services are not properly managed. Lack of trained personnels and relatively weak organizational structure are the major obstacles to the development of a programme which has a significant and measurable impact on the growth rate. Once these obstacles are removed additional financing will be needed. As to the success and popularity, M.S. Haque says, "Two years of the plan period have just finished and there are, at present, about 1600 family planning clinics in the country; roughly 1025 in West Pakistn and 575 in East Pakistan. The attendance at the clinics, however, has not been as good as hoped and during the year 1961, from January to December, the total number of visits in West Pakistan were 117,000 and in East Pakistan 107,000".[9] There is little comparable experience by which to judge Pakistan's programme, although one would count it as a success of a reduction, for example, of the birth rate by 10 points from 45 per 1000 population to 35 in 10 years. It is much too early to expect a reduction in the birth rate of Pakistan. The current programme must be intensified and expanded if significant results are to be achieved at a relatively early date; but the major initial decision has been made..... to try to bring about a reduction in the rate of population growth through family planning.[10]

Pakistan today is in exactly the same position as the western countries were in the early stages of the Industrial Revolution. It is somewhat significant that we have not as yet been able to device the ways and means of avoiding the dangers, attached to such economic and social changes. It requires collaborative work by the demographers and other social scientists to help in the formulation of suitable policies.

Some thirtyfive years ago John Maynard Keynes wrote, "The time has already come when each country needs a considered national policy about what size of population, whether large or small than at

---

9. Haque, M. S. "Family Planning in Pakistan".
10. Qureshi, M.L. Population Growth and Economic Development with special Reference to Pakistan, Institute of Development Economics, Karachi.

present, or the same, is more expedient. And having settled this policy, we must take steps to carry it into operation."

What is the population policy of Pakistan? What could be the optimum size of Pakistan's population? The question of quantity would normally continue to be the major problem. But it is fact that the most desirable quantity of the population is the one that attains the maximum production, highest standard of living, political stability, economic security and adequate freedom and leisure for the pursuit of cultural values. The question that arises now is how we can be both self-sufficient and raise our standard when our population is growing first.

The solution of the problem of growth of population in Pakistan can be effected in two ways: by the rapid economic development of the country and by checking the birth rate. The first way i.e., the rapid economic development is discussed here. As it has already been mentioned in this section, there exists the possibility of relieving East Pakistan which is thickly populated by encouraging the inter-wing migration to West Pakistan, which is sparsely populated.

For the economic development of Pakistan, Agriculture in the country, has to be improved and also the industrialization of the country is to be carried on in a rapid scale.

AGRICULTURE

From the point of view of the irreducible requirements of decent human existence, our resources as they are available today are behind our needs. As for food production alone, all our efforts are directed towards making our country self-sufficient at the present low standard of nutrition. The total agricultural structure is based on the primitive system but the situation does not mean, however, that there is no scope for improving the agriculture in East Pakistan. With modern methods of agricultural science of erosion-preventing and soil reclamation, consolidation of holdings, improved methods of cultivation, proper manuring, and the irrigation and drainage system, the cultivated land could probably be made to double its present yield; and some, at least, of the uncultivable waste could be brought under profitable cultivation.

INDUSTRIALIZATION

While it is obvious that Pakistan is bound to remain an agrarian economy for many decades to come, Pakistan's industrialization is important in the solution of her population problems for, at least, two reasons. First, it could increase the productivity of labour and create an abundance of badly needed commodities and services and transform the present economy of near-scarcity into an economy of sufficiency, if not of possible abundance. But here again, it could only do so if sufficient capital and skill are available to overtake the population increase. Secondly, and this is perhaps more important for East Pakistan, industrialization could encourage the development of new urban patterns of living which often leads to the control of the birth rate. It has been proved in countries like U.K., U.S.A., and Japan that industrialization and high standard of living have been accompanied by a declining fertility.

POPULATION DYNAMICS IN EAST PAKISTAN

Population, food, and Inter-Continental Ballistic Missiles are the main problems facing mankind today. Money and man-power are lavished on projects concerned with the development of nuclear weapons but there is little evidence that most governments take the other problems seriously. Their importance is bound to increase as the rate of world population growth goes beyond thirty million per year at which it now stands and as the natural resources are further depleted.

The growth of human population is strongly influenced by social and cultural factors which are much less important in other species. For all that, Homosapien is an animal and many aspects of his relationship with his environment, with other species, and with other members of his own species should be open to biological analysis.

A Problem of First Magnitude : The population problem has become one of the most fundamental of all human problems. It affects every aspect of man's social life—individual, national and international. It affects the health and happiness of individual families ; it affects the material prosperity and social progress of nations ; and it affects international security and peace, for the problems of population pressure are connected with issues of Peace and War.

In our subject there seems to be a definite difference between the outlooks of the biologist and the sociologist. The biologist tries to work from the law of organic nature, which he derives from a study of the whole animal kingdom including man, whereas the sociologist tries to derive the principles from the observation of the ways of life of human societies only.

A purely biological growth is liable to give incomplete and sometimes, even misleading results. If we are to understand the changes that actually take place it will be necessary to consider the social rather than the biological aspects of the problem. Human demography lies on the border line between the biological and social sciences ; but it has more in common with the latter than the former.

GROWTH OF POPULATION

To many countries of the world today,—free and colonial, developed and underdeveloped—no socio-economic issue is more grave or more urgent than that of population growth. Whether the problem takes the form of tremendous pressure of population on a country's available land and other resources or conflict between a high-fertility cultural milieu and a desire for a higher standard of living, or the degree of technological conditions in many countries are such that rapid population growth militates against the rising standards of living.

Staggering Statistics : The world's population is now larger than it has been before. According to reliable estimates the population of the world has increased from 456 million in 1650 to 2,350 million in 1950 and is increasing by some 30 million a year. The population of the world has reached three thousand million before the mid of 1962 and is growing at an annual rate of about 1·7 per cent. It is estimated that over 100 million babies are now being born every year and some 50 million people are dying. The resulting yearly increment of about 50 millon is as large as the entire population of Italy.

Population growth is most rapid in economically and technologically underdeveloped areas of Africa, Asia and Latin America where well over half the world's people live. At least two thirds of all the babies born each year are born in these areas. Pakistan is now the 6th largest country in the world from the population point of view. The total population of Pakistan now stands at 93,812,000 (1961) while it was

World Population Growth

Year	Population In Millions
1650	465
1750	660
1800	836
1850	1,096
1900	1,551
1929	1,820
1930	1,988
1937	2,147
1947	2,330
1950	2,350

75,866,000, ten years ago. The population of East Pakistan has jumped up from 42,063,000 (1951) to 50,844,000 (1961) giving rise to the density of population from 762 to 922. The position is not so alarming when we look at the density of Pakistan's population which according to the recent census stands at 256. Average number of persons living per sq. mile in West Pakistan is only 136. One of the most striking features of the Pakistan's population is that the country is most unevenly populated. While the western part of our country is very much scantily populated the Eastern Zone has abnormally thick population.

The following tables give a complete picture of the changes in the population structure of East Pakistan in comparison with the other parts of the country :

Area, Population and Literacy, 1961

Locality	Area Sq. miles	Population (1,000's)	Persons per sq. mile	Literates Number (100's)	Literates Percentage of total Population
East Pakistan	55126	50844	922	89360	17.6
West Pakistan	300839	40815	136	47726	11.7
Federal Territory (former) of Karachi	9564	2153	225	6741	31.3
Pakistan	365529	93712	256	143827	15.3

6—

Population by sex in 1951 and 1961

| Locality | Population (1000's) | | | | | | Percentage increase over preceding census |
| | 1961 | | | 1951 | | | |
	Male	Female	Total	Male	Female	Total	
East Pakistan	26522	24322	50844	22039	20024	42063	20.9
West Pakistan	21748	19067	40815	17445	15138	32583	25.3
Federal Territory of Karachi	1215	838	2053	696	524	1220	76.5
Pakistan	49485	44227	93712	40180	35686	75866	23.9

Apart from the staggering total of East Pakistan's population and the rapid pace at which it is growing, there is one other disturbing factor in the present day's demographic situation, and that is, the unevenness in the growth of the population, both on the national and local basis. And perhaps the most disquieting feature is that a great majority of East Pakistan's population has a poor standard of living. Despite the great advancement of modern science and technological skill around the world, a majority of East Pakistan's population is denied even the bare necessities of civilized existence.

Nowhere the situation is more difficult than in Eastern Zone of Pakistan where the population problem has become alarming in recent years. East Pakistan's population problem arises primarily out of an extremely high fertility accompanied by a relatively high but declining mortality. The resulting increase in population, which amounts to nearly 878100 a year, apart from its very low survival value, need not constitute for us a problem if in East Pakistan the level of living were high enough to absorb the additional population without reducing the existing standard of living. But our level of living is so low that any further addition to the number of poor families may well be disastrous, and as they are so numerous it may be generalised that the population as such will find further increase a great problem.

Asset That is Liability : The net addition of 878,100 a year on a grand total of 50844000 in East Pakistan can be an asset and become really a resource if an over-whelming majority of the population, not to speak of every man, woman and child, enjoyed the irreducible minimum requirements of decent human existence in terms of food, clothing, shelter, education, health, employment and leisure for re- creation. But this is not so in East Pakistan, and what is worse is the well-known and depressing qualitative aspect of our population problem. And as the quality of the people is related to the quantity, it cannot be improved in the context of the quantity. Hence the danger in the number of East Pakistan's teeming millions is not only to her overall economic and social development but also to her place in the national life and the modern world.

Pakistan vs. Population : The real problem which East Pakistan is facing is not the rate of increase but the net addition to the existing population every decade. Because of the massive number of the exi- sting population, even a modest rate of increase of 10 or 15 per cent constitutes the problem because it nullifies all the efforts to improve the admittedly very low standard of living of the East Pakistani people. All programmes to increase the production of food and other com- modities and services to give a better per capita share to the existing population are either deferred or frustrated as the increasing popula- tion overstrains the capacity of education, public health, sanitation, and rural development. Thus in the present circumstances, efforts at raising the standard of living in East Pakistan and the increasing growth of population are incompatible.

SOCIO-ECONOMIC PROBLEMS

Prof. Jullian Huxley has "recently described the rapid increase in the world's population as a "population explosion" arising from a world modification of the incidence of births." We, in East Pakistan are experiencing our full share of that "explosion".

Social Problems : The demographic situation in any region is the product of its peculiar social characteristics, affecting in their turn births, deaths and migration. The population problem in East Pakistan would be very different if the social institution of early marriage, universality of marraige and the joint family and other institutions and attitudes resulting in a high birth rate and sex ratio in favour of males, did not exist. But as these institutions with a socio-religious tradition and cultural sanction behind them exist and condition the lives of an over-whelming majority of the people, the demographic problem has become what it is today.

Early and universal marriage are the dominant features of the East Pakistani social scene. Here the girls attain the puberty between the ages of twelve and fifteen and though often, physically and emotionally immature they are physiologically ready to bear children. Particularly in the rural areas the girls marry as soon as they reach the puberty and begin bearing children early with no adequate spacing between child births—all this resulting in exhaustion and premature death. Early marriages, ill-advised pregnancies and deliveries, and high maternal and infant mortality—all seem to go together.

The second factor is the universality of the married state. Every one in East Pakistan, sooner or later, gets married. It is a religious duty. As an individual's economic security is not usually a prerequisite to marriage and as there is no individual choice, by and large, in obtaining a partner, there is no economic or emotional deterrent to marriage.

The Vicious Chain : The social ban on widow-remarriage, among the Hindu population of East Pakistan is yet another reactionary feature of our society. The East Pakistani demographic situation is, to a considerable extent, the product of its social institutions, for one undesirable social institution leads to another, and so on, in an endless chain. The practice of "social sterilizing" the widows among the Hindus, results in a considerable disparity in age between the husbands and wives. Since most widowers remarry and since they do not marry the widows, they have to seek their wives among the girls much junior to them. This unequal age combination itself leads to an increasing number of widows, for the old husband soon passes away, leaving behind his young wife,—a widow, and of course, she cannot marry. The disproportionate sex ratio and the resulting deficiency of women keep up the customs of early marriage and consequently the growth of population.

Among all the demographic factors, the rate of fertility is the most important. The high almost stationary birth rate and the comparatively faster rate of fall in death rate in East Pakistan envisage the population, growing at an increasing rate for, at least, within this century.

It would be of interest in this connection to observe the position of East Pakistan in the demographic transition types recongnized in human fertility pattern by several demographers.

1) In the first type, both the birth and the death rates are high and nearly equal, resulting in stationary or very slowly increasing population. This pattern is being wiped out and is now found in only certain African countries.

2) In the second type, the birth rate remains high, while the death rate begins to decline resulting in a moderate population growth but with the potentiality of rapid growth. Most of the underdeveloped countries in Asia, including India, China and Pakistan fall in this type.

3) In the third type, the high birth rates continue without any tendency to fall while the death rates remain fairly low, resulting in what has been termed the "population explosion". The growth of population is very rapid in this set-up. Ceylon, Malaya and Formosa in Asia, and some other countries in Latin America fall in this category.

4) The fourth type is marked by declining birth rates and low death rates with a consequent slowing down of the rate of population growth. USSR, Canada, Japan, etc., fall in this type.

5) In the fifth type the birth rates have declined substantially and with the low death rate, the rate of population growth is moderate. The U.S.A. and some Western European countries are of this type.

The factors leading to high fertility in East Pakistan may be enumerated as follows :

1) Early marriage.

2) Lower mortality rates.

3) Improved economic condition and higher level of living, leading to more children (Urban phenomenon).

4) Promotion of widow remarriage and withdrawal of social ban on widow remarriage.

5) Relaxation of existing religious and cultural taboos, restricting sexual intimacy.

6) Absence of family planning as an intensified and vigorous system.

Births Defeat Deaths : The population growth during the last century has been conditioned, to a considerable extent, by the high but fluctuating death rate. Though the death rate in East Pakistan shows a gradual declining tendency, yet the position here is about 30 deaths per thousand per annum—higher than what the death rate should have been in East Pakistan. The death rate rises distressingly during the bad years when the rain fails, crops wither, famine and epidemics break out and natural calamities appear. Despite the infantile, maternal and overall mortality rate the average annual addition to the population of East Pakistan continues to be above 8 lakh.

Economic Problem : Five million fifty one lakh, and thirty four thousand or even six million people in East Pakistan need not constitute a problem if all were provided with a fair share of the irreducible minimum requirements of a decent human existence. But our standard of living is very low compared to what it could be.

The first, in modern times to study the correlation between the population and food supply was "Malthus" whose law stated that as human population tends to multiply faster in geometrical progression than the food supply which increases in the arithmetical progression ; unless the population growth is checked, a time will come when there will be no food for all.

Population has always tended to increase faster than the food supply. Hence there has never been sufficient food for all the people. Before the last World War it was estimated that two thirds of the people in the world suffered from malnutrition and many from sheer hunger. The position is much the same today. A great part of the entire population in East Pakistan is close to the famine level. The problem of population has to be considered in relation to the means of subsistence, primarily food as almost 80% of the population is dependent on agriculture for livelihood.

Unreliable Provider : Our agriculture is still so dependent on the vagaries of the monsoon that no thoughtful person can set store by the bumper crop of last year. East Pakistan's agriculture is characterized by the primitive methods of farming, subdivision and fragmentation of land (which renders mechanization impossible, even granting the necessary capital for machinery is available) lack of irrigation and consequent dependence on the uncertain deluge of the monsoon or drought—all these leading to uneconomic holdings and to an excessive dependence by the people on land for living. The primitive technique of East Pakistan in farming is responsible not only for the yield per capita, even when compared with other Asian countries such as Japan and China, but also for the gradual deterioration of land, soil erosion and progressive deforestation. By and large, agriculture for many of our farmers has become an uneconomic and frustrating way of life and not a successful business proposition, which it ought to be.

Another factor which makes the population growth in East Pakistan a problem is the industrial backwardness. There are innumerable causes for industrial backwardness in East Pakistan, of which most important are as follows:

1. Neglect of the British Government before partition.
2. There are a few business leaders in Pakistan.
3. Lack of coal, iron and some other minerals.
4. Lack of private enterprise.
5. Shortage of sufficient technical hands.
6. Lack of cheap power.

Due to the above factors it is a fact that the industrialization that has taken place in East Pakistan during the last decade has not helped to ease the population pressure. The percentage of population gainfully employed in modern industry has been a very small percentage of the total population.

PREVENTIVE MEASURES AND FAMILY PLANNING

Some thirtyfive years ago John Maynard Keynes wrote : "The time has already come when each country needs a considered national policy about what size of population, whether larger or smaller than at present, or the same is more expedient. And having settled this policy, we must take steps to carry it into operation."

For East Pakistan a Population Policy : What can be a population policy for East Pakistan? What could be the optimum size of East Pakistan's population? The question of quantity would continue to be the major problem. The most desirable quantity of population is the one that attains the maximum production, highest standard of living, political stability, and economic security. The question that arises now is how we can be both self-sufficient and raise our standard of living when our production is growing. We cannot run with the hare and hunt with the hounds.

Solution of the problem of growth of population can be effected by two ways,—by rapid economic development in East Pakistan and by checking birth rate.

Agriculture In East Pakistan : Our resources as they are available today are behind our needs. As for food production alone all our efforts today are directed towards making our country self-sufficient in this respect. The total agricultural structure is based on the primitive system but the situation does not mean, however, that there is no scope for improving agriculture in East Pakistan. With modern methods of agricultural science the cultivated land could probably be made to double its present yield, and some of the so called uncultivable waste could be brought under profitable cultivation.

Industrial Growth : It is believed that East Pakistan is bound to remain mainly an agrarian economy for many decades to come ; her industrialization is important in the solution of her population problems for, at least, two reasons. First, it could increase the productivity of labour and create an abundance of badly needed commodities and services and transform the present economy of near scarcity into an economy of sufficiency. She could only do so if sufficient capital and skill are available to overtake the population increase. Secondly, industrialization could encourage the development of new urban patterns of living which often lead to the control of the birth rate.

Migration : The scope of the possibility of internal migration as a method of relieving the pressure in East Pakistan is much wide. We know that the two wings of Pakistan show a contrasting picture in density of population. While the Western wing is very scantily populated the East wing has the credit of carrying the weight of 922 persons per square mile. In order to relieve East Pakistan of her population problems, to some extent, the inter-wing migration should be frequently undetaken and should be carried out in a systematic way i.e., to relieve that parts of East Pakistan first, where the density of population is relatively high.

There are several factors which discourage the inter-wing and regional migration from East Pakistan and within it. The primary factor is the physical feature which separates the two wings of Pakistan by a big gap of more than one thousand miles of a foreign territory.

The poor mass of the East Pakistani agriculturists cannot afford to spend a considerable amount of money for trying their lucks in the western wing. Besides this consideration, several other factors of social, economic and religious nature, can be cited to explain the traditional immobility of the East Pakistani population and the slender volume of internal migration.

The economic reason of this immobility is simple. As the majority of the people are wedded to an agricultural life and since land is the chief source of sustenance, the average East Pakistani peasant cannot possibly leave the farm on which he was born and where he works. It is not that agriculture in East Pakistan is such a paying proposition that it renders the emigration to urban areas unattractive, but that there is an absence of a better calling elsewhere to take its place. In East Pakistan, agriculture is not just an occupation ; it is a way of life to an overwhelming majority of the population. Then there is an incredibly large rural indebtedness that chains the peasants to their mortgaged homesteads.

Certain social factors also contribute to the essential home living character of the East Pakistani people. Caste, language and the diversities of the regional and communal mores render severance from home, village or town uncomfortable. Thus the internal migration offers no substantial relief from the population pressure. And the partition of the country, which has already forced upon both Pakistan and India communal migration, renders the prospects of further inter-wing and regional migration dim, unless the Government plans in a systematic and well planned way.

Family Planning : The last and the most important solution to our population problems is the Family Planning or the birth control or the planned parenthood. The question of birth control has not been ignored by the Government of Pakistan. The Government of Pakistan is making systematic endeavours to propagate the benefit of planning the families as a remedy to the population problems.

Dilemma Resolved : Family planning is one of those significant human discoveries that resolve an acute dilemma in terms of human emotions, instincts and passions, arising from the dual aspect of the sex impulse in human beings. The increase and decrease of human population revolve on the axis of the two impulses, desire for mating and desire for offspring. If human beings want mating, as well as, its natural consequence,—children—both impulses work harmoniously and there is no problem. But, sometimes, for economic, health and social reasons, people do not want the children but do not want to renounce mating. Acute problems of emotional strain and, sometimes even, the physical impairment arise in intimate human relations when husbands and wives desperately want mating, but definitely do not desire children. Birth control is an answer to this conflict. The term 'Birth Control' was, first of all, used by Margaret Sanger, and has come into popular use, despite its scientific inexactitude.

Used, Abused But Little Understood : Despite the importance of birth control, or perhaps because of it and the power inherent in it, the subject has always been and is, even today, discussed with the greatest possible ignorance, bias, prejudice, and preconceptions. It is still denounced and discouraged by certain national Government and by the Roman Catholic Church. It is declared illegal in certain nations and states and is even debarred from discussion in certain groups. Mankind has been controlling the population, in one way or another, mostly by such method as celibacy, delayed marriages, abortion or infanticide for a long time. But birth control, however, in its modern sense is only a century old. Only within the last half century satisfactory methods have been developed. And though perfection is yet to be attained, safe and effective means are at our disposal today. There are several objections brought against birth control. Immorality is the foremost objection. Morality, as we know, is a matter of customs, and varies from age to age and from one culture to another. Morals are man made and as such they can never be static or absolute. In all cultures the codes of morals change with the changing needs and outlook of the people. Pearl S. Buck pleading for birth control points out *"If we are not able to live under the codes of our forefathers, it is not because we do not want to, but because life has changed so that we cannot, and we want help"*. An American advocate of birth control once put it in reply to the charge that it is immoral. *"Of course it is immoral, but it is socially useful. Therefore, one proposes to make it moral."*

Some contend that birth control is unnatural. But we know that, civilization itself can be summed up as the bold and daring interference with the nature. The nature can never be allowed to take her own course because it will lead us to the same most primitive level of existence. Today, in most civilized countries, the youngmen and women often refrain from marriage for economic reason. It also gives rise to prostitution and other vices. Birth control will be a positive help in that situation, as it will increase the legal, normal, and happy marriages and reduce immorality.

The importance of the Islamic view towards family planning is obvious, but there is a controversy on this point among the different schools of Islamic thought and version. Some are of the opinion that birth control is basically a moral crime and it is an offence against the 'shariat'. But others follow the 'fatawa' of the grand Mufti of Egypt who issued the following text on the 25th January, 1937: *"It is permissible for either husband or wife by mutual consent to take any measures.........in order to prevent conception"*.

It is desirable to lay stress, as well as, to spread the knowledge of cheap and safe methods of birth control. Birth control clinics should be established and other necessary measures should be taken on this behalf to prevent the use of advertisement of the harmful methods.

THE FUTURE

It is impossible to predict the future with any degree of certainty. It seems probable, however, that in the next fifty years world population may be between 5,000 and 6,000 million and the East Pakistan's population might be doubled by that time at which level it may tend to become stabilized and it also seems that with modern science the earth's resources can be made to support that number with a high standard of living. But the future depends on the trends of the scientific and technological achievements which might be applied to destructive ends in war or to constructive ends in developing the potential wealth of the earth for the benefit of the whole human family. The future depends on how soon the economic and political thought among the leaders in all countries can be adjusted to the new age so that they can co-operate in bringing it about. When that revolution in thought occurs, the shadow of war will fade before the bright hope of a new age of peace and prosperity which science has made possible.

It is a fact that science has now reached the stage when it can either free the world from hunger, poverty, fear, and drudgery or eliminate the life.

IMPACT OF SOME ASPECTS OF POPULATION CHANGE ON SOCIAL LIFE IN EAST PAKISTAN

In writing this section, we have to depend mainly on the facts, figures and informations, available in the censuses of undivided India and 1951 and 1961 censuses of Pakistan. In using the data from the censuses of undivided India, we have had help from Kingsley Davis' book on "The Population of India and Pakistan".

We have begun with the study of rural-urban migration of East Pakistan and impact of this migration on various spheres of social life in the province. In comparison with many large world regions, East Pakistan contains a higher proportion of population, classified as rural or agricultural. Since the partition of India in 1947 there have been important streams of migration from rural to urban areas.

Generally the economic considerations motivate the people to migrate from one area to the other. The important reasons which account for intensive migration to urban areas is the over-population in rural areas and the employment opportunities in cities and towns.

In East Pakistan 94·8% (according to 1961 census) of the population, living in villages depend on agriculture. This high percentage of people in rural areas puts a heavy pressure on the available means of subsistence and thereby forcing the people to migrate to the cities and towns for better economic opportunities.

RURAL-URBAN GROWTH OF POPULATION

The distinction between an urban and rural population is based on the definition of what actually constitutes an urban population. The standards used for distinguishing an urban area differ from region to region and would seem to be based on the prevailing condition of the country. According to 1961 census definition, urban areas in Pakistan include Municipalities, Civil lines and Cantonments, not included within Municipal limits, etc., and any other continuous collection of houses inhabited by not less than 5,000 persons which the Porvincial Director may decide to treat as urban for census purposes. The

Provincial Directors were given further instructions to look for pronounced urban characteristics e.g. common utilities, roads, sanitation,
schools and specially non-agricultural occupation of the people in
deciding the urban character of a place. Thus as a special case, a few
areas which had urban characteristics but had less than 5,000 population were also declared urban areas.[1]

Migration from rural areas has given much impetus to the urbanization in East Pakistan. The relative proportions of the population of a country living in rural and urban areas respectively reflect
the degree of industrialization achieved by it. Urbanization gives
stress on the demographic factor, density and congestion. Over the
last 10 years there has been increasing trend towards urbanization
which has involved radical shifts from rural to urban areas. The
unequal rate of growth in the two sectors of Pakistan's population
is reflected in the changes in their proportion of the total from one
census to another. In 1901 census only 5·1 percent of the total population resided in the urban places. In 1941 and 1951 the size of the
urban population was 7·9 percent and 10·4 percent respectively. But in
1961 census it became 13·1 percent. It indicates that urbanization
is getting momentum in recent years. The 1961 census of Pakistan
shows a sharp contrast between rural and urban growth of the population of Pakistan. The speed of urbanization is not equal in East
and West Pakistan. East Pakistan's painful progress in urbanization
gives a dismal picture of the province. According to 1961 census of
Pakistan, East Pakistan has 5·2% urban population, while in West
Pakistan the percentage of urban population is 22·5%. From the percentage of urban population in both the wings of the country it can be
said that by 1961 Pakistan has emerged as semi-industrial country, especially the western part of the country. But compared to the developed
countries in the world, the degree of urbanization in Pakistan is very
low, especially in East Pakistan.

IMPACTS OF THE RURAL-URBAN MIGRATION OR MOVEMENT

In East Pakistan we can see two general types of movements i.e.,
recurrent and non-recurrent. Recurrent movements from country to
city and city to country comprise all those movements that are rou-

---

1.   1961 Pakistan Census Bulletin No. 2. p. 13.

tine and repetitive. They might also be called functional, for it is by this type of movement that the functioning of a community is carried on. The recurrent movements are expressive of the rhythm and timing of community activities. This type of movement involves no break with the past, no disruption of an established order of the East Pakistani society. They are the means by which an existing equilibrium is maintained. They are the basic and the visible manifestation of stability.

On the other hand, non-recurrent movements from country to city and city to country are those movements out of and without return to a given context of life conditions. They follow from an alternation of fundamental conditions which require a readjustment of population in a modified or entirely new structure of relationships. In the shifting and sorting of population which ensures non-recurrent movements in East Pakistan may take the form of a complete displacement of some portion of the total population for resettlement elsewhere, of local redistribution of some individuals in a different alignment of relationships or of an influx of individuals from other localities. Such movements are, therefore, symptomatic of change ; they involve a transition from one pattern of organization to another. Non-recurrent movement is the means by which change is effected and the most accessible and measurable evidence of change. It is to this type that the term migration is usually applied and it is, of course, this type of movement in East Pakistan with which we are primarily interested in this section. Although in East Pakistan the migrants to city are the families permanently settled majority of them can not totally cut off their connections with the village. The village remains their home. They go back to their village-home periodically to visit their relatives, to help with the harvest, to take part in the social ceremonies.

This phenomenon of rural-urban migration has important and significant effects on social life of East Pakistan. In the first place, it can be said that the frequent movement of the city workers to the village is a financial and intellectual gain for the rural areas. The savings, the workers bring home after several months' absence are valuable addition to the local capital formation. Furthermore, as the migrants have the direct contact with the city, they help in diffusing the urban intellectual ideas, the urban conception of individualism, efficiency, attitudes towards life, the standard of living, and values of education. The emigration to the city presumably drains off the surplus population and thus lowers the population pressure on the villages. But the purpose is frustrated by the fact that the emigration to the city attracts the able-bodied workers, leaving the young dependents, the old and the morbid to carry on agricultural production in rural areas. As a result of the urban-bound migration the villages are gradually becoming poor in leadership and initiative of any kind. This factor is vital for the deteriorating conditions of the rural areas. in East Pakistan. For social, economic, political and educational progress, good leadership is necessary. It is they who stimulate the rural people to work for the development of the village and start or direct those institutions which create better life of the community. But the continuous flow of the rural young people to cities and towns results in the social, political and economic stagnation in the rural areas. Today a village is a vacuum and the indigenous culture cries and dies in this vacuum because of the lack of communication and inter-action between the village and the city or town. This segregation and isolation between the rural and ruban population is a hard blow to the national cause.

   Now we shall try to discuss the impact of rural-urban migration upon the East Pakistani society. There are a host of problems of social readjustment, emerging as an effect of rural-urban movements of the people. The migrants, living in a completely new environments with new values and code of life, working in new surroundings with varied experiences, require to change many of their habits, practices and values and enter into a completely new set of relationships to adjust themselves to the new situation in life. In the process of this adjustment, some significant changes in the old and traditional values of the migrants take place. This may stimulate them to adopt new ideologies in life. In this process there is the risk of weakening or losing some of the finer elements in the culture of the migrants when their own cultural values are weakened and they can not fully adopt the new cultural values of their new environment. They, for the period of transition, are in anomic conditions. This anomic con-ditions create the problem of maladjustment for the migrants. From a survey report prepared by Prof. A.F.A. Hossain it appears that probably a majority of the workers are more or less maladjusted to the factory life. The symptoms of maladjustments among the factory workers are probably much more numerous and marked than the symptoms which indicate adjusment. The most important sources of maladjustment are in matters of working conditions, food, housing, sanitation and contact with one's family.[1]

Internal migratory movements create social problems. The shift of many people from one social and cultural setting to the other brings forth maladjustment. The rural-urban movements contribute to many social and pathological problems in East Pakistan.

PROBLEM OF ACCOMMODATION

The urban areas with high density of population face the acute problem of accommodation. Most of the cities and towns are over crowded. The cities and towns in East Pakistan are burdened with high density of population. The absence of good number of housing estate and multi-storied apartment houses, compels the bulk of the population to live in one or two roomed houses without any sanitary facilities. Old Dacca city provides a good example of unhealthy conditions of urban housing. It is not true that over crowded living is confined only to the urban areas because many rural areas exhibit the gloomy picture of unsanitary over crowded housing arrangements.

From the 1951 census it can be seen that for 4,20,62610 persons East Pakistan has a total number of 1,66,69077 rooms. The average number of persons per household is 4·82 persons in the proportion of 1·62 adult males, 1·45 adult females and 1·75 children.[2]

In urban areas the number of persons per household varies from 4 to 9. Generally the big cities and towns have more people living in one household. As for example the Dacca and Barisal munici- palities have 7 and 9 persons per household respectively.[3] These figures reflect the tremendous pressure of the population on dwelling space.

---

1. Hossain, A.F.A. Social Integration of Industrial Workers in Khulna. Dacca University Socio-Economic Research Board, 1961.

2. Census of Pakistan, 1951, vol. 3, pp. 47-48.

3. 1961 Census of Pakistan.

Due to migration of large number of people from rural areas, the town and city population is growing to an uncontrollable magnitude. This unchecked population increase in the urban areas is responsible for the appearance of the slums, disappearance of open space and the construction of temporary structures here and there. This has made the habitation unhealthy and overcrowded. Prof. A.F.A. Hossain's report on a survey shows that in East Pakistan 3 to 5 factory workers share a room with an area of 100 square feet, average floor space per person being 19·3 square feet. Maintenance of health has some connections with the housing system. Overcrowded houses have a harmful effect on the health of the family members and create the delicate problem of the maintenance of privacy.

FOOD PROBLEM

There has been great concern about the growth of world population especially in relation to the food supplies. Robert Malthus painted a picture of a world where the increasing population would outstrip the food supply. But the subsequent revolution in technology and transport and the growth of capital has greatly increased the productivity. This has discredited the gloomy forecast of Malthus. But his ghost still haunts the South-East and Middle-East Asian countries. Malthus' conclusion on populaton growth fully applies to East Pakistan because of shortage in food supply, low standard of living and tremendous population growth of over 2% a year. Compared to other countries in the world agriculture in East Pakistan is primitive in nature. The output per acre is very low. This low agricultural production is primarily due to uneconomic holdings, following sub-division and fragmentation, wrong process, followed in the rotation of crops, lack of marketing and irrigational facilities, primitive agricultural techniques, poor manures and seeds etc. The problem of low productivity of agriculture has been aggravated by the rapid growth of population.

According to a report of the Department of Food, exports of gram which were over 3 lakh tons in 1950-51 have been replaced by the net imports of over 16 lakh tons 10 years later; but the per capita availability of grain for domestic consumption has hardly increased. The import of food grain in the pre-1956 period is considerably lower

7—

than during the post-1958 period. Before 1956 imports of food grain were mainly due to lower level of production. But from 1956 onwards the pressure of population was felt and the rise in the level of agricultural production lagged behind the increased demand for food by the increasing population of the country. At present the production and population curves are far too close together. The margin for increasing consumption is very narrow ; and the accumulation of capital, a vital requisite for further production increases in future is even more severely restricted.[1]

The increase of population at an annual rate of nearly 2.16% is, to a great extent, responsible for food problem in East Pakistan. East Pakistan has to feed her growing population in exchange of her hard earned foreign exchanges. Even she has to extend a beggars hand to other nations for feeding her starving millions. But foreign aid cannot and must not be a permanent reliance. To become truly independent and establish a secure base for higher standard of living, East Pakistan must build up her own savings, investment and productive capacity at a faster rate.

EFFECTS ON ECONOMY

Population is related to economic activity in two fundamental ways, (a) as a labour force it produces goods and services and (b) as a consumer it creates the demand for such goods and services. In order to establish an equilibrium between demand for and supply of goods and services, a country should have a desirable size of population for the maximum utilization of her resources. She must see that the rate of her population growth does not go ahead of the rate of her economic growth.

The economy of East Pakistan is primarily agricultural. Most of the people (about 80%) are directly dependent on agriculture for livelihood. As the agricultural and other resources are limited in East Pakistan, the accelerated growth of population is one of the major obstacles to the economic development.

PROBLEM OF UNEMPLOYMENT

The high rate of population growth is one of the important factors which gives rise to the problem of surplus man power in East Pak-

---

1. Economic Survey of Pakistan, 1961-62, pp. 7-8

istan. There is a heavy population pressure on land in East pakistan.
The overwhelming majority of the labour force is engaged in
agriculture in both the wings of Pakistan. According to 1951 census,
labour force engaged in agriculture is 84·1% in East Pakistan and 66%
in West Pakistan. On the other hand, the labour force engaged in industry is not significant. In East Pakistan the per capita land is a
little more than half of an acre. It has been estimated that a per
capita minimum of 2·5 acres of agricultural land is indispensible for
the support of each man.[1] Now in East Pakistan there is little land to
keep the total supply of agricultural labour employed at a high level
of productivity. The shortage of land compared to the rapid population growth forces the people to migrate to urban areas, where they
seek employment. But with the limited scope in the industrial
labour field, the demand is much below the supply of labour forces.
Consequently, the country faces the problem of widespread under-
employment and unemployment.

PROBLEM OF CAPITAL FORMATION AND INVESTMENT

Economic development in East Pakistan is retarded by demographic forces. For sound economic development, saving and accumulation of capital are necessary. But the rapid growth of population
in the province hinders the capital formation by aggravating the burden of dependency and, thereby increasing the consumption. The
high mortality rate hits at the root of the social investment of the
country. The low level of capital formation in this region is partly
due to low per capita income and wide unemployment and under-
employment. The rapid growth of population restricts savings when
there are many dependents in the families to feed. Different type of
models, constructed for the under-developed countries with a growing
population, show that a moderate rise in per capita ncome requires
savings ranging from 15 to 25 P.C. of the national income.
But the rates of savings in East Pakistan fall considerably
short of the above range (15 to 25 P.C.) due to rapid growth of
population.

It is true that in the process of economic growth greater use of
capital equipment is necessary. But if the population goes on

1. 1951 Census of Pakistan.

increasing, the same amount of capital equipment is thinly spread over a large aggregate of labour force. This factor prevents the intensive use of capital equipment, retards the process of increasing the productive efficiency of labour and thereby slackens the rate of economic growth. This is evident from the targets, set in Pakistan's First Five-Year Plan. The plan anticipated the increase of national income by 15% and on the basis of an expected 7·5% rise in population, per capita income was expected to be increased by 7%. But after the plan period national income rose only about 2%. In view of the normal increase in the population, per capita income grew very little.

If the existing standards of living are to be maintained, the real income must increase. Income investment ratio in Pakistan is about 1 : 4. Present rate of capital formation is 6·7% i.e., sufficient only to absorb the year to year addition to the population. In other words, almost nothing is left for keeping up existing production capacity intact. According to the estimate of Collin Clark Pakistan must save 12·5% of her national income for both the purposes stated above. It does not seem possible for East Pakistan to increase its rate of savings out of the current income, particularly in view of its expanding need for food and other necessities as a result of rapid population growth.[1]

PUBLIC HEALTH AND POPULATION

According to the definition of the World Health Organization, health is a state of complete physical, mental and social well-being rather than only the absence of disease and infirmity. However the discussion of public health in relation to population trends was restricted to the problems of mortality and morbidity. Morbidity was emphasized because of its importance in connection with the wastage of manpower.

Balanced diet requires, at least, 2,500 calories per day for an individual. But the food value of the average daily diet of the people of East Pakistan does not exceed 2000 calories. This is, due to, the alarming growth of population in East Pakistan without proportionate increase in food production.

---

1. First Five-Year Plan of Pakistan.

The under-nourished people of East Pakistan are the centres of epidemic diseases. 50 million rural population which constitute 96% of the total population are living in sub-standard health conditions of overcrowding, malnutrition and disease. Millions of the people in the province can not do any productive work because of chronic diseases.[1]

PRESSURE ON EDUCATIONAL INSTITUTIONS

In East Pakistan, like many other underdeveloped countries in the world, there has been significant reduction of child mortality due to improved public health measures and the introduction of modern treatment and medicine. As a result, there are more and more children in the country. The proportion of children under 10 years of age in the total population of the country increased from 28·4% in 1951 to 35·1% in 1961. With such a high percentage of children in the total population there is bound to be a great economic strain on education development programmes i.e., construction of new educational institutions and supply of trained teachers and other facilities for a healthy atmosphere of education. In East Pakistan especially in the urban areas, it is a great problem to give education to the children owing to dearth of seats in schools and colleges. During the years 1954-59, while the number of primary schools remained almost static (26,000) the number of students increased by 6,00000.[2] Consequently the educational coverage of the primary school children will continue to be the most formidable problem if the present demographic trends (population explosion) continue.

IMPACT ON FAMILY

The institution of family in our country is under great stress due to the rapid growth of population. The size and structure of our population is affecting the size, composition and functions of the family.

The present family size in East Pakistan presents an interesting picture. The high income groups tend to have a small family, while the low income groups tend to have a large family. As accurate statistical figures are not available, the number of families, having

---

1. Asia and Far East Seminar on Population, 1955 p. 25.
2. Report of the Directorate of Public Relations, Govt. of East Pakistan, 1961.

the burden-some size cannot be ascertained. But it can be assumed that 95% of the population of East Pakistan have big families.

The structure and form of our family reveal an unfortunate situation. In almost 95% of East Pakistani families, there are about 7 to 8 members with one earning member. Here many young couples do not mind having many children because of their fatalistic attitude. On the other hand, they consider the childern as the blessing of heaven. So they are not dismayed at the arrival of new baby, no matter whether they are able to feed it or not. It is important to mention that there is high old age dependency in the families in East Pakistan because of the traditional social values that the old parents should be supported by the sons. Too many children with high old age dependency rate add disastrously to the crushing burden of the grim struggle for existence of the bread earner. Thus, the earning member of the family,—the productive manpower of the society is subject to a prolonged stress of the family burden. This family burden is gradually but inexorably sapping his life blood, crippling his ability and thwarting his hopes, desires, emotions and ambitions. Due to the population explosion, the family with many dependents are failing to perform its normal function and thereby giving rise to problems of marital unhappiness, divorce, parental neglect, maladjustment and delinquency of children.

CRIME AND BEGGARY

The present demographic trends have great influence over the pathological problems in East Pakistan. The growth of industrial estates, towns and cities, in the absence of rural industries, aggravates crimes in urban areas because of the shift of population from rural to urban areas. This has occurred mainly for economic reasons and accentuated unemployment in large cities. What is more interesting in this urbanization process is that the dependents are usually left behind in the villages. The people of the economic productive age group (15-50 years) come to cities in search of employment. But when they are unable to find a job they face uncertainty and take resort to criminal activities. As regards beggary, the people especially the weak and the old turn to begging when they fail to find jobs, thereby overcrowding the roads and streets in the cities and towns in East Pakistan.

In conclusion we may say that the population problem in East Pakistan is a vital question for the government and the people alike because the solution of many other social, economic and political problems of the country depends on the sound solution of the population problem. From our study we have seen that the demographic changes in the province are influencing the various spheres of life of the community in East Pakistan. This is important to know for the future sound social and economic planning of the country.

Bibliography

Agarwala, S. N. *India's Population* : *Some Problems in Perspective planning* (Proceedings of a Seminar) Asia Publishing House, Bombay, 1960.

Davis, K. *The Population of India and Pakistan.* Princeton University Press, 1951.

Hossain, A.F.A. *Human and Social impact of technological Change in Pakistan.* Oxford University Press, Pakistan, 1956, vol. I.

Hawley, A.H. *Human Ecology,* A *Theory of Community Structure.* The Ronald Press Company. New York, 1950.

Philips Harold, A. *Population in its Human Aspects,* New York, 1956. and Henderson, D.

Thomson, W.S. *Population and Progress in the Far East.* The University of Chicago Press, Chicago, U.S.A. 1959.

United Nations. *The Determinants and Consequences of population Trends.* New York, Population Division. Department of Social Affairs U.N. 1959.

Chandrashekhar, S. *Population and Planned parenthood in India.* George Allen & Unwin Ltd.London 1955.

Journals and Reports

Economic Survey of East Pakistan. Published by the Ministry of Finance, Govt. of Pakistan, Rawalpindi, 1962.

The Sixth International Conference on planned parenthood. Proceeding Report of 1959, New Delhi, India.

The Pakistan Development Review., Published by the Institute of Development Economics, Karachi 1961.

Census of Pakistan, 1951.

Census of Pakistan, 1961.

CHAPTER 6

FAMILY PATTERN AND MARRIAGE IN PAKISTAN

The institution of family refers to a group of persons united by marriage, kinship or adoption, constituting a single household and interacting in roles of husband and wife, father and mother, son and daughter and brother and sister. It is important to discuss the family pattern in Pakistan because family is still one of the basic institutions in different societies. It is the fundamental agency of socialization and social control.

In Pakistan the vast majority of families are extended or joint in nature. But it can not be said that Extended or Joint family system is the only system of family in Pakistan. There are single or nuclear type of families, specially in urban areas of Pakistan.

In the rural areas of Pakistan the striking majority of families are joint in character. Such families, generally consist of brothers, their parents, sisters, wives and children and in rare cases, other relatives. The head of the family is the eldest male member or some other responsible male member of the family. The rest of the members have to abide by the decision of the head of the family. But it may be mentioned here that the authority of the head of the family is decreasing day by day. Leaving aside these extended families, we have another form of family which is called the single family. But if we think that this single family system is the same as that in the western societies, we shall commit a mistake. Our single family system is different from that in the United States. Almost all the families in the western societies are nuclear, consisting of husband, wife and their unmarried children. After marriage the young men generally leave their parents' house and live in a separate residence. Most often, they have new houses to live in. In this way they have developed the system of Neo-local residence. Their families have little connection with their parents' family.

These families are purely single or nuclear in form. Of course, there may be some exceptions. In Pakistani society the number of single families is much less than that of joint families. But the single families in Pakistan are not of pure nuclear type of western societies. In most cases, they are connected with joint families. It is very difficult to get families, consisting of only the husband, wife and their unmarried children.

In Pakistan, generally, after the death of the father, each brother takes his due share in the whole property and begins to live separately. This is the case, frequently found in rural areas of Pakistan. But it often happens that the deceased father left one or some of his sons and daughters unmarried. So, after his death his elderly and married sons become separate ; the younger and unmarried brothers and sisters live with them either by rotation or permanently with one of them. The mother may be alive and she, often, lives with one of her sons permanently or with all of them by rotation. There are other relatives who may be working as disturbing elements in forming purely single or nuclear families. Many times a widowed sister, with or without her offsprings may live with her brothers who live separately. A widowed daughter may live with her parents who formed a single family. In this way if we analyse the family in more details, we shall see that there are many factors which go against the formation of nuclear or single family in rural Pakistan. Although, in many cases, the young men of some illiterate families begin to live separately after their marriage because of frequent quarrels with their parents and some other family disturbances, it is found that they remain connected with their parents' families in many respects. Above all, they do not leave their parents' house. They live in the same house in a separate room. What they think to be most important for living separately is to have the separate management and arrangement of gathering, preparing and taking food. When they have done it, they think, they have become separate. This is more or less the case in the rural areas of Pakistan.

The case in the urban areas is different. In the urban areas the percentage of single families is higher than that in the rural areas. But compared to extended or joint family, the percentage of single or nuclear family is low even in urban areas. So, in urban areas too the majority of families are extended or joint in character. The reasons for the existence and persistence of joint family system may be traced in the present economic structure of Pakistan. The structure and functions of the institution of family in Pakistan are the product of our agrarian economy. Unless the whole economic base of our country is changed, there will be little changes in the structure and functions of our families. Of course, there may be some minor or insignificant changes in the family pattern of our country. Education, possession of wealth, contact with the advanced and industrialized western countries, religious attitude and beliefs, influence of geography etc., are the factors which are responsible for these minor changes in the functions and structure of our family.

CHANGING FAMILY PATTERN IN PAKISTAN

It can be observed that in most of the countries the family is changing and going through readjustments. The question is whether Pakistani family is also changing and going through readjustments. There are some scholars who are of the opinion that family is almost breaking down and, most probably, in future there will be no family. To them, gradually the state and other associations are taking the responsibility of performing many functions of the family. At present, many things are being done outside the family. This cannot be the indication of complete break-down of family life. It is a fact that some bonds of family life have become loose especially in the urban areas of Pakistan. Many changes have taken place in the roles of the members of the family due to various factors. The roles of family members have been changed by the mother, working outside the home for wages, by adolescent members of a family, earning as much as the father, by the father, commuting to the city or by a member of the family going away from home for higher education. The roles of family members in the city are different from the roles of their forefathers in the country. Also the changing functions of the family have altered the positional arrangements and relationships of various members of the family in Pakistan.

So, we find that changes have occurred in various aspects of our family. But from this we can not conclude that the family is breaking down. It is rather going through readjustments to cope with the changing economic, political and social structures of Pakistan.

Due to industrialization and urbanization, changes are taking place in the structure and functions of the family in Pakistan. The propagation of Family Planning is also bringing about some changes in the family life of our country. The Family ordinance has also got impact on the family life in Pakistan. It is often said that the family is no longer the economic unit in pakistan. This should not mean that the family has lost its economic functions. Many people, leaving their families in the rural areas, go to the cities and towns for earning. They earn in the town and, now and then, visit their homes. They are attracted to the towns by the increasing facilities for earning and, in short, by the modernization and new inventions of the towns. Whenever the rural people get a chance, they try to go to towns and industrial areas for jobs because of the inadequate yield from cultivation and the disguised rural unemployment. The educated people mostly live in the urban areas. The culture of the towns and cities is different from that of the village. Due to migration of the village people to the towns and cities and the frequent visits of the urban people to the village, some changes are taking place in the rural families. In this way some cultural, social, economic and structural changes have occurred in the rural family. Thus in every function of the family of Pakistan there have been more or less changes in recent times. But the changes are not like those in the western countries. The changes that took place in the western families centuries ago, are taking place now in our family system. So, it can be said that in course of gradual technological and industrial development, our family system may assume a different form in future. The educational functions of the family in Pakistan have changed considerably due to increasing facilities, extended by our government. In all other functions, such as economic, political, recreational etc., there have been some changes. The psychological and security functions of the families in Pakistan are still very important.

Thus if we analyse the various functions of the family in Pakistan, we shall see that the family is the most important institution in our society inspite of the fact that it has undergone many changes in various fileds such as marriage, structure, Patterns, relations, functions etc. According to Southerland and Woodward, "The family is a cultural and universal institution, varying in details of structure but, rooted firmly in the nature of man and in human experience." So we can be sure that family in Pakistan or in any other place cannot break down completely. There are changes towards a new pattern which may replace the old one.

MARRIAGE SYSTEM IN PAKISTAN

Marriage is generally considered to be a social institution. It may be defined as a relation of one or more men to one or more women. The relationship, established between the males and females by marriage is governed by the laws and customs of the society. It involves certain rights and duties both for the husband and wife. These rights and duties vary from culture to culture. They cannot be brought to the fold of the general definition of marriage. But there is something common in every marriage i.e., the right of sexual intercourse. Theoretically men and women can be united through marriage bond in the following four ways : (1) Monogamy is the marriage of one man to one woman. It is the most widespread form of mating ; (2) Polygamy is a type of marriage in which two or more women are married to one man ; (3) Polyandry is a form of marriage in which several men are married to a woman, and ; (4) Group marriage was mostly prevalent among the primitive people. It is hardly found in today's world. It is a system in which one group of men are mated to a group of women.

The marriage system in Pakistan can be classified as follows:
1) Negotiated marriage.
2) Cross-Cousin marriage
3) Exchange marriage
4) Court marriage.
5) Forced marriage.

In case of the negotiated marriage, it takes place between two families by negotiations through a third man or a party, generally known as "Ghatak." This system may also include child marriage and widow remarriage. In our rural areas there is no, hard and fast, rule in measuring the age limit of marriage, though generally in case of the girls, it falls in between 13 and 17 years and in case of the boys in between 16 and 20 Years.

In case of the cross-cousin-marriage, it takes place between two families formerly related. Usually the marriage takes place between two cousins i.e., between the boy and his mother's brother's daughter or the girl and her mother's brother's son etc. This may be either because of economic factors or to strengthen the former relationship. Child marriage and widow remarriage may also take place in this system.

The exchange marriage means those marriages which take place without observing any such important rites and rituals. This is mainly done to economise the expenses. In this system the bride-groom will arrange the marriage between his sister and his brother-in-law.

The Court marriage means those marriages which are permitted by law but, not by the guardians of either the bride or the groom. This is in vogue mainly in the urban areas and sometimes, among the educated class of the rural areas.

The Forced Marriage is not a very common type of marriage in Pakistan. But, sometimes, it happens that the bride is forcibly taken away from her parents' home by the bride-groom and his party.

Adults are to be married ; it is rather universal. The child marriage is also not very hard to be found. Endogamy, which means that a man is bound to marry a woman of his own caste is fully prevalent among the Hindus and among the Muslims like jolahas, Kulus, Tatis etc.

The rural people generally believe that boys and girls are to be married whenever they attain the reproductive capacity. To them the age for attaining the reproductive capacity is 12 years, in case of the girls and 16 years, in case of the boys.

In case of the urbanites, there is no general marriageable age limit because here most of the boys and girls are imparted education and, in many cases, higher education.

Marriage among the Muslims in Pakistan, like that among the Muslims the world over, is a civil ceremony and is not a sacrament but no less sacred. It is invariably solemnised by a "Kazi" or a Marriage Registrar. Marriages are always arranged by the parents of the persons concerned, and in the absence of the parents the nearest aged relation takes the responsibility. From the case studies that have been made by Prof. A.F.A. Hussain, it appears that the majority of the girls are still married before they are 14, possibly at 11 or 12 only". One important reason why early marriages are supported is that the family and not the individual, being the social unit the wife has to merge herself into her husband's family. Such adjustment to a new family is obviously much easier for a young girl than for a more mature one. In case of the boys, the age of marriage is generally over 16 years. There is evidence that the age of marriage, particularly among the males, has been increasing steadily. The successive census figures show a reduction of the proportion of married persons in the total population between the ages 10 and 39. Thus among the Muslim males between 10 and 39, the proportion of married persons fell from 65.13 percent in 1931 to 53.80 percent in 1941 and to 47.74 percent in 1951. Among the Muslim women between 10 and 39, the proportion of married women fell from 80.31 percent in 1931 to 77.01 percent in 1941 and to 75.40 percent in 1951.[1] This is probably, due to economic difficulties and the unwillingness of the young persons to shoulder additional financial burden at an early age. One or two cases are on record where a young man has fled away from his home in the village to escape a marriage.

Marriage is a matter of considerable negotiation between the families through a go-between. Marriages are generally arranged between the families in the same or in neighbouring villages, sometimes, with close relations such as cousins. The family status which, in practice, depends on a number of complex factors and indicates the traditional position of the family in the village community is often a very important factor which is taken into consideration in marriage negotiations, particularly in the choice of the bride. In the choice of the bride-groom much emphasis is given on his economic condition. Money [the amount to be spent and not necessarily the amount to be paid in cash] and property are also important considerations in marriages. In some districts marriage among near relations, such as, cousins is quite common and is often, due to, property considerations. Other things remaining the same, the amount of money to be spent usually in the form of ornaments by the bride-groom's family is often a deciding factor in the contract of a marriage. Education which is, sometimes, taken into account is not probably a significant considerations in the arrangement of rural marriages.

---

1. Census of Pakistan, 1951.

The bride-groom's family generally makes the gifts, namely, clothes, ornaments etc., for the bride, as well as, provides a feast for the bride-groom's and the bride's friends and relations, while the bride's family arranges the wedding feast for its own people, as well as, for the large party which often accompanies the bride-groom as wedding is solemnized at the bride's house. At present, among the Muslim peasant families in Pakistan the expenses, incurred by the bride-groom and his family are generally heavier than those, incurred by the bride's family. A dowry is fixed to be paid to the bride by the bride-groom under the law of Islam and this is incorporated in the marriage contract. The 'Mahar' is payable only if demanded by the bride and in the great majority of cases, is not paid at all.

Islam does not recognise the caste system among its followers. In theory, a Muslim belonging to any profession can marry a Muslim in any other profession. However, some of the agricultural and artisan groups, which are considered socially inferior, are as strictly endogamous as the Hindus. The Jolahs constitute such a group. Even a well placed Jolah would find it extremely difficult if not impossible, to marry in a peasant family, nor would a Jolah be anxious to give his daughter in marriage outside his caste like group. This caste tendency was the result of the influence of Hindu caste system. The system of arranged marriage is the predominant form of marriage in Pakistan. But with the increase in education and also under some influence of the western countries, love and civil marriages can occasionally be seen in Pakistan. In this type of marriage the bride or the bride-groom is not selected by the parents or by other relatives. They choose themselves and come into mutual contact with each other. They then, go to their parents or guardians for their opinion. If the parents of the bride-groom are willing, the proposal is sent to the bride's parents. If they accept the proposal, the ceremony is solemnised by the "Kazi" at the will of the guardians of the bride and the bride-groom. In this case, the process of marriage is like the settled marriage. But in case, the bride and the bride-groom fail to get the consent of their parents, they go to the court of law and register their names as husband and wife in presence of a first class magistrate and two witnesses. This system of marriage is known as civil marriage.

Widow marriage is another form of marriage which is very common among the Muslims in Pakistan. It is permissible in Islam. A Muslim woman who lost her husband by death, is allowed to marry even her brother-in-law. The Hindus generally do not practise widow marriage. When a very young Hindu girl looses her husband, she has to spend her whole life as a widow.

Taking the number of wives into account, we find that monogamy is the common type of marriage in Pakistan. In this system a man is married to a woman. Polygamy is permitted by Islam, provided the husband can give equal treatment and attention to his wives. But it is rarely practised due to economic consideration of the husband, the social disapproval and the indirect discouragement by the government in the 'Family ordinance'.

The Pakistani culture has got a profound relationship with the prevailing pattern of marriage in the country. The joint family system is predominant in Pakistan. In this system every member of the family forms a part of the family and has got certain responsibilities and obligations to the other members of the family. Unlike the western countries, in Pakistan a son feels it his duty to maintain the parents in their old age, as well as, to give education and food to his younger brothers and sisters, if the parents are unable to manage their expenditure. He also has the obligation to get the younger brothers and sisters married if the parents are not economically capable of doing so.

A bride in Pakistan has to do her duties not only to her husband but also to her father-in-law, mother-in-law, brother-in-laws and sister-in-laws. In some cases, specially in the villages, it is considered that the bride has got her primary duty to the old father and mother-in-laws. The parents, therefore, feel it their duty to choose a bride for their son after giving a proper consideration of the family back-ground, heritage and economic conditions of the bride's father's family so that she can live happily in their family and do her duties to all members of their family. This can only be attained by arranged marriage and hence, thes ystem of arranged marriage has got the maximum popularity in this country and it may be said that this pattern of marriage i.e., arranged marriage has got a profound relationship with the culture in Pakistan.

Bibliography

Folsom, Joseph, Kirk. *The Family and Democratic Society.* Published in England, 1948. Routledge and Kegan Paul Ltd., London.

Burgess, Ernest, W. and Locke, Harvey, J. *The Family—From Institution to Companionship.* [Printed in the U.S.A.] American Book Company, New York.

Bottomore, T.B. *Sociology—A Guide to Problems and Literature.* (First Published in 1962.) The English Language Book Society and George Allen and Unwin Ltd., London. Part III—*The Family and Kinship.*

Ogburn, William, F. and Nimkoff, Meyer, F. *A Hand Book of Sociology.* Fourth Edition (Revised) 1960. Routledge and Kegan Paul Ltd., London. Chapter XXI and part seven.

Young, K. and Mack, Raymond, W. *Principles of Sociology.* [Published in India.] Eurasia Publishing House Ltd., Ramnagar, New Delhi. Chapters 6 and 20.

MackIver, R. M. & Page, Charles, H. *Society—An Introductory Analysis.* Macmillan and Co. Ltd., London 1962.

Loomis, Charles, P. and Beegle, J. Allan. *Rural Sociology—The Strategy of Change.* First Printed, January, 1957 [Printed in the U.S.A.] Prentice Hall Inc, Engle Woodcliffs N.J. Chapters 3 and 14.

Nazmul Karim, A. K. *Changing Society in India and Pakistan.* First Printed in 1956. Oxford University Press, Dacca. Pakistan. Chapters I, III and VII.

Russel, B. *Marriage and Morals.* First Published, March, 1959. Bantam Books, New York. Chapters XIII and XV.

Afsaruddin, M. *Rural Life In East Pakistan—A Study of Five Selected Villages.* First Edition, May, 1964. Social Science Research Project. Department of Sociology, University of Dacca, East Pakistan. Chapters 2 and 7.

Afsaruddin, M. (ed.) *Sociology and Social Research in Pakistan.* First Editon, September, 1963. The Pakistan Sociological Association, (East Pakistan unit), Dacca, Pakistan. Chapter 3—*Family and Kinship in a Hindu Village of East Pakistan,* by Bessaignet P.

Dube, S.C. *Indian Village.* First Published in 1955. Routledge and Kegan Paul Ltd., London. Chapter V.

8—

Dube, S.C. *India's Changing Villages*. First Published in 1958. Routledge and Kegan Paul Ltd., London.

Hussain, A.F.A. *Human and Social Impact of Technological Change in Pakistan*. Oxford University Press, Amen House, London. 1956.

Maron, S. *Pakistan : Society and Culture*. Human Relations Area Files. New Haven, 1957.

Westermarck, E. *The History of Human Marriage*. Macmillan and Co. Ltd., London. 1921.

Chapter X, The Frequency of Marriage and the Marriage age.

CHAPTER 7

THE MEANING OF SOCIAL CONTROL AND ITS AGENCIES IN PAKISTAN

INTRODUCTION

It may be said that social order is the result of social control. In other words, social control is fundamentally connected with the problems of orderliness and regularity of human society. Order, without control cannot be found in human society. Social control is purposive in society. Efforts and contrivance are needed for it. It is a product of greater or lesser degree of intelligence and it can not be taken for granted that it must be maintained. There is always deliberate restraint of some conduct and deliberate stimulation and eliciting of other conduct. The order is maintained in the society only by an elaborate system of social control.

DEFINITION AND MEANING

Social control has been defined by various scholars in different ways. It refers to something by which the society is kept under control. T.B. Bottomore says, "The term 'Social Control' may be regarded as referring to the aggregate of values and norms by means of which tensions and conflicts between individuals and groups are resolved or mitigated, in order to, maintain the soliderity of some more inclusive group and also to the arrangements through which these values and norms are communicated and instilled". From this definition there appears a distinction between the types of social control and its 'agencies' and 'means'. According to Bottomore, customs, opinion, law, religion, morals and education are the types of social control. Social control should not be confused with personal leadership. When one person tries to control the behaviour of others, he is generally thought to be exercising leadership rather than social control.

According to MacIver social control is the way which the entire social order coheres and maintains itself. To study social control we should seek out the ways in which society patterns and regulates individual behaviour and, at the same time, the ways in which the patterned and standardized behaviour, in turn, serves the social organization.

PURPOSE OF SOCIAL CONTROL

The purpose of social control is to bring about conformity, soliderity and continuity of a particular group or society. The general purposes of the agents of social control can be designated roughly as (1) exploitative;---motivated by some form of self interest, direct or indirect ; (2) regulatory ;—based upon the habit and the desire for behaviour of customary type ; and (3) creative or constructive,—directed towards social change, believed to be beneficial.

MEANS OF SOCIAL CONTROL

The means by which the individuals or groups induce or compel conformity to their preferences in conduct, are numerous and varied. In considering these means one should bear in mind that the significance of institutions and agencies of social control depends largely upon the cultural or social setting. The relative efficacy of the means of social control varies with the changes in the social organization and life values of the group. For instance, in a static society, custom is a powerful means of influencing the responses of individuals ; but in a dynamic society the influence of tradition is less significant.

MAJOR AGENCIES OF SOCIAL CONTROL IN PAKISTAN

Laws and Customs : Almost all social and political rules or laws originated in Pakistan, as in other places, first in customs or folkways of long standing and are based upon the existing conception of justice and right in Pakistani Society. Law controls, to a great extent, the behaviour and activities of the people of Pakistan. This is also true for other countries in the world. By giving punishment to the offenders and protection to the good citizens, law maintains the order in our society and controls the activities of the people. In Pakistan there are many customs which always play their important roles to bring about conformity in the observance of some of the values in our society. As for example, the custom of respecting the aged members in the family controls the behaviour of the members in the family. The deviancy is always discouraged. The deviants are sometimes, punished and forced to correct their behaviour.

Government : Various agencies of the government of Pakistan have become the primary instruments of social control. The legal, traditional and political powers of different departments of the government of Pakistan can control our society. These powers are very wide, extending over almost all the phases of Pakistani society and can be used to suit the purposes of the government. For example, the East Pakistan police is such a department of the government of East Pakistan as has great power to control the society. The police is there to execute the legal orders or decisions of the judiciary.

SOME RELIGIOUS AGENCIES

(a) Religion

The universal function of religion is the interpretation and control of man's relation to the forces of his physical and social environment. We find no exception to this function in Pakistan. Islam is the predominant religion in Pakistan. Through the universal function of Islam, it is controlling our society. Every aspect of life of the Muslims of Pakistan is being controlled by Islam. The conception of heaven and hell in Islam also controls the social behaviour and activities of the people. Other religions such as Hinduism, Buddhism and Christianity in Pakistan, are also working as most important agencies of social control in their respective religious groups.

(b) Ritual and Ceremony

In our Pakistani society, ritual and ceremony, especially when they are elaborate, repeated and associated with mysterious powers and strong emotions can easily shape the behaviour of the people.

(c) Beliefs and Knowledge

All religious institutions in Pakistan depend upon the beliefs, knowledge and training to exert their influence upon their members. Whenever there is a little scientific knowledge to contradict the beliefs prevalent in Islam or in any other religion in Pakistan, the existing beliefs readily control the social behaviour.

(d) Mosque, Temple, Pagoda, Church etc.

A mosque has a very important role to control the behaviour of the people of Pakistan who are the followers of Islam. The religious sermon, given by the "Imam" of the mosque after the congregational prayer on Friday, goes a long way to control the behaviour of the people. In Pakistan, sometimes, the "Imam" in consultation with other religious leaders gives the exemplary punishment to the offenders of his area. Similarly a temple, a pagoda and a church have the control over the Hindus, the Buddhists and the christians respectively. The people obey the rules and regulations of their respective religious institutions of worship, such as mosque, temple etc., and thus their behaviour is controlled.

(e) Mullahs or Clergymen

The Mullahs have tremendous influence upon the people of the rural areas of Pakistan. They also have the influence upon the urban religious minded people. There are two or more 'Paras' in a village and there is generally one Mullah for each 'Para' or for two 'Paras'. The Mullahs have extensive control over the people of their respective 'Paras'. They settle many disputes, especially those which are of religious nature. Thus they control our society to a great extent. They often work as physicians by giving a "Tabiz" to the people to cure various diseases. The Christian clergymen, with their religious power and prestige in the society also exercise a great influence over their followers, thereby controlling their religious and social activities.

(f) Peers, Priests and Religious Scholars

There are many 'peers' in Pakistan over whom the Muslims have great reverence. The peers are the religious guides. There are religious guides in other religions too. In every religion the religious guides have enormous influence upon their respective followers. The peers have many disciples called the "Murids". They influence and control every aspect of the life of their disciples. They give "Fatawa" on various aspects of life and their disciples obey those "Fatawas" or rules very sincerely. In Hinduism the Brahmins or the 'Thakurs' do exercise this power of control over the Hindu society. In Buddhism the "Bhikhoos" and in Christianity the Clergies give the people religious teachings which control their behaviour and activities.

(g) Religious Books

The religious books such as the Koran, the Veda, the Bible etc., also have control over their respective religious communities. For example, the activities of a Muslim is largely regulated by the teachings of the Koran and Hadiths.

(h) Fakirs, Dargahs and Mazars

There are some other minor religious agencies of social control in Pakistan i.e., Fakirs, Dargahs, Mazars etc. These agencies control the society to a considerable extent.

In the development of scientific knowledge and techniques for control over the forces of physical and social environments, it often appears that the religious institutions in Pakistan are gradually losing their influence in controlling the individual and social behaviour. With the advance of science and practical knowledge, those religious organizations which have continued to exercise effective social control, are gradually trying to discover and apply practical methods of religious principles to life.

MARRIAGE AND FAMILY

The laws and social customs of our society like other societies, regulate the behaviour of the individual in family relationship. In Pakistan a wife may not be forced to testify against her husband in criminal proceedings ; a husband is responsible for the support of his wife and children and the sons who have attained their maturity are responsible for the support of their invalid parents. In the family the children are given training for their future life. Marriage is also an important institution of social control. The sexual, reproductive and emotional behaviours of our people are controlled by marriage.

EDUCATION

An important aspect of education as an agency of social control in Pakistan is the control of schools through the teachers. The schools have significant control over the behaviour of the students. The schools, colleges and universities train the students in such a way that they learn to control themselves and become aware of the rules, regulations and the discipline of our society. Besides these schools and colleges there are many educational organizations and institutions that influence the young, as well as, the old. These include the Adult Education Programmes, Boys' Scouts, Girls' Guide, Madrasa, Church schools.

SOCIAL CLASS

A social class which has excessive power in comparison with other social classes of Pakistan, uses that power to control the members of less fortunate classes. In our society where power is derived chiefly from the ownership and control of wealth, we find many evidences of class-control. The ownership and control of the capital and wealth have given power to certain sections of the people of Pakistan to maintain a high degree of control over other sections of the population.

LEADERSHIP

The Basic Democrats and the village headmen are the leaders in the rural areas of Pakistan. They are very important for social control in our rural areas. They settle most of the disputes in the villages. The Basic Democrats are also the leaders of their respective areas in the urban society. Besides these people, there are other leaders in our country. All these leaders have control over their respective groups.

ART AND LITERATURE

Art, in its many forms, has been used for social control throughout the history of mankind and among all the people. Since the dawn of civilization, literature has played a similar role. The social control function of art and literature in Pakistan as in any other place, may be either unconscious or planned. Through art and literature the norms, values, traditions etc., are communicated to the people. This, to a great extent, regulates the social and cultural life in Pakistan.

RECREATION

Recreation both as a means and an agency of social control is used universally. It is an important means to train the children for social membership in the society of Pakistan. For the adults, it is not only the satisfaction of basic human need but also the deliberate instrument for influencing the people.

PUBLIC OPINION

Public opinion is a composite opinion, formed from varying opinion held by the public which can be mobilised on some particular issue and directed toward some kind of decision. Today, its formation in Pakistan upon word-symbols, emotionally loaded generalities make an impression on the masses. These are used to maneuver the public into taking a stand on an issue without examining the facts surrounding it. Thus public opinion also works as an important agency of social control in Pakistan.

PRESS

The press in Pakistan exerts control over the public to which it appeals and, in turn, it is controlled by them. The chief interest of the press in Pakistan is, in general, to bring about uniform and favourable reactions to the advertised goods and services. Other purposes are to create a public opinion in favour or against a political, economic and social issue. Like some other agencies of social control, the press seeks to exert its influence over the largest possible groups of people in our country. The press works as a means of social control in Pakistan through news papers, journals, magazines, advertisements, government publications, booklets etc.,

RADIO

Today our police, fire and forestry, our commercial and military aircraft stations,—all utilise air waves in performing their functions and duties. Today radio has become a very important means of social control both in urban and rural areas of Pakistan through its various programmes.

PUBLIC CRITICISM AND OSTRACISM

Public criticism is one of the most important agencies of social control in Pakistan. Bad activities are criticised by the public. Sometimes, people are afraid of doing things because of public criticism.

In the rural areas of Pakistan the anti-social elements are ostracised by the people. The ostracised persons are debarred from enjoying the normal privileges, offered by the society. They are not allowed to attend any public functions. The community services are not given to them. Sometimes, the people stop talking with the ostracised persons. It becomes very difficult for them to live in the community. So the fear of ostracism controls the activities of the people.

MOTION PICTURES

There can be little doubt about the influences which Dacca, Karachi, and Lahore have exerted and are exerting upon the cultural and social life in Pakistan. Many of the styles of today have been diffused from these cities. Many of our stereotypes and symbols have been formed by the movies, screened in the country. In our society, especially in the urban areas, we find many people imitating the behaviour of the cinema actors and actresses. Through the motion pictures, sometimes the social, cultural and moral values of Pakistani society are taught to the people.

Bibliography

Bottomore, T.B. *Sociology—A guide to Problems and Literature.* English Language Book Society, London 1964.

Green, Arnold, W. *Sociology—An analysis of life in Modern Society.* Third Edition. McGraw Hill Book company, New York 1960.

Hertzler, I.O. *Social Institutions.* Nebraska, U.S.A. 1946.

MacIver, R.M. and Page, Charles, H. *Society—An Introductory Analysis.* Macmillan and company Ltd., London 1962.

Roucek, joseph, S., and Associates. *Social Control.* Second Edition, New Delhi, January, 1965.

CHAPTER 8

URBANIZATION AND INDUSTRIALIZATION IN PAKISTAN

One of the outstanding features of our society is the urbanization of population and the growth of urban centre in an increasing rate. With this development the people of some parts of the country are becoming more and more city minded. Before we discuss the urbanization in Pakistan we shall try to examine the meaning of urbanization. By the concept 'urban' we mean the collection of people living in close proximity to one another in permanent compact settlements. In the words of Hatt and Reiss "Urbanization is the process of population concentration in which the ratio of urban people to the total population in a territory increases ; the process of urbanization inevitably involves a multiplication of the point of population concentration in a given territory."[1] According to 1961 census of Pakistan, "All municipalities, civil lines, cantonments and any continuous collection of houses inhabited by not less than 5000 persons were treated as urban areas."[2]

Different definitions used by different writers and sociologists may vary from country to country in their characteristics. In modern times urban communities have developed as a consequence of the development of commerce and industry. As a matter of fact, without trade, industry and commerce no town can grow because they presuppose the non-agricultural people who buy their food which will come from within the country or from abroad.

In Pakistan the movement of population towards the city and town is, to a great extent, the consequence of poor economic conditions in the rural areas and the lack of opportunities to earn to meet the bare necessities of life. Excessive pressure on land has resulted in the poverty

1. Hatt & Reiss. Cities and Society.
2. Census of Pakistan, 1961.

of the people which became the cause of their movement to urban areas. In other words, the movement to urban areas has been mainly due to the push towards them by the adversity at home rather than the pull towards them by the prospects of relative prosperity.

The pattern of urbanization in Pakistan is different from the countries of the West. A large number of city and town dwellers in Pakistan are from outside the country. They are mostly businessmen (merchants) and evictees (muhajirs). Another characteristic of the population structure of the towns and cities in Pakistan is that a large number of city and town dwellers do not have their permanent house there. They live in rented houses. There are few large and medium sized towns in Pakistan. According to 1951 census, there were only two cities Dacca (pop. 273,459) and Chittagong (pop. 143,264). There were only three towns with the population between 50,000, and 100,000, i.e., Narayanganj. (pop. 68,373), Barisal (pop. 89,278) and Saidpur (pop. 61,018). Fourteen towns had the population between 25000 and 50,000 and only twenty had the population between 10,000 and 25,000. The remaining twentysix towns had the population under 10,000.[1] The total number of towns was sixtyfive.

The proportion of the provincial population, living in towns of less than 10,000 has remained almost static in the last fifty years. But a steady tendency towards the increase of population in the towns over 20,000, rather than in those between 10,000 and 20,000, has been found. In 1901 to 1911 and 1911 to 1921 it was noticed that towns with 20,000 to 50,000 were growing faster than the 5,000 to 10,000 category.[2] The cities and towns in Pakistan may be classified into the following categories:

Country towns : These towns owe their existence largely to local marketing, trade and transport. They are mainly rural in their characteristics and mostly serve as collecting centres for local products and distribute the consumer goods and necessities of life in the neighbourhood. In some instances, administrative centres fit into these urban areas. Many such towns grew during the last few decades

---

1. Ahmad, N. Economic Geography of East Pakistan. London, Oxford University Press, 1958.

2. Davis, K. The Population of India and Pakistan. Princeton University Press, 1951.

but developed little urbanism. There are many examples of such towns in many districts in Pakistan. Muktagacha (Mymensingh), Rajbari (Faridpur), Naogaon (Rajshahi) are some of the examples.

Jute Collecting and Trading Centres : This is a class of small urban centres, many of which have grown up in comparatively recent times with the expansion of jute cultivation and its collecting trade in the last sixty to seventy years. Other distributive and market facilities have grown up around jute trade. In this category may be mentioned Bhairab Bazar, Narsindi etc.

Administrative Centres : A number of towns varying in sizes owe their growth and importance primarily to the fact that they are the administrative centres of a district or a subdivision. Several of them are old towns with historical significance ; but many of them are comparatively new in origin. Dacca, Lahore, Rawalpindi, Islamabad, Montogomery, Sylhet, Mymensingh, Rajshahi, Bogra etc., may be cited as examples of administrative centres.

Communication Centres : Several towns in Pakistan have good communication advantages through the river or rail transport. But some of them are primarily notable as communication centres such as Parbatipur, Saidpur, Sirajganj, Ishwardi, Chandpur and Barisal etc.

Industrial or Commercial Centre : Narayanganj, Dacca, Chittagong, Khulna, Chalna, Karachi etc., are the important industrial and commercial centres in Pakistan.

Static or Decaying Towns : There are some towns whose importance or utility has decreased in recent decades owing to various adverse factors such as river action, disease, bad climate and the general deterioration in their ecological conditions. During the last eighty years their population has either actually declined or, at best, increased very slightly. Domar in Rangpur and Sherpur in Bogra may be cited as examples.

Sea Port : There are some sea ports in Pakistan. Their main function is to handle the exports and imports of our country. Karachi, Chittagong, Khulna, Chalna may be mentioned as examples of sea ports.

Health Resorts : In both the wings of Pakistan there are some health resort centres. These are the centres where the people go for recreation and good health. Muree, Abotabad, Cox's Bazar,

Shitakunda etc. are some of the examples of this type of towns.

Military Establishment : There are some towns in Pakistan which originated because of the existence of some military institutions. Kakul, Sargoda, Lowertoppa etc., are some of the towns of this category.

River Ports : In Pakistan specially in East Pakistan, there are some good river ports to handle the local movement of goods and population. Goalanda, Chandpur, Sirajganj, Barisal etc. are some of the examples of this type of towns.

The important factors for the growth of cities and towns in Pakistan are the following : (a) The expansion of commerce and industry ; (b) The increase in agricultural surplus ; (c) The development of transport and communication ; (d) The Improvement of sanitary and health conditions of cities and lastly ; (e) The growth of population.

It has been observed that if there is industrial development in a place there will be increase in trade and commercial activities. This will increase the population of that area because the people will come to work in the factories, mills and industries. So in this way that area will be urbanized. The surplus in agriculture also encourages the rural people to come to the urban areas in Pakistan. Poverty, sometimes, forces the people to move to the urbanized area. It contributes much to the number of population of cities and towns. The better transport and communication are also responsible for the growth of urban areas. The introduction of some modern techniques in transportation and communication in Pakistan is no doubt helping in the growth of urbanization. Health and sanitary conditions are important factors for the urbanization in Pakistan. In our rural areas, thousands of people die of cholera, small pox and other epidemic diseases. The fear of these epidemics, sometimes, push the rural people towards cities and towns if they can manage a job there. The most important factor for the growth of urbanization is the population growth. It will be observed that most of the urban areas except a few have increased their population size. The rate of growth, in most cases, has been above the provincial rate of growth. This is in keeping with the general trend towards urbanization. Among the rapidly increasing urban areas it may be convenient to include only those urban areas which have shown an increase over 50% since 1951. The figures given in table-1, can be treated as rapidly growing urban areas in East Pakistan.

Table 1.[1]
Rapidly Growing Urban Areas in East Pakistan

Name of cities and towns	Population 1961	Population 1951	Number of Increase	Percentage of Increase
Dacca.	5,56,712	3,35,928	2,20,784	65·72
Narayanganj	1,62,054	68,373	93,681	137·01
Khulna	1,27,970	41,409	86,561	209·04
Jessore	46,366	23,867	22,499	94·27
Lalmonirhat	22,001	9,073	12,928	142·49

The urban population as a whole has been increasing during last sixty years. It has gone up to 22·52% in 1961 against 9·77% in 1901 and 17·82% in 1951. It is found that as many as 30 cities and towns, having more than twenty thousand population have shown an increase of more than 50% during the last decade.

In West Pakistan some cities like Peshawar, Quetta, Dera Ismail Khan, Kohat etc., have the high percentage of urban population. Besides these Karachi, Lahore etc., show the highest percentage of urban population.

According to 1961 census the urban population in Pakistan is 13·1% and in East Pakistan the percentage is 5·2. It can be observed that Rahimyar Khan in West Pakistan has shown the highest increase of 192% urban population and Khulna in East Pakistan shows the highest increase of 209·04%. This is due to the industrial and commercial expansion. Lyallpur has registered an increase of 154% of urban population. The other towns like Haroonabad, Burawala and Kanpur show the increase of 125%, 123% and 60% to 100% respectively. The overall increase in the urban population and the growth of new urban areas are, to some extent, counter balanced by the declining towns and cities. In West Pakistan Thatta, Lasbela and Kharan

---

1. Census of Pakistan, 1961.

128   SOCIOLOGY OF PAKISTAN

show the lowest percentage of urban population. Jheelum and
Shialkot have also shown the decrease in urban population. In East
Pakistan Parbatipur, Thakurgaon, Saidpur and Barisal municipality
have shown the great decrease in urban population.

Table 2.

Decreasing population in some urban areas in East Pakistan

Name of towns	Population 1961	Population 1951	Decrease in Number.	Percentage of decrease
Parbatipur	27,188	32,410	5,222	16·11
Thakurgaon	7,039	9,849	2,810	28·53
Saidpur	60,628	61,018	390	0·64
Debhata	4,042	5,461	1,419	25·98
Barisal	69,936	89,278	19,342	21·66
Bajitpur	12,097	13,105	1,008	7·69

Various categories of Pakistani towns appear to have four main
functions :

(1) The towns handle local trade ; serve as collecting and distributing centres and ; provide commercial contacts between the rural
community and the neighbouring area.

(2) As administrative centres with or without commercial function,
the towns contain educational institutions and often possess the bank-
ing and credit facilities and professional services are centred in them.

(3) Some of the towns prepare or semi-process local raw materials for their manufacture elsewhere into exportable goods. These
activities include jute baling, leather tanning, oil pressing etc. They
also manufacture various products on a cottage or small-scale
industry basis, using available local raw materials and the individual
skill of the rural crafts.

(4) Many of the towns serve as important communication centres
either on rivers and railways or on roads. They have multiple facilities.

The first mentioned function is practically common to all towns ;
while the second and third functions represent a high degree of material

development and economic organization. In addition there are a few larger centres engaged in some sort of modern manufacturing though other forms of activities are also present. This category represents a greater accumulation of capital and some kind of modernization of productive forces. However, this development is only in its infancy in Pakistan, but holds the same hope of economic betterment of manpower and greater utilization of natural resources.

URBANIZATION AND INDUSTRIALIZATION IN PAKISTAN

According to the Pakistan censuses of 1951 & 1961, any place where 5000 or more people are living is called the urban area. To the demographers and census experts, population is the main criterion to determine the nature of the place.

Sociologically, urbanism is considered to be a process by which a rural area turns into an urban area giving a distinct way of life, associated with industrial civilization. Both social and demographic factors combined together constitute a sound definition of urbanization. A place is called an urban area where there should be a good sized population with the distinct type of life, associated with industrial development.

Pakistan is predominantly an agricultural country. About 87% of the people depend on agriculture. Agriculture is the main occupation of the people and most of them are living in rural areas. But now our society is in a state of transition. For a better standard of living there is an effort towards industrialization. Without industrialization rapid and true progress of a society is not possible. Rapid changes are being observed in our social structure because of the second world war, partition of India in 1947, inflation, influx of refugees, urbanization and similar other forces. The age-old traditions are breaking down under the impact of modern age. Modern world is the world of industrialization. At present, urbanization is highly correlated with industrialization. Pakistan is also going to be urbanized with the development of industries, factories, mills etc. Of course, urbanization is possible without industrialization. Hence the cities may be pre-industrial in nature. Industry played no important part in the growth of this type of cities. Even now pre-industrial characteristics of cities are found in Pakistan.

9—

Urban growth can be divided into the following three stages:
1) Urbanization in pre-British India.
2) Urbanization in British India.
3) Urbanization in modern India and Pakistan.

The history of urbanization started in pre-British India. The Pre-British period was divided into two : (1) Ancient India and (2) Medieval India. Urbanization, according to some sociologists, is possible without industrialization and the best example for this is the medieval period. The cities grew in pre-British India, was a non-industrial phenomenon. The Little Republic (self sufficient village) was the main hindrance in the growth of urbanization in pre-British India.

In British India, urbanization expanded because of the introduction of trade and commerce. True urbanization began after the Industrial Revolution which helped the establishment of mills, factories and industries.

Under-developed countries sometimes become industrialized through colonization, essentially an exploiting process and enclave industrialization i.e., an isolated company sets up a model industrial community but the rest of the country is little affected by it.

The economy of Pakistan at the time of independence, was basically agrarian in character. Out of the total of 1219 factories of cotton, jute, iron, paper, glass, cement, sugar etc., only 49 factories came to Pakistan. 61 % of the income came from agriculture. The pattern of land tenure in Pakistan at the time of independence, was semi-feudal in character. The Zamindary system was abolished in 1950 and land reform was introduced by the Martial Law Govt., in West Pakistan in 1959. This reform was non-radical in character. One of the most important characteristics of West Pakistan's economy is the cottage industry, run by small artisans and craftsmen. Thus, Pakistan inherited semi-feudal characteristics namely, stagnation, low social mobility, primitive technique in agriculture and industry, low rate of urbanization, low standard of living and lack of educational facilities.

Technological changes in most of the underdeveloped countries in this era mean the breaking of the stagnation of the feudal economy and a take-off into the capitalistic structure of the economy. But the capitalism in underdeveloped countries is sponsored by public and private sectors. This is called a mixed economy. Pakistan's movement towards industrialization is also of the same nature. The stages of industrialization of Pakistan are the following :

  (1) 6-Year Plan (1949-'55)
  (2) 1st. five-Year Plan (1955-'60)
  (3) 2nd. five-Year Plan (1960-'65)

By this time a significant change has taken place in our economic structure. 53 % of national income comes from agriculture and the rest from the industries.

The pace of technological change in Pakistan has been quickened in the period after the partition of August, 1947. The few existing industries consisted of cotton textiles, jute, general engineering industry, railway workshop, rice mills, sugar manufacturing etc.

The existing industries at the time of the partition were mainly run by the Hindu capital and enterprise. A number of these industrialists went over to India. Others reduced the scale of their enterprise ; while most of them faced an acute difficulty in obtaining their raw materials which they, previously, imported from India and also in marketing their products in Pakistan.

Several factors have been responsible for quickening the pace of economic activity in Pakistan in recent years. With the partition there came a dislocation of the external trade of the country. The areas comprising Pakistan which, previously obtained most of their requirements of manufactured goods from India, found themselves cut off from the supply of those commodities. Similarly, India which had formed the natural market for a number of Pakistani products previously, became an increasingly inaccessible market for this country for a number of reasons. Apart from administrative obstacles to trade, the introduction of tariff barrier and the law of exchange control, Pakistan's decision not to devalue her currency in 1949 and India's non-recognition of the fact ;—all contributed to the meeting of requirements of manufactured goods from the countries other than India generally at a high cost. Our country had to seek markets in the countries other than India.

With the partition there was an influx of Muslim businessmen from India to Pakistan. Many of them who had experience of trade and possessed capital readily took up the export and import business which has been very lucrative due to the general shortage of goods and the policy of import control by the Govt. of Pakistan. Very few of the businessmen possessed any experience of industry in India. The more enterprising among them started the industries and this process has been aided by Govt., measures such as acquisition of sites for industries and making them available at low price rates, liberal tax concessions for new industries and transport facilities. The Government of Pakistan established an Industrial Finance Corporation in 1949 to give medium term and long term loans for the development of industry.

Industrialization has also been facilitated by the large-scale influx of Muslim workers from India many of whom had experience of industrial work in India. In this way, Pakistan is going to be industrialized and also to be urbanized.

West Pakistan is more urbanized than East Pakistan. The main reason is that West Pakistan is much more industrialized than East Pakistan. She possesses a large number of mills, factories, workshops etc. Of course, the percentage of people living in urban areas in Pakistan is increasing day by day. But in East Pakistan the increase is slow. The small proportion of town and city dwellers in this province can be explained by several significant features of her economic geography i.e., the predominance of rural paddy culture, main dependence on agrarian resources, limited means of communications and too meagre development of modern industry. Towns have grown up and flourished, in most cases, as administrative centres and in geographically suitable locations for inland transport and commercial facilities. There is no particular concentration of them in the province.

IMPACT OF INDUSTRIALIZATION AND URBANIZATION

Although Pakistan has been traditionally rural, there are undeniable evidences that a change is under way. The acceleration in the growth of cities, the correlation between the size of the city and the rapidity of growth, the trend toward industrial and commercial expansion, development of female employment in urban industries and the consequent normalization of the sex-ratio,—all indicate that urbanization in Pakistan is likely to gain a momentum as it goes forward.

If urbanization is coming on a large-scale, a fundamental revolution will inevitably occur in the Muslim society. The city is the diffusion centre for modern civilization and as it comes to dominate the country side, the new will come to dominate the old. The city has, so far, led in the growth of literacy, in the education of women, in the decline of caste, in the reduction of fertility and in the development of political awareness.

Urbanization in Pakistan faces many obstacles in its growth. Despite the presence of modern industry, modern transportation and modern ideas, the cities have a sprawling insanitary, unplanned and neglected character. Further more, even though modern ideas are in circulation, the extensiveness and persistence of ignorence, disease, overcrowding and stratification are present.

An awareness of urban problems exists. The cities are becoming a more acceptable place to live. Kingsley Davis rightly says, "Urbanization in India and Pakistan as it accelerates, promises to become gradually more humane, but there is likely to be a long period when the gains it makes in this direction will be offset by the losses, contingent upon the faster rate of growth itself."

Pakistani society is in transition. With the achievement of independence in 1947 there are manifold changes in the country. The whole structure of our society is going to have a new character and new shape. Changes are found in the social, economic, political, cultural and educational aspects. Industrialization and urbanization are becoming rapid in Pakistan. There are many consequences of the process of industrialization and urbanization in Pakistan. They are the following:

1. Breaking up of joint family.

2. Increasing contact with the urban centres results in wiping out prejudices and superstitions.

3. Cosmopolitan approach towards life and living.

4. Tendency towards secular approach of life ; religious intolerations are being instigated by the interested quarters.

5. Shift of the centre of community life from the mosques or temples to the schools, class or other government or non-government organizations.

6. Declining impact of the religious authorities on social life.

7. Increasing social mobility.

8. Emergence of the working class. The working class people of Pakistan own some land in the villages.

9. Increase of crimes and juvenile delinquency in the urban areas.

10. Increase of industrial dispute.

11. Development of transportation is helping the movement of population.

12. Spread of westernized education has increased considerably since 1947.

13. Urbanization is bringing the industrial workers together who are now infused with class consciousness.

14. Education and the spread of commerce and industry etc., have encouraged the growth of a middle class in contemporary Pakistani society. This middle class is accelerating the social change at a rapid speed. In political agitations the middle class is playing the vital role.

15. The contemporary Pakistani society is undergoing changes under the pressures of a rising capitalist class. The capitalists in Pakistan are accelerating the industrialization which is bringing about other social changes. The old feudal social structure is being changed by the capitalist.

16. Change in social stratification.

Urban social class:

(a) Upper class : Capitalists, industrialists, big contractors, big businessmen, high govt. officers.

(b) Middle class : Govt. officers, intellectuals, lawyers, doctors, engineers, petty merchants etc.

(c) Lower class : Factory workers, rickshaw-pullers, labourers etc.

Rural Social Class :

(a) Upper class : Big owner-farmers, rich village headmen, wealthy Basic Democrats, village aristocrats etc.

(b) Middle class : Owner-cum-tenant farmers, village doctors, priests, school teachers etc.

(c) Lower class: Landless labourers.

17. Media of communication such as radio and other media of information are helping the cultural diffusion.

18. Printing press and publications and films industry are growing with urbanization.

19. Tendency towards obscurity of our contemporary arts.

20. Change from fatalistic out-look to materialistic out-look.

21. The transition from the compact and intimate world of the village to the highly impersonal and anonymous world of the city.

The areas which constitute Pakistan were neglected by the British entrepreneurs. After the independence things have changed. Pakistan is undergoing rapid industrialization. The govt. initiative and enterprises of E.P.I.D.C. and W.P.I.D.C. have facilitated her industrialization. Response to industrialization from the private sector is also quite satisfactory in certain spheres.

Urbanization is also increasing with industrialization. The rapid industrialization is materially bringing some new social problems. As the socio-economic structure of Pakistan is changing and with this change there is also concomitant rise of new social problems. The following problems are caused by urbanization and industrialization in Pakistan :

1. Housing problem.
2. Unemployment and poverty.
3. Disintegration of families.
4. Juvenile delinquency.
5. Prostitution.
6. Gambling.
7. Crime.
8. Drug addiction.
9. Deaths and diseases.
10. Alcoholism.
11. Change in attitude to morality.
12. Insecurities of the old.
13. Occupational hazards.

Housing Problem : Overcrowded slums are found in the cities because of the lack of housing estate. To extreme overcrowding, there is a notable absence of sanitary facilities and other conveniences. The urban housing conditions are little worse than those in the country because this region has rural slums, scarcely equalled elsewhere.

Unemployment and poverty : Unemployment and poverty are the two important social problems which are related to many socio-economic reasons. Unemployment and poverty are mainly due to lack of economic growth and the introduction of the new types of instruments of production. The old traditional cottage industries are being wiped out by the machine-run large-scale industries. This throws the labourers, engaged there out of employment. This will bring poverty to the people of the country.

In industrialized Pakistan new types of unemployment will be created by the social disorganization, division of labour and specialization. Unemployment in industrialized Pakistan will fundamentally be caused by a lack of balance between supply and demand of labour.

Disintegration of Families : The family in this country meant not only the husband and wife but also a number of dependents, including even the distant relations. This traditional joint family was intact in Pakistan until the recent times. But an investigation in the "Human and Social Impact of Technological Changes in Pakistan" reveals that the joint family system is slowly breaking down in the urban areas. When a young member of a family educates himself and accepts an employment in the urban areas he takes his wife and children with him. This is the genesis of the disintegration of joint family system in our country.

Juvenile delinquency : The children, as well as, the adults may become bad citizens. The recent statistics of the western countries reveal that the rate of the crime in the age group of 7-21 years is on increase. The criminals in this age group are known as juvenile delinquents. It is mainly due to the disorganization of family. In cities and towns, sometimes, both the husband and wife go out for earning their wages. As a result, the children are neglected. They suffer from emotional instability. In Pakistan the problem is not yet serious. Nevertheless, the number of the offenders between the age group of 7-21 years is increasing.

Prostitution : Prostitution as an institution has persisted in the urban life for a long time. It is not the institution of recent origin. The glamour of the city life used to attract many girls to the urban areas. It is an institution, relatively compact in the urban centres of the industrial civilizations. In the present day world, it is an institution which refers to the type of reciprocity that exists between the customer and the prostitutes. The type of reciprocity is highly mobile and easy-going in the city life. The city life possesses the hybrid of human personality. The factor of anonymity also helps the professional to get a high frequency of reciprocity with the customers. The main factor behind the development of the profession of prostitution in the urban life of Pakistan is poverty.

Gambling : It is the most universal phenomenon and connected with urban life. With the urbanization of Pakistan it is being institutionalized.

Crime : The good place of criminals in the city life is the fringe or the zone of transition. Many people in this zone do not share the established values of the society. From the point of view of the value, they are the marginal people of urban life. There develop the various types of criminals,—Pickpocket, blackmailer, house breaker etc. They commit crime through the institutional organization. It refers to the various criminal associations, organizations and institutions— all of which are coherently organized and conducted under the rigid leadership in order to carry on the business of crime as an occupation. Very often, the organizations are so well equiped that they challenge the protection of the public system.

Drug Addiction : The chronic patients, society girls, juvenile delinquents, criminals and the prostitutes are the drug addicted population of urban life.

The patients take the medicine for the cure of the disease. But after the cure of the disease they can not give up the habit. The process of addiction in this case is psychological. Due to the contrasting way of life caused by the uneven distribution of power, wealth and social status, there are certain classes of people who have to lead a miserable life. Among these classes society girls are the most typical to have usually undergone a deep psychological strain and complexes. In order to escape from the hard realities of life the depressed classes take the drugs to be disorganized. It is almost an universal phenomenon in modern city life.

Alcoholism : Alcoholism is similar to drug addiction in that it is either the cause or the effect of mental disorder. The problem of alcoholism is psychological as well as social. It is found in an institutional form in the city. It is prohibited officially and constitutionally in the Islamic Republic of Pakistan. But with the influence of western culture and civilization and also with the development of urbanization and industrialization, it is increasing day by day. It is sufficient to mention the costly hotels with "Bar" in Dacca, Karachi and Lahore.

Change in attitudes to morality : The social background of Pakistan is still conservative. But industrialization will shatter this conservatism. Employment in factories take the workers away from their homes. They are away from their wives. So there is a tendency among the workers to indulge in cheap recreation. Immorality in the industrial areas in Pakistan has not yet taken any drastic shape. This problem may be tackled with reinforcement of moral education and better recreation facilities.

Insecurities of the old : The industrial workers are thrown out of employment after a certain stage of their life. It is due to physical inability and mental infirmity. The older generation may drift to pauperism and beggary which mean additional social problems. In the western societies the problem is being solved with old-age pensions and other beneficial schemes. But in Pakistan, so far, little has been done for the social security benefits.

Occupational hazards : Occupational hazards are the fatal and non-fatal accidents, industrial accidents, automobile accidents and home accidents. The automobile and industrial accidents are increasing day by day. The industrial hazards constitute a great social problem. When a man dies in such an accident he leaves his family and other dependents helpless, who may become vagrants or criminals because of the sudden break of their normal livelihood and education.

Bibliography

Ahmad, N. *Economic Geography of East Pakistan.* London, Oxford University Press, 1958.

Afsaruddin, Md. *Juvenile Delinquency in East Pakistan.* Dacca, 1963.

Arnold, F.B. (ed.) *Pakistan: Economic and Commercial Conditions.* London, H.M. Stationary office, 1954. (overseas economic survey)

Akhtar, S.M. *"Economic Institutions".* Pakistan Review 9 (2) Feb., 1961.

Ahmad, K. *"Our Economic Problems"* in Voice of Islam 6 (2-3) Nov.-Dec. 1957.

Davis, K. *The Population of India and Pakistan.* Princeton University Press, 1951.

Hatt, K. P. and Reiss, J. A. *Cities and Society.* New York, 1961.

Hussain, A.F.A. *Human and Social Impact of Technological Change in Pakistan.* Oxford University Press, vol. I. Pakistan, 1956.

Hussain, A.F.A. and Farouk, A. *Problems of Social Integration of Industrial Workers in Khulna with special reference to the problem of industrial unrest,* Dacca. Dacca University Socio-Economic Research Board, 1961.

Karim, A.K.N. *"Changing Patterns of East Pakistan Family".* (In Women in New Asia. Paris, Unesco, 1963, P.P. 296-322)

Khan, A.H. *Towns of Pakistan, Ancient and Modern.* Karachi, Bashir Ahmad, 1950.

Khan, F.K. and Masood, M. *"Urban Structure of Comilla Town",* Oriental Geographer 6 (2), July, 1963. P.P. 109-139.

Ibrahim, R. *"Industrialization and Culture"* in the Pakistan Development Review, vol. V. Karachi, 1965.

Newman, P.C. *"National Planning, Industrialization and the Economic Development"* in the Pakistan Economic Journal vol. IV, 1954.

CHAPTER 9
GROUP LIFE IN PAKISTAN

MEANING OF A GROUP

A social group consists of two or more persons who have a common goal and a common point of interest. The members share the experiences of each other. To describe a group in a different way, it is an aggregation of persons whose relations with each other are important to demand the attention of the members who have common interests and objectives and also the attention of those who do not participate in these relationships. According to Selznick and Broom, a group refers to any collection of persons who are bound together by a distinctive set of social relations.

IMPORTANCE OF GROUP IN SOCIAL AND CULTURAL LIFE

Man has always lived in some sort of groups. From the very beginning of social life man has felt the necessity to live and carry on his various types of activities in the association of human beings. In this world of competition, conflict and challenge he can survive and face the challenge only by cooperating with his fellow beings to meet his biological and social needs. As man nowhere lives in complete isolation, the common sharing of experiences of those in human association would leave the imprint of group life upon him. During his formative period a child is very much influenced by the association with others in the collective task of making a living and securing a shelter. From his very childhood man always lives in a group, sharing the activities, ideas and points of view of other members in the group.

CLASSIFICATION OF GROUPS

There are always various types of groups in the society. When a society is highly differentiated there are many groups to cope with the division of labour. These groups may be large or small, permanent or temporary. The following are the major types of groups:

Primary Group : It refers to intimate face to face association, cooperation and sympathy. It is fundamental in forming the social nature of individual. The specific types of primary groups that Prof. Cooley had in mind, were the family group, the play group of children and the neighbourhood.

Secondary Group : In this type of group the bonds of sentiment and sympathy are less apparent. The contacts are more likely to be casual, impersonal and fleeting. A club can be cited as an example of a secondary group.

Pressure Group : It is an association formed for protest or conflict purpose. It is organized formally to combat some other types of groups, to oppose some practices or to promote some particular idea or plan of action.

In-Group : It is an association with which the individual is identified both psychologically and physically.

Out-Group : It is a group with which the person is not identified. In his study of the primitive, society Sumner mentioned that the members of his in-group were quite different from those of the out-group.

GROUP FUNCTION

The members or, at least, a part of them act together in some types of enterprise. As members of a given group they may work to promote some idea or objective in political, economic, religious, recreational, educational, scientific and literary fields. A group has got certain psychological functions. It may provide for the person some degree of security or prestige. It may also serve as an outlet through which emotional expression may be channalized. It influences the process of socialization and personality development of the individuals.

RECENT TRENDS IN GROUP LIFE IN PAKISTAN

In a primitive tribe, individuals are linked together for the most part by primary type of group relationship. But as the complexity of the society has increased and as the accomplishment of more of its tasks has required the development of large-scale organizations, a greater number of secondary types of relationships are evolving and many of the old primary relations and the groups within which they are expressed have been disturbed or displaced. The so-called secondary groups are showing an increase in number, especially in urban areas. The development of civilization has primarily meant the technological change, the economic expansion and the rapid growth of urbanization with all its by-products. All these have, no doubt, the effect of breaking up of old social units. But they are also responsible for the emergence of new social pattern with new values. Now let us try to make some observations on the present trends of group-life in Pakistan and find out the causes responsible for the changes. Pakistan is mainly an agricultural country. The great bulk of the population lives in villages. In comparison with industrialized countries there are very few industries here. But it is a fact that industrialization and urbanization are gradually heading up in Pakistan and there is a gradual increase of urban population and number of industries. The percentage of literacy is increasing. Thus the growth of urbanization and industrialization, the increase in literacy and employment of women, the changing status of women in the family and cultural diffusion etc., have led to the gradual breaking up of traditional primary groups in Pakistan.

While there are numerous primary groups in Pakistani society, there is gradual increase in secondary contacts. (In rural areas, however, the great bulk of human association occurs in primary groups. It is only in the urban and semi-urban areas, we see the phenomenon of increased secondary contacts.) One reason for this trend may be the decreased amount of time being spent in primary groups and the corresponding increase in the secondary type of participation. With the complex net-work of social mechanism groups are becoming more and more specialized. Not only the individuals but also the groups are becoming increasingly devoted to specific purposes and functions. These groups have grown up because of the new and even basically changed needs of people under modern urban conditions. Many of them have arisen as specialized groups. Thus the family which, at one time, supported many of the needs of its members is giving way to various specialized groups such as school, nursery, laundry, hospital etc. As for example, the function formerly performed by the family doctors are now divided up among dozens of specialized kinds of medical groups, working in hospitals, laboratories and special clinics for almost every organ in the body, each organization, having some specialized sort of functions for meeting the health needs of the person. It is probable, of course, that the opportunity is thus provided for better health of many people, but the kind of group interaction characterized by the family doctor and his patient is slowly but surely declining and in its place are arising those specialized groups in which a person participates as a member-participant, perhaps a few times in life or may be not at all.

There was a time, when people were cradled in small local groups in which everyone was interested in his neighbour's activities and they were highly concerned about each other's coming and going, loves and hates, sorrows and miseries and loss and profit, but now the individuals are attaching more and more value and importance to secondary contacts. Life for the child still begins in the most primary group of all,- the family. For the child there is still the play-ground. But as the child gains the adolescence he begins to transfer to secondary group situation in which strangeness and anonymity are the characteristics. This, for many, begins as they enter the large city high school or in case of rural young people as they enter into large consolidated high school. The transfer to the work world too is, for most young people, a long step from a life surrounded by primary group influences. The transition takes place when the young people of rural areas migrate to the cities or towns, seeking work and this breaks the connection with the customs, folkways and mores in intimate local neighbourhood. They are to adopt their lives to daily contacts with strangers in the urban areas where mobility is very high. As a result, the neighbourhood bond breaks up and causes life to loose its intimate character. Nevertheless the rural life today best typifies the primary group experience ; while urban life best typifies the secondary group experience. But urbanization has increased man's secondary group experience to an enormous degree. Adult life for many is spent in secondary groups though everyone tries to build around himself a primary group in whatever situation he is placed. In the rural areas neighbourhood groups of relatives often go together for special days and celebrations. The entire group members know each other and talk of their common life and problems,—the

harvest of the year, the children etc. All in the group face the same
daily routine. Even the smallest incident relating to the affairs of all
youngsters is not only the concern of the parents, but also of the aunts,
uncles and neighbours. The youngsters are subservient to their
relatives and neighbours. There we have some restrictive form of life.

The city-life has contributed much to the growth of individualism
among the city-dwellers. Today, group life in the city in Pakistan has
relieved man, to some extent, from the restrictive inhibitions of the
intimate group and made it possible for individualism to flourish.

In an anonymous city life in Pakistan, a man may follow his own
inclinations, not being too seriously disturbed by what others think of
him. Because of the increasing number of secondary groups in urban
areas, people have a new path to walk on. They experience a considerable change in the social values when they come to live in larger social
aggregates where contacts are, for the most part, casual rather than
intimate.

In this mobile urban community where the locality no longer binds
a man to his long acquainted neighbours and relatives, a man can go
on his own way without much scrutiny of his former neighbours. It is,
of course, true that this tendency is less apparent in rural communities.

CAUSES OF THIS TRANSITION

All that we can effectively say is that Pakistani society is undergoing a change and more and more groups are becoming secondary
in nature, especially in urban areas. Modern industrial civilization rests
on non-primary form of groupings where the relationship is mostly
formal in nature. Pakistan has also experienced the impact of industrialization and as a result, the growth of large-scale associations
and organizations are causing the disappearance of the neighbourhood
group feeling. the intimate family relationship and the spontaneous
play group. What seems to matter in the 20th century is the phenomenal growth of secondary groups. In our city-life the intimacy of the
neighbourhood has been broken up by the growth of an intricate mesh
of wider contacts which leave us strangers to the people who live perhaps in the same house. Due to improved system of communication
the people are no longer satisfied in their local associations. In the cities
where the old life has been disorganized by the influx of strangers,

a neighbourhood does no longer seem to be a distinguishable unit of social organization. For example the people nearby, may not know them personally and have no regard for other's opinion.

Modern communication through radio, newspaper etc., is breaking the psychological unit which was the feature of the past. We see that the people in the city feel no interest about their next door neighbour. People of the like attitude do tend to segregate into territorial publics in the city, but the modern life in the city tends to destroy real neighbourhood solidarity. Modern communication has impact on primary group in many ways. The family and the play group are showing the effects of the mobility of their own members and of the community about them. The activities of the members of a household, especially in urban areas are now done away from home. Many women now work outside their home. The agencies, drawing the children outside the home are increasing. People of different age groups flock to the cities and towns from the rural areas for various facilities, such as education, employment opportunities etc., in different governmental agencies. A good number of adult population is moving to urban areas for employment in governmental agencies, companies, factories etc. Thus the traditional family system is losing its integrity.

What all these mean is that the primary group is gradually changing. Facing the decline of the old spontaneous face-to-face association, we have been driven to set up other less intimate groups, such as neighbourhood club.

No matter how informally such organization may be conducted and no matter how much familiarity may spring up between the members, they are still an ad hock organization, set up for a purpose with rules and formal regulations. It is becoming increasingly difficult to maintain the primary group relationships in the metropolis like Karachi, Dacca and Lahore. However, the reliance upon primary group exclusively in such a situation would merely bring about the decay of those basic interactions and the unity of sentiment and purpose, necessary for the maintenance of the family as a unit. Thus the secondary type of group is inevitable to grow up in such communities.

Bibliography

Bottomore, T.B. *Sociology*. George Allen & Unwin Ltd., London 1962.

Bessaignet, P. (ed.) *Social Research in East Pakistan*. Asiatic Society of Pakistan, Dacca 1960.

Gisbert, P. *Fundamentals of Sociology*. Orient Longmans Ltd., Bombay 1957.

Griffith, P. *The British Impact on India*. London 1952

MacIver, R.M. *Society*. Macmillan and Co. Ltd., 1962.

Selznick, P. and Broom, L. *Sociology (A Text With Adopted Readings)* Row, Peterson and Company, New York 1956.

Carr, L. J. *Analytical Sociology*. Harper & Brothers, New York 1948-1955

CHAPTER 10

SOCIAL CHANGE AND SOCIAL PROBLEMS IN PAKISTAN

MEANING OF SOCIAL CHANGE

Social change refers to the modifications which occur in the life pattern of a people. According to Nordskog, "Social change means simply the process of becoming different in any sense." In the opinion of MacIver social change is a process responsive to many types of change, to changes in the attitudes and beliefs of men and to changes that go back beyond human control.

Society is never static ; it is always dynamic. In most of the contemporary societies the change is relatively rapid. Generally, social change implies the modifications in the social structure. It is impossible to analyse the structure of modern societies without constantly referring to the changes that are taking place in behaviour, status, roles, institutions, values and other pattern of relationships, existing among the members of the society. The concept of social change has the basic implications for a dynamic society.

Hence it is important to know the extent of the changes in the structure of a society. In Barber's words, social structure merely defines some pattern picked out at any moment from the endlessly continuing process of social interaction. Social change, therefore, means, (a) that given individuals, groups, associations, communities, classes, values, status, roles and institutions assume different positions in the social structure, (b) that the assumed positions are subject to change with the passage of time.

CHANGES IN PAKISTAN

Under the present situation we consider Pakistani society a transitional one. As the process of social change is not of equal nature and speed in our urban and rural areas, we shall deal separately with the changes in the urban and rural areas.

CHANGES IN URBAN AREAS

Economy: After the partition of Indo-Pak subcontinent we find many changes in the economic field of Pakistan. Before the partition in 1947 the main centres of production were the villages i.e., the economy was based on agriculture. But after independence Pakistan gave full importance and attention to industrialization. Many factories and mills were set up in different parts of the country. Due to this industrialization many changes are taking place in the economic spheres of our country. Although predominantly agricultural in nature, the economic structure of Pakistan is becoming more and more industrial and urban. This change from the agrarian to the industrial economy is sociologically significant because with these changes in the economic structure there are many other changes in other structures of our society. Due to this change the distinction between different economic classes i.e., upper class, middle class and lower class is becoming prominent and the conflicts of interest are creating many serious problems. Specialization and division of labour are emerging in the society. The labour classes in Pakistan are organizing themselves through trade unions to fight for their cause. To cope with this transformation of our economy, the number of banks, markets, insurance companies and commercial farms is increasing in Pakistan. The emergence of some industrial values which are, sometimes, in conflict with our old traditional values is very significant.

The foreign trade of Pakistan has expanded much during these 18 years. There are also changes in the land tenure system which has given the ownership right to the tenants.

POLITICS

After independence, Pakistan has become a democratic country. After 1947 many changes have been introduced in our political field. These changes are mainly found in the structure and functions of the state and government. But the major structural-functional changes in the state and the government have been introduced by President Ayub Khan by giving the country a new form of democracy, called the Basic Democracies. Another significant development in our political field is the emergence of many political parties with different aims and objectives. This has made the people politically conscious. They show interest in both national and international political issues.

SOCIAL

Family : There are considerable changes in the pattern of family life in the urban areas of Pakistan. The joint family system is breaking down and the single family system is gradually becoming predominant in the urban areas. The concept of individualism is developing among the members of the urban family. With the break down of the joint family, the relationship between the parents and the children is becoming informal and democratic in nature. In some of the urban fami lies where both the husband and wife work outside their home the children are mostly deprived of parental care, sympathy and affection. There are changes in the nature and type of family recreation. Most of the urban families are attracted by the outside recreational centres like club, theatre, movies, cultural shows, danceparty, picnic etc.

Marriage : In the urban areas there are changes in marriage pattern. Although the arranged marriage is still the predominant form of marriage, the incidence of choice-marriage is increasingly found in our urban areas. There is simplicity in the ceremonies of urban marriages because of the economic consideration. The introduction of the Family Ordinance has brought about changes in family relationships and marriage patterns in Pakistan. This ordinance has given the women proper status and has indirectly discouraged the practice of polygamy among the Muslims.

Role And Status : Role and status are the two related terms in sociology. The status of the urban people in Pakistan is largely determined by their roles in economic, political, administrative, cultural and social spheres. Like other countries of the world, the urban people of Pakistan are to achieve their status by proving their worth in their activities. This is the result of the industrial economic structure, towards which Pakistan is going fast. The independence itself has helped to change the status and role of the urban population in Pakistan. With the partition of India in 1947, many people in Pakistan engaged themselves in the small-scale trade, farming, large-scale investment in business and industries. Many high Governmental posts, previously occupied by the Britishers and the Hindus were filled up by the Muslim urban educated people. This caused a significant change in the class affiliation of the people in Pakistan. A strong middle class emerged in our society.

Class And Caste : The Concept of social structure can not be objectively analysed without the understanding of social stratification. There are two phenomena of social stratification : (1) Class and (2) Caste. In Pakistan, due to the change of economic structure the class affiliation of the people is changing. As for example the Nawabs, Zamindars, Jotdars and Talukdars do not have the same status as they previoulsy used to enjoy. Flexibility in class affiliation, class characteristics and class relations can be observed in the urban areas. Among the Hindus flexibility in some characteristics i.e., interdining, untouchability is found in the caste system. The modern technology is breaking the rigidity of the caste system in the urban areas.

Education : Change is also taking place in the educational sphere in the urban areas of Pakistan. Education for the children is desired by every class of people in our society. During the British period the purpose of education was to create a number of officials to help the British Administration in ruling the country. But after the partition of India in 1947 many changes have been introduced in its structure and function. Now, different educational institutions are giving emphasis on our national and cultural values.

Recreation : Changes are also taking place in the field of recreation of our society. The nature of recreation has changed a lot. In the urban areas the recreational facilities of the people are increasing beacuse of both the public and private endeavours. With the growth of urbanization and industrialization the recreational activities are being taken away by various commercial recreational concerns, associations and secondary groups. The urbanites go to the club, theatre, cinema etc., for recreation. Changes can also be found in the housing and consumption pattern, health, sanitation and medical care and dress pattern in the urban areas of Pakistan.

CHANGE IN RURAL AREAS

Economy : There is little change in the village economy of Pakistan. The village dwellers are to depend upon agriculture for their livelihood.

There are some changes in agriculture. In some areas of Pakistan there is mechanization of agriculture ; manures are supplied to the cultivators; insects are destroyed by spraying medicine to improve the conditions of agriculture in Pakistan. The Government of Pakistan is trying hard to bring overall improvements in the field of agriculture by introducing various measures. They are supplying good seeds and trying to bring about a change in the method of cultivation. The introduction of the works programme is also responsible for some changes in our rural economy.

POLITICS

In our villages, certain political changes are observed. Now-a-days the rural people are becoming conscious about their political rights and privileges. They often discuss the national issues. In the village administration changes are very prominent. The village Union Board has disappeared and in its place the institution of Basic Democracies has been introduced.

SOCIAL

Family And Marriage : In rural Pakistan the joint family system is still predominant. There are very few single families. No important change is found in the structure of the family. But there are changes in the functions of the rural family due to the impact of urbanization and industrialization which are attracting the rural people to the urban areas. The system of arranged marriage is the usual pattern of marriage. Changes are visible in the factors, responsible for the selection of the bride and the bridegroom.

Role And Status : There is very little change in the status and role of the villagers because of the lack of opportunities available to them. However, some minor changes have taken place in the economic role of a number of villagers. This change has given them a different status in the society.

Recreation : In the recreational aspects of our rural life some changes have taken place. In early times "gossip" was an important source of recreation for the rural people. 'Jatra' (village opera) and 'mela' (fair) were two other important sources of recreation. Boat race and cattle race were very popular among the villagers. But today we find the addition of transistor radio and village club for the recreation of the villagers. There are other areas such as consumption pattern, sanitation and health and dress pattern where minor changes are taking place.

FACTORS RESPONSIBLE FOR SOCIAL CHANGE IN PAKISTAN

There are many factors which are directly or indirectly responsible for social changes in Pakistan. If we analyse the factors or circumstances, responsible for these changes we find the following :

1. Partition of India in 1947 itself is responsible for the changes in different areas of social life. Since the partition certain dynamic forces are at work in the society which tend to move the social structure and institutions into a new phase.

2. Technology and scientific inventions have great influence on our social life and their introduction and impact bring about the major changes in the structure and functions of the society.

3. The growth of urbanization and industrialization is largely responsible for the social changes in Pakistan. It is said that agriculture leads to conservatism and industrialization to modernization and liberalism. With the introduction of industrialization there occurred changes in attitude, occupation and mode of living of the people of Pakistan.

4. Commercial activities and international trade are also the causes of social change because they are always the important factors for the growth of urbanization and development of cities and towns in Pakistan.

5. The change in the economic structure of the country is responsible for the changes in other structures and sub-structures of Pakistani society. As for example, the transformation of agricultural economic structure to the industrial economic structure, is responsible for the changes in our political, educational, religious, recreational and family life.

6. The spread of literacy is another factor for the changes in our society. The secular intelligentia,—the manipulators of symbols, who shape the slogans and doctrines by which the new ways of life are rationalized and institutionalized.

7. The ideology of different political parties in Pakistan is also influencing our attitudes, life and social values.

8. The impact of highly developed countries is responsible for social changes in our country. These developed countries provide the underdeveloped country like Pakistan with money, technical equipments and technicians.

9. Trade unions and cooperative movements play their significant roles for social changes.

10. Mass media of communication is playing a significant role for the social change in our country. Different agencies of mass media of communication i.e., radio, press, cinema, transistor etc., help the people to change their attitudes and outlook.

11. Migration is indirectly responsible for social change because of the interaction between the migrants (sometimes, with different culture) and the local people.

12. One of the most important factors, responsible for social change is the cultural diffusion. Some of the culture complexes and traits of the western societies are penetrating in our culture and mode of living.

SOCIAL PROBLEMS IN PAKISTAN

Meaning of Social Problem : According to P.B. Horton, a social problem is a condition affecting a significant number of people in ways, considered undesirable and about which it is felt something can be done through collective social actions. This definition has four distinct ideas (1) a condition affecting a significant number of people, (2) in ways considerd undesirable, (3) about which it is felt something can be done and (4) through collective social action.

The following are some of the ideas of the people about social problems :

(1) Problems are not natural and inevitable ; (2) Problems are not abnormal but they are the normal results of our social arrangements ; (3) Problems arise from social arrangements and not from bad people and the badness of the people involved should usually be viewed as symptoms or results rather than causes of the problem ; (4) Problems are genuine and they are not illusions created by wild talks ; (5) Many people do not really want certain problems to be solved ; (6) Most problems do not solve themselves or die out as time passes ; (7) Getting the facts will rarely solve a problem

because people hold different values and want different outcomes ;
(8) Problems can not be thoroughly solved without major changes
in present social institutions and practices.

According to Dryden, a social problem is any condition that causes
strain, tension, conflict and frustration and interferes with the fulfilment
of a need. The dimensions of a social problem are psychological in
the sense of emotional or intellectual disturbance and material in the
sense of extent, incidence or distribution. Strain or anxiety is a dynamic
element in the problem. A problem situation compels those affected
to seek a 'solution'. It calls for relief through modifications of the
environment through social changes in the situation.

The impact of any one individual on most of the social situations
of his life is relatively limited. Each of us was born into a pre-existing
society with its pre-existing associations, forms, categories and processes
and its pre-existing culture of language, customs, institutions and so on.
As children we are not even aware of these things. Even as adults
we find ourselves caught in all kinds of social conditions that have
developed without our consciously desiring them. There are such
undesiring things as housing shortages, depressions etc. A hundred
other unwished contingencies arise. These force us to readjust to our
social world. In primitive life, in the middle ages before the coming
of the western ideas, customary response to such contingencies would
have been submission ; reliance on supernatural aid. But since the rise
of modern western civilization, a different attitude has come to prevail.
Modern western man takes it for granted that man ought to dominate
his environment, even this social environment, instead of letting the
environment dominate him. These contingencies that one can not
any longer handle on the basis of habit and routine are what we call
problems. The word 'problem' comes from a Greek word 'Problema'
which means something 'thrown forward' or thrust on attention. And
what is thrown forward or thrust on attention in the case of social
problem is the failure of a social situation to meet our preferences
or values. A problem then according to Lowell, J. carr, exists
whenever we become conscious of a difficulty, a gap between our
preference and reality. When that consciousness of a difficulty
involves enough persons to constitute a challenge to the 'status quo'
we speak of a social problem. How many individuals are enough to

constitute a challenge depends on many things,—who they are, how effectively they can dramatize the issue and so on.

As a developing country Pakistan is facing various problems. Before independence, when we were under the British rule we did not feel much about these problems. But after we attained a separate homeland in 1947, we became more conscious of these problems. Until and unless something is done by the whole nation to do away with these problems, it would not be possible for us to develop our underdeveloped social and economic structures. Many of these problems which were not existing before the British rule, are the products of the western capitalistic influence. Among the problems the most grave one which the whole nation faces is the population problem. Though it is not a social problem in the sense of other problems like juvenile delinquency, beggary, crimes etc., but still it is the major problem of Pakistan which exerts strain, tension, conflict and frustration among both the intelligentia, as well as, the general masses. Practically various other social problems are more or less the result of this increasing growth of population. Other major social problems which this developing country faces are (a) Prostitution, (b) Beggary, (c) Juvenile delinquency, (4) Unemployment, (e) Student unrest, (f) Refugee and (g) Crimes.

POPULATION PROBLEM

Population problem is not only confined to a particular region like Pakistan, but it is considered as an international or global problem. This problem of population growth is dangerous in Asia, especially in South East Part and in Latin America. Pakistan's two great neighbours,—India and China are also facing an unbelievable population pressure.

According to Malthusian theory of population, the growth of population tends to be faster than the food supply. According to this theory population has the tendency to grow in geometrical progression (1,2,4,8,16) while the food supply on arithmetical progression (1,2,3,4,5,). Consequently at any given time the size of a population is limited by the amount of available food. Most of the population exists at a minimum subsistence level, barely staying alive and ready to be wiped out by a variety of possible calamities. According to Malthus, the growth of population would be checked by two measures.

The positive checks refer to those means of population limitation which operate through deaths by war, famine, diseases etc. The preventive measure checks through the preventing of additional births which depend upon the primary will power of human being. He meant that people should marry late. Thus, in this way the increasing growth of population would be checked.

But this theory of population limitation is not effectively applicable in our country. Here the birth rate is so high that a few positive measures have little effect on the increasing growth of the size of the population. Moreover the Malthusian supposition that in a highly populated area the birth rate will be low among the poor class because of malnutrition is falsified because in our country it can be found that the poor people have the maximum number of children.

Population growth was, however, in equilibrium for sometime in the past in united India. The death rate was even higher than the birth rate because of poor diet and epidemic diseases. But since it was surpassed by higher birth rate, the population grew moderately and steadily. Every few years a calamity of one sort or the other would suddenly increase the death rate and wipe out the population increment that had been accumulating.

There were three decades when population in India hardly grew because of two great famines, one in 1876-78 and the second in 1898-1900 and other one is the influenza epidemic of 1918, killing a total population of 15 Million. But besides these three great calamities the population was increasing somewhat rapidly.

Now we should turn to a consideration of some of the demographic data of Pakistan. From this it can be seen that Pakistan has shown a steady rise of her population. Pakistan had in 1901 a total population of slightly more than 4 crores. According to the census report of 1951 her population became 76 million. About 56% of her population i.e., 42 million lived in East Pakistan and 44% i.e., 34 million in West Pakistan. Thus the statistics between these two periods showed an increase of approximately 66.7% or an average of 1.03% per annum. East Pakistan increased her population during that period by about 18% against 9% during 1901-'11, 5% during 1911-'21 and 7% during 1921-'31. The 1941-'51 decade was less favourable to the population growth due to partition and famine in East Pakistan. Among the countries of the world Pakistan stood 7th in size of population. Based on a total area of 365000 sq. miles the average total population density in 1951 was 208 persons per sq. mile. It has therefore the 5th highest density among the 10 most populated countries of the world.

According to 1961 census, the total population of the country was 93·8 million though the unofficial record showed the population of 100 million. West Pakistan with relatively large area of 310 thousand sq. miles contained only 45·8% of the total population, whereas East Pakistan with an area of only 55 thousand sq. miles contained 54·2% of the total population. Pakistan, thus, has the 6th position in the world in size of population. The increase of population during the last decade has been 27·1% in West Pakistan and 20·9% in East Pakistan.

The agricultural density by which is meant the total rural population per sq. mile of cultivated land exceeds 1200 in East Pakistan and 700 in the former Punjab. This gives East Pakistan perhaps the highest population density in the world for an agrarian economy with the possible exception of Java.

This increasing trend of population in Pakistan poses a great problem. If this rate of population increase goes on, by 1969 the population is supposed to be 10 crores 16 lakhs. The population will gradually be increasing more as the death rate comes down because of western medical facilities. Thus the low death rate on the one hand, and high birth rate on the other will help the population grow very rapidly.

Pakistan specially East Pakistan is an agricultural country. The area under crops in both the provinces is 54 million acres which is little less than one-fourth of total area of the country. The cultivated area amounts to just under 0.6 acres per capita. Of the total cultivated area, over 80 percent is under food crops, mostly rice and wheat. The yields per acre are very low, with the serious result that Pakistan is not producing enough food to feed her large population and the population is growing at an alarming rate.

Agricultural statistics show that the area under food crops increased from approximately 40·5 to 44·7 million acres from 1948-'49 to 1961-'62 and the production of food grains increased from 14·4 million to 16·5 million tons during the same period. Assuming 4·5 maunds of food grains as an average per capita consumption per year, a population of 100 million would require 18·5 million tons ; while the estimated food production is only 16·5 million tones, thus leaving a deficit of 2 million tones per year. Thus the country is facing a grave food crisis and this crisis would be more acute in the future unless and until the production is increased on the one hand, and the population growth is checked on the other.

This unusual growth of population is sure to have serious consequences on the economy of Pakistan. Because of the low production and high birth rate, our per capita income is as low as 56 paisa which is unable even to meet the minimum subsistence level. The per capita income depends upon the resources, technology and economic organization, as well as, upon the population.

In this grave situation we need a planned population policy for raising the standard of living. Planned parenthood is needed to decrease the birth rate. There are many sociological, economic and psychological hindrances to birth control in Pakistan, but from the foregoing analysis it becomes clear that these barriers should be removed. If Pakistan does not solve these problems and does not sharply reduce the birth rate in the near future, the standard of living will inevitably decline and the present multitude of socio-economic problems will increase and become more severe. The problem of population can be solved only in relation to other problems such as utilization of human and material resources, spread of education and training, improvement in man-power planning, creation of employment opportunities, intensification of the programmes of family planning and health centres. In fact, training and use of human resources should be the essence of our planning.

JUVENILE DELINQUENCY

Another important problem, Pakistan is facing is the problem of juvenile delinquency. Practically it is not only a problem of Pakistani society, but a problem of many societies of the world. Any society, undergoing a change in its structural-functional aspects is bound to face the problem of dislocation and disequilibrium in the social, cultural, political and economic life of the community. As Pakistani society is experiencing a rapid change both in its basic and super structures due to industrialization, many changes are taking place, which resulted in the emergence of new problems of which juvenile delinquency is one. It is regarded by many sociologists as the by product of the transition of the bulk of the population from the status of peasant class to that of industrial labour class.

The delinquents are the maladjusted children who have been defined as "children, suffering from emotional disorder". To Shulman, "juvenile delinquency spells the loss of control of family and society over a portion of the growing generation". According to Burt, a child is to be regarded as technically a delinquent when his anti-social tendencies appear so grave that he becomes or ought to become the subject of official action. In a broad sense, it refers to the anti-social acts of children and of young people of under age. Generally when the boys and girls between 7 to 21 years of age commit crimes or other anti-social activities, they are considered as juvenile delinquents. In our country the distinction between crime and delinquency is made on the basis of age. But there is a great legal flaw in the fixing of age. An offender is considered juvenile or adult on the basis of his age at the time of conviction and not at the time of commission of the offence.

Now we are to see how juvenile delinquency is a problem in our society. Nothing is problem which affects only an individual of the society. Juvenile delinquency is a problem because it not only affects some juveniles but a significant number of people of the society. The young boys and girls constitute the significant part of a nation upon which the future of the country depends. If a significant number of this young generation deviates from the right path by indulging themselves in some harmful anti-social activities, the whole nation will face a serious crisis. Everybody should give a serious thought to save this valuable generation for the sake of existing values and for the existence of our society.

In Pakistan this problem is not yet as dangerous as in the Western countries. The delinquents can be identified by observing their abnormal behaviour, non-adaptive personality, dissatisfied life, frustrated feeling, hostile attitude to the existing norms of group life, antagonistic nature against the established values and authority system, deliberate habit of violation of the existing laws and regulations for an orderly collective life and other types of abnormalities. In Pakistan the juvenile delinquents are generally associated with stealing, murder, pick-pocketing, fraud, truancy, fighting, sexual offence, although the sexual offences and murder are insignificant in comparision with other western societies.

Many social thinkers in our country are of the opinion that delinquent activities in the rural areas are associated with property. In the towns and cities of Pakistan, they are found to be engaged in anti-social activities. They are occasionally found addicted to liquor, gambling and prostitution. In addition to this, in Dacca, Karachi, Lahore, Chittagong and in other towns and cities of Pakistan we find special type of juvenile offenders known as 'Teddy.' It is a product of industrialization and urbanization of our society. These delinquents share some common habits and practices. They wear drain-pipe pants and make such offences as fighting on the street corners, at cinema halls and recreation centres, insulting the passersby and teasing the policemen, crowding at cross roads and loitering here and there, gazing at girls, teasing them by throwing insulting and dirty words and following them in a controlled manner, absenting from home till late at night, rush driving of motor cycles and violating the traffic rules and other abnormal behaviours. They occasionally carry knives, small sticks etc. They are also, sometimes, found with girl companions. They commit sex offences, theft, damage public and private properties, gamble and drink. They see the cinemas of violence, fighting and criminal characters. The following table shows the number of delinquents in East Pakistan from 1948 to 1962.

Table
Delinquents in East Pakistan, 1948-'62

Year	Number of Juvenile Delinquents
1948	2,513.
1954	5,336.
1958	6,142.
1959	8,042.
1960	4,686.
1961	3,085.
1962	2,443.

It can be seen from the above figures that the number of juvenile delinquents decreases considerably from 1959 to 1962.

In our country the girl offenders are less in number. The U.N. report holds, "In Pakistan girl delinquency is negligible when compared with boys." This may be due to the family customs and organization as the girls lead a much more sheltered and protected life.

This problem of juvenile delinquency is largely an urban phenomenon. Because of the transition of our traditional society to semi-industrial society many of our old values and customs are changing. The disintegration of the joint family system leads to the insecurity of the children. In our cities some mother's continual work outside the home exposes their childern to emotional deprivation and increases their opportunities for becoming a delinquent. When the mother is away from home all day, not only does the child suffer from lack of family care but his future is endangered by the high expectancy of his delinquent behaviour. Broken homes which are regarded as the characteristics of the modern urban societies, are also responsible for making the children delinquents. This delinquency is also due to 'cultural lag'. In Pakistani cities the material progress is rapid ; but the traditional values are changing very slowly which resulted a gap between the traditional and modern culture. This 'cultural lag' is also responsible for increasing juvenile delinquency. Moreover, in our urban societies the children become delinquents because of bad company. Parental rejection of unwanted child also makes them delinquents. Economic status of the people is also responsible because it is found that most of the delinquents come from the low economic status group. Afsaruddin's "Juvenile Delinquency in East Pakistan" reveals that maximum number of children become delinquents because of physical punishment. Lack of recreational facilities for the children in our urban cities is also another factor for the juvenile delinquency.

Prevention of delinquency by getting at its root is the responsibility of the society as a whole. The role of the family is important to prevent juvenile delinquency because it is in the family that a child first develops its mentality. Parental education, better housing and sanitation, improvement in the physical care of children and the assumption of greater responsibility by the parents for the rearing and supervising

11—

of children will reduce the rate of delinquency in our country. Needy families should be given financial help so that the children can be well fed and be given proper education. The children should be provided with proper recreational facilities so that they can use their leisure time in playing games and in doing other constructive things. Next to home, the school is in the most strategic position in the community for the prevention of delinquency as it has close and continuous contact with all the children in the community. According to Martin, "The opportunity of the school in preventing delinquency is great because it reaches particularly all children at a relatively early period of growth." The teachers should be friendly and co-operative in developing a healthy atmosphere among them. The government has also a great responsibility in the prevention of juvenile delinquency. The law should not treat juvenile delinquents equally with the criminals. Some institutions should he established by the government where the juvenile delinquents can be given proper treatment. It should not always adopt punitive and repressive measures to check juvenile delinquent's behaviour. They should be given sympathetic considerations. Every effort should be made to improve their mental, social and economic conditions.

PROSTITUTION

Prostitution is also another important problem of Pakistan. Of all the evils, prostitution appears to be institutionalised because they are carried on permanently and in an organized manner. It is not that only Pakistan is facing this problem, but virtually there can hardly be found any society where the practice of prostitution is not carried on. It is, perhaps, one of the oldest human institutions. In the ancient times the practice of prostitution was carried on in Greece and also in Indian temples. Though almost all the countries of the world banned this practice, still it exists in all these societies because the society itself protects it.

Prostitution has been defined as an illicit sex union on a promiscuous and mercenary basis with accompanying emotional indifference. In general, it may be said that prostitution is defined by three criteria promiscuity, barter and emotional indifference.

In the cities of our country, as well as, in any part of the world a prostitute is both a socially fallen woman and a socially accepted human being. She is socially fallen because she has no home, no chastity and no status in the society. She sells her body for money and makes it her profession for livelihood. But the most tragic thing is that, though she sells her body in lieu of money, she has little share on that money because much of it goes to the hands of her mistress or to her patron. She is a socially accepted human being because society protects her and allows her to carry on her profession through its legal sanction. In many societies, especially in the capitalistic one, many self-interested persons patronise this profession because of their business sake. They use the prostitutes as the media for their economic progress. Therefore, she forms a part of the society. In our cities a prostitute is the centre of several enjoyments for those who are sex-indulgent and who have sexual dissatisfaction and perversion.

As Pakistan is gradually changing from an agricultural country to an industrial one, many values of our traditional society have changed. Before urbanization the boys and girls in the rural areas were married at an early age. But as the process of industrialization takes place, in the cities the age at marriage has increased to a great extent, partially because of economic factor. In urban areas, some poor and young women indulge in prostitution to earn their livelihood. The adolescent girls who particularly become delinquents and suffer from sexual frustration due to lack of parental care and support on the one hand and their association with bad companion on the other, are found helpless to become prostitutes. Again certain circumstances force the girls to take up prostitution as a profession though they have the desires and ambitions of a normal house wife. When the girls are raped by the sexual criminals, they cannot go back to their families as the society as a whole hates them. They find no other way but to choose prostitution as a profession. In our country the role of kidnappers in making the girls and women prostitutes is important. They, in an organized way kidnap minor girls from different parts of the urban and rural areas and make a good profit by selling them in the redlight areas. Many innocent girls are brought from the rural areas by the notorious agents on the assurance that they would be given suitable jobs or would get a chance in the movies but they are sent to the brothels against money. This role of the kidnappers is a great problem for our society.

The social problem of prostitution in our country arises from its violation of the codes and morals that regulate the sexual behaviour and the veneral diseases it, almost, inevitably spreads. The fundamental objection to prostitution is on moral grounds. The prostitutes generally consist of the economically dependent, mentally inferior and morally degraded section of women. The effects of the prostitution are found not only on moral and legal codes but also on physical, economic and social aspects. The effects of prostitution have three factors ;—the prostitute, the patron and the general public, and for this wide effect it is considered as one of the important social problems in any society.

The prostitutes spread the veneral diseases to their patrons who transmit these dangerous diseases such as syphilis, gonorrhea to their wives and children. These result in a serious crisis in the family life. The principal sources of infection are the immoral girls and women who understand little about the dangers or methods of prevention and treatment of veneral diseases.

Personal demoralization : The personal effects of prostitution apart from health are, in many respects, deplorable. The prostitutes are mostly recruited from those segments of the population that have litle social and economic resources. Prostitution plays an important part in the demoralization and deterioration of its personnel.

Apart from the branded prostitutes there are other prostitutes who are called call-girls. They, generally, move in the high circle. These prostitutes are dangerous because they come to know from their high ranking customers the most secret things of the state. Sometimes, these call-girls reside in the aristocratic residential area and thus disturb the peace of the people of that locality. Moreover, the prostitution creates a problem for the children in the deteriorated areas in which many brothels are located.

It is a basic threat to family life. It degrades the sexual function of marriage in a special sense for it undermines the capacity of men to confine their sex experience within the limits of marriage and this, sometimes, causes divorce.

Many things have been said about prostitution by the moralists, social workers and a few sociologists. Like so many vicious enterprises prostitution has been prohibited by many societies. Serious controversies have raised about its role in modern urban industrial secular society. Reformers have undertaken the task to abolish this practice without fundamental modification of the conditions that produce it and exploiters have always deffended it.

It is our duty to solve this problem though it is not an easy job. The women and girls who are kidnapped and forced to lead an immoral life, should be rescued and returned to their families if they are accepted. The young prostitutes should compulsorily be married with those who may treat them as their wives. Those who can not be married due to over-age should be employed in cottage industries on reasonable wages. The removal of one of the oldest problems of the society needs a sincere efforts by the general mass, as well as, the initiative from the government. The total eradication of the existing private brothel houses in our cities is not possible unless the local people of the area organise to fight against the same in close co-operation with the local police station. The solution of this problem needs the solution of not the superficial factors but the root causes.

BEGGARY

Beggary is another important problem in our society. The number of beggars is increasing in both rural and urban areas. It appears to be institutionalized because it is carried on permanently and in an organized manner.

The beggars earn their livelihood through begging from door to door or by showing their various physical abnormalities at some crowded areas or in the market. Majority of these beggars are blind and physically handicapped. There are some beggars who, inspite of their physical abilities accept beggary as their profession and these able-bodied beggars create different problems.

Beggary has some religious sanction in our country ; but this sanction has been misunderstood and misused. The religion directs to help only those beggars who are old and physically unable to earn their livelihood. Majority of the beggars in our country adopt begging as a profession for livelihood. These beggars develop the art of extorting money from the people by playing upon their sentiments.

Apart from their daily habit of begging from door to door, they also come round on friday and on the occasions like Ramzan ,Shab-e-Barat, Eids and Muharram etc.

Beggary is a problem because the beggars are the parasites in our society and these parasites disturb the healthy growth of our nation as a whole. The parasitic beggars create a great tension in the society as they trade on by kidnapping minor children. These children are mercilessly turned into peculiarly deformed one. These parasitic beggars earn a lot of money through these maimed and deformed children. For kidnapping the small children they organize a gang which operates through out the country. Therefore, such beggars who beg with the support of maimed children are the greatest enemy of the nation. Beggary produces a section of people who are generally looked down upon by the rest of the people of the society and thus create inequality among the members of the society. Beggary also greatly hampers the economic growth of the country as the beggars are normally dependent on the rest of the members of the socity and thereby avoid working. In this way, a section of manpower remains inactive. The kidnapping of small children is on increase in our country by these professional gang of beggars. This creates a great anxiety among the public. There should be some solution of this problem. The problem of beggary represents an unhealthy nation. Thus, the young beggars who are normal human beings should be provided with proper works either in the factories or in other organizations. The child beggars should be sent to such orphanages where they can be nourished, as well as, get the training to stand on their own foot. They should be given proper education. The old and physically handicapped beggars who are unable to earn their livelihood should be given assistance from the state fund. In our efforts to solve the problem of beggary we should first of all trace out the parasitic beggars who earn their livelihood through kidnapping the normal children of the society. They must be punished severely so that they can never be able to run such a trade. The public should co-operate with the police in arresting such parasitic beggars.

UNEMPLOYMENT

Another problem which Pakistan is constantly facing is the unemployment. It is the direct result of population pressure. Though the population grows constantly and in an alarming rate, the growth of industries is slow. For this the increasing number of people cannot be provided with a suitable job for earning their livelihood.

Unemployment is a serious problem as it may bring about total disorganization in a family. If the bread-earner of a family is un-employed, the whole family at once fell into the hand of an indefinite future. This unemployment results in the breaking of peace in a family. If a person is not economically solvent, he cannot hope to do anything for his future. The problem of unemployment is very acute in our underdeveloped country. Here the majority of the people are poor with large families. If the head of the family does not get any job for supporting his family members, he becomes very much frustrated. He finds no other way but to send his wife and children in search of jobs. Many notorious people take this as a chance for their own self interest.

The problem of unemployment is greatly felt by the young genera-tion. In our country educated youths hate to cultivate land of their own as they think it to be somewhat degraded thing. They prefer a government job or a job in industry, rather than to serve their own agra-rian economy. After having the graduation or university degree, they search for a suitable and honourable job. But majority of them hardly get the kind of job which they want. They, therefore, become very much disgusted about their lives. Due to unemployment people find no other way but to support their livelihood by doing anti-social activities,—rob-bery, theft etc. The war between India and Pakistan has also increased greatly the problem of unemployment because of the curtailment of many development projects where many people could be employed

Unlike other problems, unemployment can be solved easily. We are to develop new industries where a great number of the unemployed la-bourers would find a suitable job for supporting their childen. The fresh graduates should also be provided in different private organizations like banks, farms etc. But this problem of unemployment connot be permanently solved until and unless our population growth is checked.

REFUGEE PROBLEM

It is also another vital problem which Pakistan is facing after the independence of 1947. Many refugees from India are flocking to

Pakistan where the population is already above the limitation. This influx of refugees is posing a great threat towards the sound economic development of Pakistan. It becomes a great problem for the society as a whole to rehabilitate these people. The problem also arises about the limited number of jobs, available for the refugees because Pakistan could not yet solve the problem of unemployment of her own people. The problem becomes acute when the question of cultural and social adjustments of the refugees to the new social setting arises.

The influx of refugees also creates great tension among the Hindus and the Muslims and sometimes, this tension causes disturbance and violence. The refugee problem can be solved by rehabilitating them. They should be given economic opportunities in the country. The conflict of the cultural and social values between the refugees and the inhabitants of the receiving country can be reduced by the process of assimilation which will help the refugees to assimilate themselves with the local people.

ANTI-SOCIAL ACTIVITIES

Various types of anti-social activities are the problems not only in Pakistan, but in all the countries of the world. The anti-social activities include theft, robbery, murder, suicide, gambling, sexual offences, black marketing, pick-pocketing etc. All these have effect on individual group, community and society. These problems pose a great insecurity to the public.

The criminal activities are found both in rural and urban areas in Pakistan. Dacoities are committed in the urban and rural areas. The pick-pockets concentrate in market places, crowded streets and railway and steamer stations. Murders are frequent in our societies. Most of these murders are connected with the conflict over property right, conflict among the industrial workers and conflict over the election results. Suicides are there in our society, especially in the poor class because of poverty. Gambling and drinking of wine are also two problems which are increasing in our society. Alcoholism is a problem because the drunkard looses his rational sense and commits anti-social activities. The people, associated with black marketing hoard the essential commodities like rice, wheat, salt and thus create an artificial crisis of these things.

They sell these food grains at much higher rate which remain out of the reach of the poor people. This crisis, sometimes, resulted in violence and agitation among the members of the public.

Bibliography

Afsaruddin, M. *Juvenile Delinquency in East Pakistan.* Dacca, 1965.

Barnett, H.G. *Innovation.* New York, 1953.

Bottomore, T.B. *Sociology.* London, 1962.

Carr, L. J. *Analytical Sociology.* Harper & Brothers, New York, 1948.

Davis, K. *The Population of India and Pakistan.* Princeton University Press, 1951.

Dube, S.C. *Indian Village.* Cornell University Press, New York, 1955.

Elliot, T. *Social Disorganization.* New York, 1950.

Hauser, P. *Urbanization in Asia and Far East.* Calcutta, 1957.

Wilson, G. *Analysis of Social Change.* London, 1945.

Hussain, A. F. A. *Human and Social Impact of Technological Change in Pakistan.* Oxford University Press, 1956.

Gerth and Mills. *Social Structure.* New York, 1954.

Karim, A.K.N. *Changing Society in India and Pakistan.* Dacca, 1956.

"Some Implications of world demographic trends with special reference to Pakistan" in Pakistan Sociological Studies, 1965.

CHAPTER 11
INFLUENCE OF GEOGRAPHY AND TOPOGRAPHY ON EAST PAKISTANI SOCIETY

To understand the influence of geography on the society of East Pakistan, we should have some knowledge about the geographical features of East Pakistan. East Pakistan has mainly flat lands; but in Chittagong Hill Tracts the lands rise to about 2,000 to 2500 feet. North-wards, where the frontier approaches the hills of Assam, there is a slender strip of rising land, but the dominating physical characteristic of East Pakistan is the system of mighty rivers flowing south-wards towards the Bay of Bengal until they join the Ganges whose big delta,—an area called the 'Sundar Bans' stretches for a distance of some three hundred miles along the coast. The Jamuna which is fed by the Brahmaputra, the Meghna and the Ganges are the three greatest of the numerous broad rivers of East Pakistan. The river system is one of the great factors of East Pakistani life. Such is their size and unpredictableness that they are extremely difficult to bridge and the diversions, caused to road and railway communications are considerable and tedious for the travellers. Nevertheless, although the rivers divide the country, they are the great channels of trade and communication and in this sense they also unite her. They are certainly the most prominent features of East Pakistan.

East Pakistan belongs to tropical regions because she has warm and rainy climate. The average rainfall is about one hundred inches a year, but it is not evenly distributed. The rain falls mostly in the monsoon season from May to October. During this period heavy downpours are, sometimes, experienced. This heavy seasonal rain, and the recurring floods, sometimes, cause great havoc with the loss of life and livelihood and the destruction of property. The greatest menace in this plain is the risk that undue rain will cause the rivers to change their courses which will be invariably disastrous.

The Jungle and marsh are common and the vegetation is lush and thick. The forests produce bamboo and hardwood trees, as well as, a variety of big games. The principal cultivated crops are jute, rice and tea ; while tropical fruits grow abundantly. The soil is fertile, but the pressure on it is tremendous because East Pakistan supports a population which, according to the census of 1961, is 50,844,000. It has been calculated that in East Pakistan the average number of persons per square mile is now 922 (1961 census) and in some areas the figure exceeds 1600. The problem of feeding this population has not yet been adequately solved and a failure of the crops is enough to have a famine in the country.

GEOGRAPHY AND COMMUNICATION

Geography is directly related with the system of communication of East Pakistan. Geography has played its dominant part. East Pakistan is a land of rivers, many of which are excellent water-ways. So, inland water transport is the major means of communication in the province. There are, at present, 4469 miles of navigable water-ways. The following places are approachable by inland water-ways : Dacca, Chandpur, Narayanganj, Barisal, Khulna, Daulatpur, Bhairab Bazar, Munshiganj, Sirajganj, Mirkadim, Daudkandi, Jhalukati etc. Chittagong, Khulna and Chalna are the major ports in the coastal areas. The parts of the districts of Noakhali, Comilla, Dacca, Faridpur, Barisal, Khulna, Jessore, Kushtia, Pabna etc., remain under water about half of the year and during this time boat is the main means of communication in the rural areas for short journey and for domestic and agricultural uses. During the rainy season many new routes are opened for the motor launch which links the important places of this area. Leaving these districts aside, the other parts of East Pakistan are generally high lands and do not go under water in the rainy season. In these areas the major means of communication through the whole year for short journey and for domestic and agricultural uses is the bullock cart, though there are roads, railways and buses.

East Pakistan has 1200 miles of all-weather roads, including only about six hundred miles of superior surface roads. She has about

22,000 miles of unmetalled roads which become useless during the rainy season. The Pakistan Eastern Railway has 1713 miles routes. The major portion of railway is in metre gauge. The major rail-links are Dacca-Chittagong, Chittagong-Sylhet and Dacca-Bahadurabad on the metre gauge and Khulna-Goalanda Ghat, Darsana-Chilahati on the broad gauge. For mainly geographical reason, it has not still been possible to construct any railway line in the district of Barisal. There are some air services of the PIA in East Pakistan, linking mainly Dacca, Faridpur, Khulna, Jessore, Iswardi, Rajshahi, Dinajpur, Rangpur, Chittagong, Hatiya, Comilla etc. In the urban areas of East Pakistan bus, taxi, rickshaw, baby taxi, ekka, Tomtom, horse-carriage etc., are the main means of communication. Bicycles and motor cycles are found in both urban, and rural areas.

INFLUENCE OF GEOGRAPHY ON AGRICULTURE AND FOOD

Agriculture is the basic structure of East Pakistani society. Almost every aspect of the life of the people in East Pakistan is linked with agriculture. It is needless to say that agriculture is predominant due to geographical causes. The pattern of food consumption is also determined by the prevailing geographical and climatic conditions and by the availability of foods.

Of the total cultivable land of Pakistan, East Pakistan has over 41·5%, though only 15·1% of the area of Pakistan belongs to East Pakistan. The climate, soil and topography favour the cultivation of larger areas in East Pakistan than in West Pakistan. East Pakistan has a hot and wet climate. The main food crops of this region are rice, pulses, oil seeds, and wheat. Various kinds of fruits like banana, pineapple, jackfruit, mango, orange etc., and vegetables are found.

Rice is the staple food of the East Pakistani people. East Pakistan may be aptly called a land of rice growers. The area under rice cultivation is about 22 million acres and that under other staple grains is 1·1 million acres only. Rice grows practically all over East Pakistan except in the Sundarbans. In this province three types of rice are produced,—(a) 'Aman' (harvested in winter), (b) 'Aus' (harvested in Autumn) and (c) 'Boro' (harvested in summer). 'Aman' is the most important rice in East Pakistan. The average total annual output of rice is 259 million maunds. This province grows pulses like gram, masur and mug in over 1 (one) million acres. She leads in the productions of rape seed and mustard seed. Wheat, millets etc., are other minor food crops.

The principal food of East Pakistan is rice, fish, vegetables, meat, pulses, pepper, milk etc. Fish is abundantly found in the rivers and ponds of this region. So, naturally, rice with fish has become the main food of the people. Pulse is another important food with rice ; while meat is taken occasionally in the rural areas and almost regularly in the urban areas. Besides these, various fruits like banana, jack-fruit, pine-apple, mango, orange etc., are taken. Most of these fruits are seasonal. Tea is taken more in the urban areas than in the rural areas. Tobacco is used for smoking in both rural and urban areas.

Among the cash crops, jute is the most important. It earns, on the average, 1,000 million rupees of foreign currency a year. Jute is cultivated in about 10% of cultivable lands. Jute is produced all over East Pakistan, but Mymensingh and Dacca districts produce 23% and 19% respectively of the total jute. Tea is an important commodity of commerce for East Pakistan. There are 143 tea gardens in Sylhet, Chittagong and Comilla. East Pakistan, on the average, produces 60 million pounds of tea.

In this province sugarcane is grown mainly in the north-western districts. Dacca, Mymensingh and Faridpur also produce sugercane. Tobacco is an important cash crop which amounts to 52% of the total production of Pakistan. East Pakistan is climatically suited to the cultivation of "Pan" or betel leaf. But the distribution is influenced by topography, soil and availability of the growers of 'Pan', who are called "Barois".

GEOGRAPHY AND VILLAGE ORGANIZATION

When the main races of the subcontinent passed from the nomadic to the settled agricultural stage, they all formed groups of land holdings analogous to the present villages. Although there is no such thing as pure form of village community, the village system,—the collection of dwellings with open lands is found in East Pakistan wherever geography, topography, climate etc., permitted. In East Pakistan scattered clusters of joint family dwellings or numerous small groups of dwellings in the village are common. The geography of this part of the country has created two types of villages. In the first type each cultivator claims his own holding, having cleared it from the jungle or inherited or bought it, but the cultivators collectively have no claim over the whole estate. They may use the waste lands around the village for grazing and to procure fire wood ; but it is not done jointly. In the second category there is a strong joint body, claiming to be in higher order or class, which enjoys a superior position to the tenants and which jointly claims the entire area. This body owns the sites on which the dwellings are built and the lands on which tanks, graveyards and cattle stands are located. Others live there or use these facilities by permission. Such villages are now rarely found.

The main components of the village are the group of holdings and the aggregation of dwellings. In addition, there will be common grazing and waste lands on part of which there will be a burial ground. In some districts the villages may include old ruins. There will also be tanks, wells or canals depending on the local geography and on the manner, the area has been colonised or developed. Innumerable local and regional variations arise owing to differences in climate and physiography. Broadly speaking, there are three types of village layouts : (1) the spider web form of the indigenous settlement with the roads and paths radiating from the 'abadi' (cultivated lands) and the boundaries of holdings, laying radially and circumferentially in the intervening segments ; (2) secondly, the contour layout where the plan has been determined by rivers, hill-slopes and other natural features and (3) thirdly, rectangular pattern of the planned settlement. Between the three extremes one finds every conceivable variety due to geographical variations.

ROLE OF GEOGRAPHY IN URBANIZATION AND INDUSTRIALIZATION

Geography plays an important part in urbanization, industrialization and localization of industries. In all places, the towns and ports can not grow or flourish. To be a port a place must be suitable for the communication and safe from natural calamities as far as possible. The port or town must be easily linkable with other ports, towns and important areas of the country. For example, we may take the case of Narayanganj which is an inland river port of East Pakistan and is linked with other important ports and towns by water-ways, railways and roads. For localization of industries or for industrial set-up, the prevailing geographical conditions are important. The jute mills have, generally, been set up near Narayanganj mainly because of communication facilities and of availability of raw materials as Narayanganj is almost in the centre of East Pakistan where jute grows. Chittagong has become the most important port of East Pakistan mainly because of its geographical situation. So, geographical factors are very closely connected with urbanization and industrialization in East Pakistan.

HOUSING PATTERN AND GEOGRAPHY

East Pakistan's social life and economy are based on regional factors and it is to be expected that the housing types, like dress, language and other such features would vary considerably from region to region. In every area, indigenous qualities will be tempered or modified to some extent by the habits or ideas, assumed by more advanced classes who over the last hundred years or more, have tended to associate western tastes with their own improved economic or social status. East Pakistan consists of the lower reaches of the great river systems ; practically all of it lie in the deltoid zone. The village housing types are governed by the position, she occupies in the river systems. In the lower reaches including the delta areas, the houses are predominantly built of reeds. Further inland, they are made of mud, bamboo and brush wood with thatch of palm. In the mountain flanking of the East Pakistan delta, there are the type platform dwellings of the hill tribes.

The forms of construction directly reflect the influence of local geography and particularly, of the materials which are available. But they are also affected by the cultural traditions. Thus in East Pakistan, extensive use is made of timber construction and wood working crafts are highly developed. This is a characteristic of early Hindu architecture.

The housing types vary, but there are common features over the wide areas. In East Pakistan the dwelling is, generally, one or more separate huts. The huts are grouped around on open space. Some of them may be linked together by a bamboo fence which may be extended to enclose a yard for cattle or to maintain some privacy for the

women. In most villages, or at least in most districts, there are generally a handful of dwellings, the standard of which far exceeds the
great majority. They may be almost palatial residences of the former
zaminders in East Pakistan or they may, merely, be the pucca houses
of the village head men or the former dwellings of the Hindu money
lenders.

The distinctive features which appear to govern East Pakistani
village housing pattern are the small variation in temperature, the
monsoon, the unstable river system, the absence of permanent building materials and the cultural contacts of Bengal with the North
and the East. The high rainfall and poor drainage make it necessary
to give importance to the roof and the floor.

The use of iron sheets for the construction of roof is, probably
the most significant change that has occurred in the construction of
village houses in East Pakistan and it is certain that the change is for
the better. In the more prosperous and accessible areas, many of the
old thatched roofs have now been covered with iron sheets. The houses
of the chakmas and other hill tribes are built entirely of bamboo,
raised four to six feet from the ground by means of bamboo support.

GEOGRAPHY AND DRESS

Geography has great influence on the pattern of the dress of the
people of East Pakistan. Most of the rural people are cultivators.
So their dress pattern is related with agriculture. They usually put
on a "Lungi" and a "genji" (a vest of hosiery). At work they wear only
a "gamcha" (napkin). In summer while at home they put on only
a "lungi' and while going to some place such as market, they have a
genji or a shirt on. Shirts are most often with half sleeves, bought
ready-made in the village market. The people who cannot afford a
shirt most often wear a 'nima' or a vest-like garment. A "chaddar"
or a sheet of home-spun cloth is most common in winter. Pajama
and panjabi with shoes are ceremonial dress in the rural areas.
The dress of a Hindu in the rural areas is dhuti, genji, shirt, panjabi,
chaddar etc. The only dress of village women is a 'sari', sometimes,
with a 'blouse'. The women of East Pakistan universally wear
ornaments mostly made of silver and, sometimes, of gold. The dress
pattern of the tribal people differs from that of the general people

mainly due to the cultural and geographical factors. The dress pattern of one region of East Pakistan is as much influenced by the geographical and climatic conditions as that of another region.

The dress of urban people differs from that of the rural people in some respects. The urban pattern of dress is not as much influenced by the geographical conditions as the rural pattern of dress. The urban pattern of dress is influenced much by social, cultural and economic factors. Suit, coat, tie, pant etc., are found mostly in the urban areas.

GEOGRAPHY AND HUMAN FERTILITY

The population problem is one of the gravest problems for Pakistan. Population is increasing very rapidly in Pakistan. The total population of East Pakistan has jumped up from 42,063,000 in 1951 to 50,844,000 in 1961 giving rise to the density of population from 762 to 922 per square mile. There is no denying the fact that the geographical factors, directly or indirectly, are responsible, to a great extent, for this rapid growth of population in East Pakistan. Because of tropical climate the East Pakistani girls attain the puberty at the age of 12 and the boys at the age of 14 to 15 years. The girls may bear a child at the age of 13 or 14 years. This becomes the cause of early marriage which is one of the important factors for high fertility in East Pakistan.

GEOGRAPHY AND MIGRATION

Migration is highly dependent on geographical, as well as, economic conditions of a country. In East Pakistan we find little mobility. The geography of East Pakistan is playing an important role in migration. A considerable migration of population between different parts both on a seasonal and long term basis, can be seen in this province because of her different climatic conditions with different degrees of pressure of population in relation to the means of livelihood. A large number of seasonal agricultural labourers from the districts of Noakhali, Faridpur, Tippera and Dacca is attracted by the district of Barisal during the harvesting seasons. Noakhali and Tippera are the two districts of exceptionally high population pressure. From these two districts there is always exodus of people to the industrial

12—

areas. As Noakhali and Chittagong are the districts in the coastal areas, the people from these two districts become sea-faring. Many people from the districts of Tippera, Mymensingh, Dacca etc., have settled in the districts of Dinajpur and Rangpur which have the low density of population.

East Pakistan is a land of rivers. Many river-side people have to migrate as a river begins to dissolve its banks. The coastal areas of East Pakistan are often damaged by the frequent cyclones. So the people of the coastal areas want to migrate to interior places.

INFLUENCE OF GEOGRAPHY ON FAMILY AND MARRIAGE

The majority of East Pakistani families are joint in nature. The joint families are found mostly among the agriculturists. Our agriculture is not yet mechanised. So, naturally more hands are needed for working in the field and for other household activities. This phenomenon partially explains the existence and persistence of the joint family system in East Pakistan. Polygamy is still practised by some rural agricultural people, although the most common system of marriage is monogamy. In many cases, such people marry more than one woman mainly as an additional hand to work in the family.

OCCUPATION, ECONOMY AND GEOGRAPHY

As East Pakistan is an agricultural country, the main occupation here is cultivation and the economy is agricultural. About 90% of the working people of East Pakistan are directly or indirectly engaged in agriculture. Industrially East Pakistan is still backward. So the number of industrial and factory workers is not significant. There is no doubt that the geographical condition has made cultivation the predominant occupation of the people of East Pakistan. In the rural areas the influence of geographical factors can be found on many other occupational groups. As for example fishermen, boatmen etc.

GEOGRAPHY AND, ECONOMIC AND SOCIAL STRUCTURE

The economic life of the people of East Pakistan is largely governed by geography. The geography of East Pakistan has created a characteristic economic life. The economic life of the people is based on agriculture.

Being influenced by geography, the village system in East Pakistan produces some kind of grains which can be stored in sufficient quantities to feed the cultivator's family and the domestic animals and to leave some surplus which can be used to support the temporal and spiritual overlords for his protection and to feed the specialists on which his technology depends.

The social organization, stemming directly from these economic potentialities which are largely the outcome of the geographical factors, is a body of cultivators who may or may not have landlords sitting on their necks and acting as patrons to a body of artisans and menials.

The geographical conditions of East Pakistan are so, that agriculture has become the important structure of the East Pakistani society. The most important group in villages are the cultivators. This does not mean, however, that they take precedence in the village society. Social position depends on status in relation to land, religion and government service. The landlord, the peer, the shopkeeper and many government officials, who happen to stay in the area take pride in the place. The landlords represent only a small proportion of land-owning class. Nevertheless, they weild enormous influence in the village. The majority of the agricultural people fall into the category of tenant cultivators or agricultural labourers.

Bibliography

MacIver, R.M. *Society.* London, Macmillan and Co. Ltd., 1957.

Bottomore, T.B. *Sociology.* George Allen & Unwin Ltd., London 1962.

Ahmed, N. *Economic Geography of East Pakistan.* London, Oxford University Press, 1958.

Dani, A.H. *"Race and Culture Complex in Bengal"*, in Bessaignet, P. (ed.) Social Research in East Pakistan. Asiatic Society of Pakistan, 1960.

Holmes, W. *"River life of East Pakistan".* Pakistan Miscellany—2, 1958.

Jafri, A. H. *"Geographical Basis of Economy of East Pakistan."* Proceedings of Pakistan Science conference, 1950.

Rashid, A. *" Eastern Pakistan".* Pakistan Quarterly 1 (2) 1949.

CHAPTER 12
PATTERN OF CULTURE IN EAST PAKISTAN

In the opinion of E.B. Taylor, one of the early anthropologists, culture had a meaning more immaterial and less utilitarian. He defined it as that complex whole which includes knowledge, beliefs, arts, morals, laws, customs and any other capabilities and habits, acquired by a man as a member of society. In other words, culture is the direct expression of our nature ; in our ways of thought and action, in art, religion, morality and recreation. It deals with interests and values conceived as ends, to which various actions and objects are directed as means.

East Pakistan has a complex culture, the constituents of which are drawn from very different sources. In this connection the influences on East Pakistani culture from Arabia and Persian are significant. To these two factors, we may also mention the influences from the Hindu culture and from the Western culture and technology. It is known to all that the influence of Arabia on our culture is very much pervading. Inspite of the influence of western thought for the last many years, one of the striking features of our national life is the tradition bound attitude towards life.

East Pakistan is mainly an agricultural country with a population predominantly rural. It is natural that in a land of such over-whelming rural population, the villages exercise a great influence upon the social life of the country. In villages religion govern not only the people's ways of life, but also their thinking and attitudes to a very marked degree. The essence of Islamic faith is a belief in one God, in Mohammad as the prophet, and in the holy Quran. The Quran and Hadith, containing the teachings of the prophet, prescribe detailed instructions regarding personal conduct and manner which are observed by all devout Muslims. Islam enjoins on all persons, above all, prayer

3ctj gh

five times a day at prescribed hours, fasting during the holy month of Ramzan, payment of Zakat and Hajj or pilgrimage to Mecca (for those who can afford it), prayer in congregation on Friday and attendance in funerals. The Religious rites and rituals are, undoubtedly, observed with much more seriousness in the villages than in the urban areas. The religion of Islam teaches charity, benevolence and hospitality.

The standard of education in the village is low. Literacy among the women is almost half of that among the men. Attendance of students at school in the rural areas is often very irregular and education for children is considered by the farmers as wastage of time and energy. With the increasing pressure of population on land and the consequent increase in the employment necessities elsewhere, political consciousness seems to have grown among a section of people resulting in the increasing demand for education in rural areas. Female education is hardly encouraged and its significance rarely understood by the villagers. The general consensus probably is that women may have education only upto the elementary stage, and should acquire ability to read the holy Quran, although Islam favours the education of the Muslim woman.

CULTURE CHARACTERISTICS IN EAST PAKISTAN

Housing Pattern: A sociologist, entering a house would be able to say whether the house belonged to a Hindu or a Muslim. The Hindu houses are more neat and clean than the Muslim houses specially in the rural areas in East Pakistan. Though the religion of Islam gives much value to cleanliness, the Muslims of East Pakistan are not very careful about it. Flower gardens are more common in the Hindu houses than in the Muslim houses, specially in our rural areas. The Hindus need flowers for the purpose of offering them to their Gods every morning. Hence every Hindu family having idols, must have some flower plants. Possibly the relative unpopularity of flowers among the Muslims in East Pakistan is a reaction of its over-popularity with the Hindus. The newly converted Muslims possibly tried to be different from the Hindus and developed distaste for flowers.

The Muslims who raise flower garden prefer roses. Rose is identified with the Muslim culture. The Hindus do not offer roses to their deity. Rose is considered to be a forbidden flower to gods, idols and deities.

The houses of Muslim middle class families have two clear cut parts;—outer house and inner house which is called "Vitar Bari."

The 'Vitar Bari" is normally walled for the observance of pardha (vail). The Hindu houses, normally, do not have such clear cut division as the Muslim houses because they are not very particular about the observance of Pardha (vail). The outer house of the Muslims is usually better organized because the guests normally stay in the outer house unless they are very close friends and relatives.

The Muslims in East Pakistan are particular in having curtains with the doors so that pardha is observed. If the curtain is beyond the means of a rural Muslim family, he would raise a construction of jute sticks so that the inner parts of the house and the movements of the inmates are not visible to the outsiders.

The house-hold utensils also demonstrate the difference in habits between the Hindus and the Muslims. The Hindus like copper and brass plates, cups and other utensils ; while the Muslims prefer meals in china clay plates. The poor use alumunium and earthen plates and cups.

The "Sikkahs" i.e., hanging materials of three or more jute ropes used for hanging the pots and vessels are found both in the Muslim and Hindu houses.

A Sociologist, entering the Hindu house especially in the rural areas would, at once, notice the pictures of Hindu gods and goddesses ; while the Muslims make the display of the picture of mosque, kaba or the tombs of the Muslim saints.

As regards the home manners the Muslims prefer to wear some clothes even when they are inside the house ; while the Hindus prefer remaining bare bodied in the house. Personal privacy is given much importance among the Muslims. Al-Quran enjoins even on the husband and wife to seek permission before meeting each other at certain hours of day and night.

Both the Hindus and the Muslims of East Pakistan are equally hospitable. If some one wants to drink a glass of water, the Hindus would offer a glass of water with something else. If they are not rich enough to offer anything else they would offer, at least, one spoonful of molasses along with the glass of water. Equally the poor Muslims would offer one piece of betel with a glass of water and also would offer the Hukka*

Dining : In taking their meals the Muslims would begin with an expression of gratitude to Allah for His kindness and put the first morsel of rice into the mouth with great satisfaction. The Hindus would begin in the name of God and offer the first morsel of rice to God. They will not eat the first morsel of rice ; but keep it and at the end of the meal they offer this to the birds or animals like cats and dogs. Both the Hindus and the Muslims want to earn the pleasure of God, but in a different way.

The plates of the Hindus are much bigger in size. All the items of curry are brought together in a big plate. But the Muslims would not take all the items at the same time. They would take the items one by one.

Food Habit : Though rice, vegetables, fish and meat are the common items of food for all East Pakistanis, the taste and preference of the Hindus and the Muslims are different. Beef is popular with the Muslims, but forbidden for the Hindus with whom the popular item is tortoise and crabs which are tabooed to the Muslims.

Vegetables are very popular with the Hindus. They know the technique of preparing it. The Hindu widows are to take vegetables for the whole life. For that reason they have mastered the art of vegetable preparation. The vegetables are cooked with varying combinations and proportions of items. The Muslims also take vegetables whatever the type of preparation may be.

Milk is given much importance by the Muslims, as well as, the Hindus, but the association of religious values with cow-milk made its appeal stronger to the Hindus. Cow-milk is considered sacred to the Hindus.

In meals, served on feast and formal dinners for the guests, the use of ghee (melted butter) is common among the Muslims. 'Polao' 'Korma', 'Birani' etc., are very common in the Muslim houses. The warmth of love and affection is displayed through the use of 'ghee' in the Muslim houses. The Hindus do not give so much importance to 'ghee.' The guests in the Muslim houses are served with different

---

*Hukka—Hubble-bubble used for smoking tobacco.

types of curries, prepared out of meat. 'Kabab', 'Kopta', 'Korma', 'Rezala,' 'Roast', etc., are the different types of 'Mughal khana' prepared for the guest in the higher middle and upper class Muslim houses. On the occasion of marriage feast, the Muslims use one curry of fish and mostly avoid fish altogather. But the Hindus serve five or six items of fish curry.

In the formal dinner the Muslims usually start together. If some one finishes his meal earlier he is supposed to wait till the others finish. It is not customary in the formal dinner among the Hindus that all should finish and get up at a time. Inspite of these differences in the type of food, served on ceremonial occasions, the people of both the communities usually take rice, dal, pulse. vegetables, fish and meat. In our rural areas fish and meat are occasionaly eaten.

Pattern of dress : The head gear is sometimes found among the Muslims in the rural areas of East Pakistan. On ceremonial occasions it is more noticeable. But the Hindus of Bengal unlike the Hindus of other parts of the subcontinent, do not have any head gear. In this respect they are different from the Muslims and the Hindus of the subcontinent. Dhuti-chaddar is the most frequently used dress of the Hindus in East Pakistan. On the other hand, the Muslims wear lungi, pajama, vest, shirt, panjabi, chaddar, nima, napkin etc. The formal dress of the Bangali Hindus is incomplete without a chaddar.

On ceremonial occasions, like marriage, puja etc., the Hindus attend in dhuti, panjabi or shirt and chaddar. The Muslims try to use sherwani on ceremonial occasions ; but are not very particular about it. It should be mentioned here that there are some changes in the pattern of dress of the Hindus and the Muslims in East Pakistan. The people of both the religious communities wear pant and shirt in the urban areas. The Hindu males now-a-days wear 'lungi', 'pajama', 'panjabi', napkin, vest etc., in rural East Pakistan. Both the Muslim and the Hindu girls and women wear sari, blouse, and petticoat.

Songs and musics : The rural Hindus are more interested in songs, music, dance etc. Among the rural Muslims, the religious taboo to songs and music is very strong. The Mullahs discourage songs and music on religious grounds. But in the urban areas the religious taboo to songs and music is not followed because the Mullah community has got very little influence over the urbanites. Both the Hindus and the Muslims have devotional songs of strong emotional appeal. Tears roll down over the cheeks when these songs are sung by the devotees. But the themes of devotional songs are different in these two communities. The Hindus have vaisnava songs, bhajan, kirtan, spiritual songs, whereas the Muslims have songs like nat, gazal, kowali, which have spiritual values.

The theme of the Folk poetry is also different in these two communities. The materials of the folk lores are taken by the Muslim folk poets from the life and society of the glorious past Muslim history, while the Hindu folk poets collect their similar materials from the vedic society and epic works.

FOLK ART IN EAST PAKISTAN

By folk art we mean generally the prevailing art among the rural low-income agrarian group. This flow of art is specially decorative and tradition-bound. In Neolithic period man's mind leaned towards illustrative art centering around pottery and weaving. Illustrative art is easy and natural in pottery and weaving. Their structure and the materials which are needed for making those articles, are suitable for the illustrative art. It is very easy to make geometric decoration by the thread of various colours. It came easily to man's mind to paint flowers, leaves, creepers on the curve body of pottery. The flow of Neolithic art is specially utilitarian in character. Its main theme is] to beautify the daily usable things. Although religious beliefs work behind this in different ways, these works are treated as folk art.

This art is mainly carried on by using simple colour and some real sketch. The materials, used to make these arts and crafts are very simple and easily available. In every country folk art developed, depending on easily available articles. Many examples of folk art are found in our country. The 'katha' is made of discarded clothes and sarees, but its artistic value is no less significant than its utilitarian value.

The love for art in man's life has been expressed through the sketch of flowers, leaves and creepers, birds, animals etc., by the thread of different colours. No expression of ideas of the rich luxurious life of the town can be found in the village clay or wooden dolls, in bamboo and cane works and in the decoration of "Sital Pati". This art is specially utilitarian in character. Its main aim is to beautify the articles of daily use.

Of course, many ideas worked behind the folk art. We find the nature of village life and the spiritual awareness in it. Religion is entangled with the folk art in our country. This can be compared with the ideas of primitive magic. The village artisans carved big eyes or bills on the head of the boat. These are not merely to further the beauty of the boat but a deep significance is hidden in them. The eyes are carved so that it can go by seeing everything and the bills of the birds signify to sail quickly like the birds and will not sink. So, we find the primitive religious ideas working behind them.

Another example of folk art is 'Alpana' (drawings on mud floor and on the court-yards). Alpana is primarily influenced by the religious ideas. Various sorts of folk arts are found in every country.

ENVIRONMENT LED TO THE ORIGIN AND DEVELOPMENT OF FOLK ART

In East Pakistan physical causes have led to various developments in different fields. The silts, brought by the rivers during the rainy season collect in the fields. This soil possesses the characteristics, suitable for pottery, doll-making and toy-making. The fertility of East Pakistani soil owes much to the periodical flood of the rivers. Both the rich alluvium, as well as, abundant rainfall in summer explains the phenomenal agricultural productivity and the high density of population. East Pakistani agriculture, depending upon the bounties of nature has created a hierarchy of nature deities in the folk mind. Thus we see invocations for rain, worship of rivers, worship of earth and harvest. To guard against drought, disease and other natural calamities, various minor deities such as 'Sitala', 'Manasa' have been evolved.

The deltoid position of East Pakistan has contributed to the development of certain special crafts such as boat-building and fishing traps, each having a unique character of its own. Apart from this, tropical rain and forest have contributed to the abundance of tropical jungles like bamboo and cane. So in East Pakistan bamboo-works and cane-works are being found in the nook and corner of the country. In connection

with these crafts and activities, various ceremonies and deities and folk
songs such as "Sari' and 'Bhatiali' have evolved in the folk mind.

The periodical 'Melas' (fairs) are traditional feature of rural East
Pakistan. These melas are spontaneous and provide a meeting ground
for the people from the nook and corner of the country, giving them
ideal opportunity for exhibiting folk entertainments, as well as, their
traditional arts and crafts.

In this manner, the close social and economic intercourse between
the different parts of the country has been maintained. Folk arts and
crafts of East Pakistan have always shared a community of interests,
never condemned to isolation and mental exclusiveness.

Folk beliefs and traditions of East Pakistan have, thus, a continuous
history and have grown through the racial elements in Bengali life and
extraneous influences. G.S. Dutt truly observes, "It was an art of
simple people, inhabiting rural East Pakistan, where a sturdy spirit
of democracy had been nurtured from the earliest possible times,
which had never been completely dominated or suppressd by external
imperial and priestly influences. Whenever any outside influence came
in its way, this sturdy culture assimilated as much of them as was
in the harmony with itself without losing its own basic character."

East Pakistani folk drama, music and dance obviously have
entangled with religion. They developed according to their own
tradition with asthetic standards.

There are certain tendencies in social and religious life that have
affected the arts and crafts of the people. East Pakistani folk art
corresponds to the following three types :

Ritualistic: It is used in the service of rites associated with some
beliefs and mystical ideas :

Utilitarian: Social customs demand the objects and the modes of
manufacture and material facilities determine the form.

Individualistic : It expresses the feelings and emotions of the artist.
Ritualistic art has been expressed in representing the abstract,
suggesting but not portraying any specific object. An illustration of a
purely abstract design of a symbolic kind is 'Alpana' design. Although
it is not representing a natural object, it certainly does represent an
idea or even succession of ideas. This may be due to ulterior motive,
either religious or symbolic. These cult objects are pre-Aryan and,

sometimes, go further back to remoter ages.

Then, there is the artistic touch with the technical processes, involved in the manufacture of utilitarian objects, including pottery, basketry, cane-works, textiles, dolls and toys. Inspite of local differences, however, these objects are mainly the variations of the same theme.

The individualistic traits have been well illustrated in the 'Kathas', 'Sikkas', and 'Pithas' made by the East Pakistani women.

VARIOUS TYPES OF FOLK ARTS IN EAST PAKISTAN

Kathas : Kathas are the conspicuous example of East Pakistani folk art. Kathas are made of discarded clothes, but their artistic value is no less than their utilitarian value. Regard for art in folk life has been expressed through them.

Kathas are generally made by the women of all classes in rural East Pakistan. The word 'katha' means embroidered work made mostly on discarded saris which are sewn together almost invisibly. Discarded saris, according to the size and thickness are arranged one on the top of the other until the desired thickness is obtained and edges are folded in. It is then filled with fine quilting work by means of white thread. Coloured threads from the borders of the saris are stitched along the border line and the surface is filled in with various designs.

Generally speaking, the embroideries in the kathas have the obverse and reverse character. Ordinarily, the designs appear distinctly on the obverse face. In the most finished types of kathas, however, the stitches are so skilfully made that the details of each design appear in the identical forms and colours on either face of the katha. Indeed, it is often extremely difficult, if not impossible to distinguish obverse face from the reverse face.

Method of carrying out the Embroidery: It is necessary to trace the design before the quilting is made, as this only forms the background. The design is usually done and held in place by embroidery stitches. As most of the East Pakistani people are Muslims they prefer to embroider creepers, branches and the leaves of the trees. They rarely embroider animals and man as it is tabooed by Islam.

Kathas are made by the women, each inventing her own design ; and it is considered dishonourable to copy another woman's work.

A particular design may be perpetuated in each family, but the women are encouraged to cultivate their inventive faculty by using their original design.

Sikkas : Sikkas are generally made of rope by the women in East Pakistan. They are used for keeping pots, bottles and earthen utensils. They are generally kept hanging. Their shape appear by knotting one rope after another. Different types of flower, leaf and creeper are designed on them by different sorts of knot. Different sorts of sikkas are found in every house in rural areas of East Pakistan. Sometimes, coloured ropes are used to further the beauty of the sikkas. Each woman has her own design and it is considered dishonourable to copy another woman's work.

Pithas : (rice cakes): Pithas are another conspicuous example of folk art in East Pakistan. Different types of designs on the pithas are the expression of the love for art in the rural areas. Different sorts of leaves, creepers etc., are designed on 'Pakan pitha,' 'Chandra puli pitha' and 'Andesha pitha' etc. In our rural areas the bride's father is given credit if his daughter knows different sorts of designs on pithas.

Textiles : From the earliest time, East Pakistani people have made the art of weaving a speciality. This industry is spread all over the province and many villages possess a number of looms. The artisans in general are the Hindu Tantubays ; while the yagis (a section of the Hindus) and the jolas (a section of the Muslims) have also a considerable influence. The Tantubays have specialized in fine weaving ; while other two communities weave coarser products.

Dyeing : The use of indigenous vegetable dyes is practically extinct in Bengal. In the district of Faridpur a yellow dye was, at one time, obtained from the flower of the 'Kusum tree,' the petals of which were dried and boiled and the solution was used for colouring the yarn. In Chittagong Hill Tracts, blue dye is still obtained from the indigo plant and red dye is obtained from the roots of the tree known as 'Rang gach'. In chittagong district, a chocolate colour is obtained from the bark of a tree which is cut into chips, left in cold water for four or five days and then boiled for at least a day.

The colour obtained from these trees is used for printing clothes in different family patterns, mainly floral and geometrical leaves, flowers and creepers.

Drawings and Paintings

(a) **Alpana** : During the progress of festivals and religious functions, the Hindu women of East Pakistan make 'Alpana' drawings on mud-floors and courtyards. They are drawn on the ground by means of small pieces of cloth wrapped around the finger, which has been soaked in the ground rice-paste. These rice-paste drawings are connected with certain rites performed exclusively by matrons (Nari vrata) and virgins (Kumari vrata) or by priests on behalf of women (Sastriya vrata).

(b) **Jadu-Patua:** The scrolls, drawn by the Jadu Patuas are relatively narrower and smaller. These pictures were originally exhibited in some of the tribal peoples of Eastern Pakistan i.e., Santals and Bediyas. According to G.S. Dutt, "Whenever a santal man, or a woman or a child dies, the Jadu Patua appears at the house of the bereaved family with a ready made sketch of the deceased, done from his own imagination. The picuture merely consists of drawings of an adult or a child or a male or a female according to the age and sex of the deceased. The Jadu Patua presents the picture completely drawn in colour with one omission only viz., the iris of the eyes. He shows the picture to the relatives and tells them that the deceased is wandering about blindly in the other world and will continue to do so until they send gifts or money or some other articles through him, viz., the Jadu Patua himself, so that he can perform the act of 'Lakasudan' or bestowal of eye sight. So, the relatives make presents of money or some other articles of domestic use to Jadu Patua for transmission to the deceased. Jadu Patua then puts the finishing touch to the picture by performing the act of 'Lakasudan' or supplying the iris of the eyes in the picture of the deceased. It is perhaps from this semi-magical practice the Jadu Patua derives his name (Judu—magic ; Patua—painter).

Pottery and Terracottas

(a) **Pottery:** The chief earthen wares, used by the common people are the cooking and drinking vessels. Dolls, toys, fruits, fishes, animals, whistles and other small objects are frequently made of earth and mud The industry is an ancient one, confined to a class of people, called kumbhakars or kumars who also specialize in making figures of the Hindu Gods and Goddesses.

Decoration : The decoration of pottery may be either plastic or pictorial. The plastic ornament consists of indentations and stamping of the clay pots. The pottery may be decorated with interlocking circles and wavy lines, zig-zag and cross-wise lines. Glazing the pots by covering them with varnish, sometimes, of contrasting colour is a late invention.

(b) Terracottas : The potters (Kumars) and women irrespective of classes make terracotta dolls, toys and idols. The objects are made by hand casting. The hand made objects are fashioned by pinching, using pellets of clay until the desired shape is obtained. Sometimes, the eye balls or the ornaments of the limbs are shown either by punctures or by grooves. The objects are baked either in slow fire of rice husks or in the sun. In rare instances they are painted. The female figures, sometimes, wear broad griddles, but are otherwise nude.

Metals

The knowledge of metallurgy is both old and wide spread in India. Metallic vessels were known in the Rig Vedic times and subsequently in the classical and medieval periods copper, brass and bronze objects were in universal use.

The manufacture of domestic articles and jewellery by precious metals like gold and silver, has always been found in East Pakistan. The uses of copper and brass, however, are almost endless ; and the articles fashioned in these metals are usually elegant, although they are, sometimes, curious and grotesque.

The graceful shaped pitchers (kalsi), betel-nut cutters (jati), small jugs (ghoti or lota), betel holders (dabar bata), bird cages (khacha), and toilet boxes are notable examples of East Pakistani metal works. These articles are incised with floral and linear designs, fish and bird pictures and figures of divinities. The ornamentation is incised with chisels, making bold, unbroken or dotted lines.

These metal works are still the monopoly of the craftsmen known as Karmakar.

Basketry : Works on Basketry and matting are done practically in all the districts of East Pakistan. The materials used for their manufacture are flexible creepers, bamboos, reeds, grasses, palm and date leaves. The old and strong shoots of plants are used for this purpose.

Preparation : Great care and skill are necessary for the preparation of the materials for basket making. The quality of finished products depends largely on the materials used. Canes, bamboos, etc., are split and then sub-divided into the desired shapes. The delicacy of the products resulting from these operations has been amply described in the proverbial Bengali Saying that these could be rubbed on the eye without hurting.

The finished products are then put into muddy-water, preferably under water hyacinths for a few days. Apart from giving durability this process is an additional protection against the ravages of wood beetles. The natural colour of the materials is changed or modified by dyeing them in vegetable colours. The juice of the 'gab' fruit is in universal use for producing a nut-brown shade in baskets.

The principal technique of basket making is that they may be either woven or coiled. The woven type is of a definite pattern made up of strands of wrap and weft. The wrap is arranged in a more or less fixed position, while the weft crosses and accrosses it, and is inter-woven singly or in pairs. The composition of the basket and its decorative designs and patterns depend on the width, colour and other features of the weaving materials, as well as, on the methods of weaving. The principal types of woven baskets made in East Pakistan are twilled-work, wilker-work and twined-work.

Ornamentation

For ornamentation on basketry works, many geometrical designs, foliage patterns and, in rare instances, human and animal forms depend upon the structure and colouring of the different strands. Coloured ornamentation is done by using materials of natural colour, dyed materials and other ornamental objects. The most striking artistic effect is obtained by simple lines, bends, spirals and geometric designs. These are adapted to the weaver's fancy and to the general form of different objects. The design of the basket is modified by breaking, bending and setting the material of different angles.

The degree of fineness of the workmanship is shown in the variety of baskets, particularly, kulas (winnowing fans), chalunis (sieves), mathals (Sun-hats), dhamas (measure bowls), and fishing traps.

Decoration of Thatched Ceilings : The decoration of thatched ceiling displays a unique craftsmanship. The beauty of the curvilinear roof of Bengali cottage architecture is renowned. The old literature of Bengali is full of descriptive references to its architectural beauties.

The frame work of the ceiling is made of bamboo and coloured strips, producing chess-board, diagonal, spiral, diamond and zig-zag patterns.

Mattings : Mats are woven of bamboos, reeds, grasses, canes and strips of palm leaves. Artistically two kinds of mats are note-worthy ; 'madur' and 'Sital Pati'

Mat of an excellent quality called, Sital Pati is found in East Pakistan especially in the districts of Faridpur and Sylhet. The superior quality of Sital Pati is judged by its gloss and its delicacy of texture. It is famous both for quality and its ornamental weaving.

In general, the decoration is limited to chess-board, diagonal, spiral, zig-zag and leaf pattern and also, sometimes to human and animal figures which illustrate mythological and social stories.

This industry is entirely in the hands of women. Sometimes the Parents received a heavy amount from the men who marry their daughters, the amount being proportional to the skill in making 'Sital Pati' mats. Sylhet is famous for Sital Pati ornamented with ivory strips and beads.

Wood Works : According to Sanskrit tradition, the worker in wood is called Sutradhar or one who holds the string. He is the principal exponent of craftsmanship in wood and is an important member of the village community.

Dolls and Toys : Wooden dolls and toys are treated as the example of craftsmanship and decoration. These are first made out of solid wood and then painted in different colours on a white background. The artist usually uses bright colour to make the object lively and uses varnish to fix the colour.

Boat Building : Bengal is famous, especially East Pakistan for the number and variety of her boats.

The boat building is undertaken after a due consultation of Panjika (astrological almanac).

The keel is first laid and the ribs are then fastened in position by nails. The 'gurras' are fixed at the appropriate height. The 'Golai', and sides of the boat are then built up.

13—

The bow of the vessel has an important decorative function in building and differs from one vessel to another. In ancient literature, references are made to seven type of bows, representing lions, baffalos, serpents, elephants, tigers and birds, especially, 'mayur' (Peacock) and 'Suka' (Mythical bird) ; and the boats were called accordingly, 'Mayur Pankhi', 'Suka Pankhi'.

Various sorts of boats are plying in the rivers and seas of East Pakistan. They vary from one another in respect of size, type, and decoration. Decoration of boats is the lively examples of surviving folk art of East Pakistan.

In our opinion the above discussion is not enough. Many folk arts and crafts are hidden in the nook and corner of East Pakistan. They are yet to be known. With the emergence of industrialization and urbanization, commercial art is getting prominence. It is a happy sign that the cammercial artists cordially receive those indigenous arts and crafts. From these folk arts and crafts we can grasp some of our cultural pattern. A rich laboratory exists for anthropologists, especially the cultural anthropologist to collect those things and study their significance in society. So, it is folk arts which reflect our lively past, as well as, the present easy and simple life of agrarian people.

FOLK SONGS OF EAST PAKISTAN

There are various kinds of folk songs in East Pakistan. They can broadly be divided into the following classes : (a) Bhatiali, (b) Bhawaia, (c) Murshidi, (d) Marefati, (e) Zari, (f) Hari, (g) Shari, (h) Baul, (i) Marriage songs, (j) Bhichchedy, (k) Lok-Gatha etc. Each kind of songs has its special significance in our society. Let us discuss, in brief, the significance of these kinds of songs.

Bhawaia: Bhawaia songs are mainly sung in North Bengal in local language. These songs originated mainly in the districts of Koochbehar, Rangpur, Dinajpur etc. They are not confined only to the districts of their origin. They are very popular throughout the whole of East Pakistan. Two examples of this type of song are given below:

> "O-rey garial bandhu rey
> Bandhu saria raite parina rey
> O-rey praner bandhu rey."

Through this song the lover expresses the view that he or she cannot remain or stay without the beloved who is addressed as "Carter" and dear friend. This is the expression of the lover in the society. The lover cannot do without the beloved.

"Je-jon prayam-er bhab janena
Tar shange nai lena dena
Khati shona charia je-jon
ney nakol shona
She jon shona chenena."

One who does not know how to love and who takes an imitated thing instead of a pure one, he does not know the pure thing and so, there connot be interchange of heart with him.

Bhatiali : This type of songs originated in East Bengal, particularly in the districts of Mymensingh and Faridpur . This is a popular form of song among the East Pakistanis. As East Pakistan is a land of river, Bhatiali songs are connected with river, tide, boat, sail etc. When these songs are sung, we remember the rivers and boats and the life of boat-men. An example of this type of song is given below:

"Ha-rey o vatial ganger naiya,
Thaku bhairey koio amaya naior nitey aiya
Rey vatial ganger naiya".

In this song, the brides in general of rural East Pakistan appeal, at least, psychologically to the boat-men to take them back to thier parents' house from the husband's home. In reality many brides of East Pakistan have to travel by boats. So, the joys and sorrows of a bride, living far away from her parents' house are linked up with these songs.

Murshidi: This kind of song is mainly prevalent among the Fakirs and their disciples. These songs depict the Fakir-disciple relationship in our society.

Example:
"Murshid path dekhaia thao
Ami j-e path chinina go,
sange kaira nao.
Murshid path dekhaia thao."

In this song the disciple requests his teacher (Murshid) to show the path and to take him to the path of salvation which is unknown to him (disciple).

Marefati : Marefati songs increase the mystical tendency of our people. Through this kind of song many people try to learn the secret of the path to God and they become too much impressed by them. It indirectly controls the behaviour of our people.

Example :
"Duarey aishachey Palki
Naiori gao tolorey.
Tolo mukhey Allah-Rasul shavey balorey"

Marriage song : This is an interesting type of song. In the marriage ceremonies of the people of our rural society, various types of marriage songs are sung. These songs give much pleasure to the friends and relatives who participate in a marriage ceremony. They are sung by the ladies working or surrounding the bride. It makes the bride easy.

Lokgatha : It is a historical type of song based on certain story. It has tremendous influence over our people. They learn many things from these songs. Pain, sorrow, joy, love, kindness, humanity, art of living etc., can be learned from such historical songs.

There are many folk songs in East Pakistan based on idea, work, performance, fact etc. These songs affect our people in various ways. They get recreation, idea, imagination from them.

Example :
"O dhan banirey dhekitey par thia
Dheki nachey ami nachi Heliya duliya."

It refers to the husking of paddy through enjoyment.

Zari gan : It refers to the historical song over the facts of life of the prophets or, sometimes, it becomes too tragic when the death of Hossain at Karbala or the sacrifice (korbani) of Ismail etc., are presented. This kind of song is too sensitive.

Hari gan : This type of song is sung generally after the cultivation is over by the cultivators in a chorus. It gives much recreation to the cultivators who are free after a long period of hard work of cultivation.

Boul song: Boul songs are sung mainly by the Hindu bouls or Baishnab or Bairagi. Generally, the singer does not have any wealth or property. With the musical instruments called 'Dotara' and 'Ektara' and a bag on his shoulder, he walks from place to place and sings. By hearing this song some people of our society become in-different to the world.

SOME OF THE CEREMONIES AND CUSTOMS ASSOCIATED WITH THE LIFE-CYCLE OF THE PEOPLE OF EAST PAKISTAN

Birth: The birth of a child in every society is an occasion for happiness. There may be differences in the attitudes and practices of different communities with regard to the sex of the child. We find in some communities great rejoicing over the birth of a male child. If we carefully investigate the matter, in most cases, we shall find that it is due to people's old believes i.e., they regard the boy as an econ-omic asset to the family and, on the other hand, the girl as an eco-nomic liability. Inspite of the changes which have taken place in our society, many people still regard the birth of a girl as a burden on the family. It may be caused by poor participation of women-folk in various fields of our social life. Moreover, the religion does not permit our women to work with men freely i.e., without 'Purdha' (vail). This almost becomes a social sanction i.e., society restricts such participation of womenfolk. The 'Purdha' system among the Muslims also greatly hinders the growth of sound economic assurance to the womenfolk of our society. Due to these hindrances and many others, womenfolk of our society rarely get any opportunity to participate in the field of various works to make themselves economically sound.

Now we shall try to enumerate the ceremonies, connected with 'birth'. Islam does not enjoin any elaborate ceremonies on the occa-sion of the birth of a child of either sex. All that is necessary is that some one should recite the "Azan" in the right ear and the 'Takbir' in the left ear of the new born baby ; and in Aqiqa ceremony, when the child is formally given a name, some animals like cow, sheep or goat should be sacrificed, (two for a male child and one for a female child). Here also we find the superiority of a male child over the female child. On the very birth we find the women in a secondary position. In case of the male child there is the further provision of Sunnat, Musalmani or Khatna i.e., circumcision which marks the attainment of "Mussalaniyat". There is another provision for both the male and female baby i.e., Aqiqa, which marks the naming of the new born baby. All these are practised exclusively by the Muslim community of our society.

Among the Hindus the ceremony of 'Annaprashana' i.e., putting of rice or sweets in the mouth of a child after teething is an occasion of rejoicing. In this celebration the Hindus invite their friends and relatives at their residence.

In present day society it has become fashionable in the larger cities to observe the birth days of the children. This is becoming more frequent and more elaborate in almost all the urban communities of our society in East Pakistan.

Death: As birth is an occasion for happiness so is the death for sorrow. Though it is difficult to say that death costs more than the birth yet in East Pakistan both among the Muslims and the Hindus the death of a person costs more than the birth of a child. The death of a person involves those relatives, he leaves behind. They have to perform a series of religious functions such as 'challisha' i.e., the feast after 40 days of death, 'Fateha' i.e., prayer for the departed soul. Apart from these, there are others like soyem, chehlum and korankhani, though all these are not strictly observed by the common people. But 'challisha' (feast after 40 days of death) is, more or less, observed by most the people of the Muslim community. The purpose of observing these practices is to show regard for the departed soul and its peace in the after world.

Among the Hindus the death of a person also involves considerable expenditure on those relations who are left behind. When an aged man or a woman dies, his or her sons have to spent heavy sums on a series of ceremonies, including a feast. This is a real hardship for the lower and middle income Hindu families. However, now-a-days it seems that these practices in both the communities is on the decline.

Marriage : Marriage is a very important event in the life of human beings. It is also an occasion for happiness, but a number of burdensome customs and economically oppressive ceremonies are centred round the institution of the marriage. Society exerts pressure on the parties to follow these customs and ceremonies even though their observance may result in poor economic condition. The Muslim marriage is a very simple affair.

The following are the main essentials for the Muslim marriage :
   (1)   Ijab-ul-Qubool (Proposal   and   acceptance)
   (2)   Shakhi (Presence   of   witnesses).
   (3)   Dower of Mohar (Token of husband's regard for his wife)
   (4)   Khutbah (Solemnity to the marriage   contract).

Of the ceremonies and functions connected with   marriage, the most important are : (1) Betrothal, (2) entertainment of 'Barat' (bridal party),   (3) 'Walima' entertainment by the bride's side when the girl goes back, for the first time, to her parents' home.

Lagni :   The bridegroom's parents take clothes, ornaments, sweets etc., to the bride's home and in return the bride's side offers a ring, sometimes, a handkerchief and other presents to the bridegroom.

Nikah : A large number of persons from both the sides of the bride and the bridegroom are invited to assemble at the bride's house at the time of 'Nikah'—a ceremony usually followed by a dinner.

Walima : A couple of days later the relations and friends of the bride-groom's side are invited by the bride's side for the 'Walima' party.

Chauthi : The bride, after staying two or three days at her father in-law's house, goes back to her parents' home, accompanied by her new relations.

Before the Nikah ceremony "Denmohar" must be settled, which is often a problem rather than a ceremony.   The "Mohar" has religious sanction. It is an essential part of the Nikah.

It is treated as a token of the husband's regard for his wife though only in theory. It has been explained by the religious 'Ulemas' that the main purpose of 'Mohar' is to give the woman a sense of security and a feeling of independence

MIDDLE CLASS CULTURE IN EAST PAKISTAN

The middle class in every country   moulds her   social and cultural structure to a great extent.   We know that the upper structure emerges out of the existing basic social structure. So culture and social structure have close relationship with each other.

To have a separate culture pattern for the urban people is of recent origin. The impact of western technology with western education and outlook and western fashions are imported by our middle class people. A great change has taken place in the middle class culture in our country. Due to economic factor and surplus population, the rural people started migrating to urban areas for which our village culture remains isolated.

SHORT HISTORY OF THE DEVELOPMENT OF MIDDLE CLASS IN EAST PAKISTAN

Going back to the ancient history of the land, the Aryans entered the Indo-Pak subcontinent about 1500 B.C., and found the country inhabited by the Non-Aryans, Dravidians and Austro-Asiatic people in the East of the country. The Tibeto-Burman people of the Mongolian race entered East Bengal at a later period after the Aryans had spread in East Bengal. It is sure that Austro-Asiatic people have left traces of their culture on the Bengali life in general. Akbar, the great conquered Bengal in 1576 A.D. By 1600 the whole of East Bengal came under the Mughal rule. During this time we find a section of people, comprising trader, soldier of less importance forming a class, but could not get into the upper class. The East India Company became the de-facto rulers after the battle of Plassy in 1757 A.D. The Muslim culture of Bengal is really a Persico-Arabico-Indian culture. Broadly speaking, the culture of East Pakistan is a product of various elements,—Austro-Asiatic, Tibeto-Burman, Indo-Aryan, Arabian, Persian, Turkish, Portuguese and English. Apart from the mixture of races and languages, the contact of different religions in East Pakistan from the earliest time uptill now has also influenced the culture of the province as a whole.

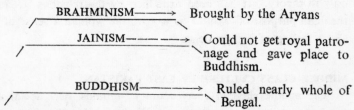

BRAHMINISM———→ Brought by the Aryans

JAINISM———————→ Could not get royal patronage and gave place to Buddhism.

BUDDHISM————————→ Ruled nearly whole of Bengal.

During these religious changes there started a class struggle which gave birth to a new class lately known as middle class. In 1201 A.D. the Muslims conquered West Bengal. During the Mughal rule in East Bengal the Muslims were limited either to the aristocracy at the service of the Mughals or to the very poor classes. The emergence of a modern Muslim middle class was further delayed after the Mutiny of 1857 by the British policy of keeping the Muslim upper classes and the Muslim population from which the Muslim middle class could be formed under strict control. After the foundation of the Congress in 1885 the Muslims i.e., the Muslim rising middle class began to be given more and more privileges in jobs and in education. The educated Muslim middle class was rapidly formed and ; such an educated class was recruited from all the sections of the society.

"The second world war and the second partition of Bengal in 1947 are now giving a new orientation to social stratification among the Muslims"[1]

The Muslims have taken the place of the Hindus in the role of the middle class. A new structure with new classes and new class relationships again comes into existence. We are heading towards the industrial culture, leaving our agrarian culture behind. It certainly influenced the rural life. The surplus population of the rural areas gathered in the urban areas. This led to the emergence of a section of new lower class factory workers. The introduction of machinecraft greatly influenced our village life.

CULTURAL CHARACTERISTICS OF THE MIDDLE CLASS

The culture of the middle class is some what different from that of the upper class or the sophisticated people of the society and the lower class. This distinction can be felt in their aims and aspirations, modes of living and thinking and in their attitude towards life and its various problems, in their income, occupation and social position and social role etc.

The middle class people are the upholders of social mobility or an open-class society. It means equal opportunity to improve one's own lot which left every individual to move freely in social space. Self-consciousness is one of the characteristics of the middle class.

Such self-consciousness was the result of intellectual thinking and progress of secular education. They uphold and emphasize the natural rights of man regardless of the class to which he might belong. They adhere to certain liberal values.

The middle class people want to lead a good life. They are

1. Bessaingnet, P. Social Research in East Pakistan. Asiatic Society, P. 241. Dacca.

sophisticated in their mode of thinking and manners and strive to maintain their standard in the society. They have money but not so much money as to afford every luxury they wish to have. Within their income they wish to live a standard life,—not far from that of the upper class people of our society. In their likes and tastes, they resemble the upper class ; but they have to satisfy their needs within their limited income which perhaps contributes modesty in their general character.

Such modesty in their general life pattern will be clear if we consider their dresses. Modesty is the primary aim of most of the middle class people. They want to look smart and tidy in their dresses. When they buy cloth they have to do it with much carefulness as to whether he would be able to wear it on more than one occasion. Some of the middle class people observe 'Purdah', but a few of them go to the extreme in their dress-style, introduced by the upper class of the society.

The pattern of residence of the middle class is different from that of the upper and lower class people. In the urban areas the middle class people especially live in colonies or flat-like apartments in residential areas with their fellows. Often, they try to improve their standard of living by changing their houses to the areas where the upper class people live. Their food consists mainly of rice, fish, vegetables and, sometimes, meat and other good foods.

Most of the middle class family both in the urban and rural areas exhibit the traditional behaviour pattern. A few upper middle class people, being influenced by the western culture are imitating their manners and ettiquette.

Marriage in the middle class society may be viewed as a means to change the status. The fathers prefer to get their daughters married in the upper stratum of the society. They have to do this by sacrificing huge amount of money to the bride groom's family as dowry. The age at marriage both for the boys and the girls are increasing in the middle class society because they prefer to have some qualification to earn before their marriage.

The middle class people give special emphasis on education of their children because, to them education is the best means for attaining a higher standard in the society. Even those who have earned enough money by trade, commerce and business realize the need of education.

Towards the education of the girls most of the middle class families hold a favourable view. But their attitudes differ as to its nature. Of course, there are a number of people who oppose the education for the sake of 'Pur dah'. But they are the insignificant minority. Their attitude to women's employment is liberal. They are receptive to different changes, taking place in our society.

The recreation of the middle class consists of several things. In our rural areas the main recreations for them are the 'Kabigan', 'Zatra', 'Puthipath' etc. Here they find intellectual satisfaction and recreation. In the urban areas cinema is the most popular form of recreation to them. Moreover, playing of football, cricket, hockey, table tennis and such other foreign games are other sources of their recreation. There are also parks, musiums and clubs for their entertainment. A very small group of people indulges in gambling, horse race and intoxicating drugs.

Due to the particular nature of middle class culture a vast majority of literature, dealing with life conditions, problems, aims and aspirations and various other aspects of life of the middle class people has sprung up in this province. Such literatures may be called the middle class literature.

The rising influence of the middle class can be traced since 1872. The influence arose from the growth of English education, especially in 1880's.

The rapid expansion of education, especially in Bengal proceeded immediately from economic motives. The increase in the population and progressive fragmentation of land were reducing the once respectable class of proprietors to increase their dependence on education as a means of livelihood.

Bibliography

Anisuzzaman. *Muslim Manas-o-Bangla Shahitya.* Pakistan writer's Guild, Dacca, 1964.

Desai, A.R. *Social Background of Indian Nationalism.* Popular Book Depot, Bombay, 1959.

Davis, K. *Human Society.* New York, 1948.

Neheru, J. *The Discovery of India.* John Day Company, New York, 1945.

Karim, A.K.N. *Changing Society in India and Pakistan.* Dacca, 1956.

MacIver, R.M. *Society.* London, Macmillan and Co. Ltd., 1957.

Ahmad, N. *East Pakistan as it is now.* Co-operative Book Society Chittagong, 1960.

Hussain, S. S. (ed.) *East Pakistan : a Profile.* Dacca, Orient Longmans, 1962.

Khan, M.A. *Muslim Struggle for freedom in Bengal.* East Pakistan Govt. Press, Dacca, 1960.

Hussain, A.F.A. *Employment of Middle Class Muslim Women in Dacca.* Socio-Economic Research Board, University of Dacca, 1958.

Mukharjee, A. *Folk Art of Bengal.* Calcutta, 1946.

CHAPTER 13

CRIME AND JUVENILE DELINQUENCY IN EAST PAKISTAN

From the legal point of view crime is an offence against the law of the land. The terms delinquent and criminal bear different significance to different countries, though both are offenders. The difference between a delinquent and a criminal rests on age. According to English law, a criminal is an adult offender of 16 years and above ; while a delinquent is a minor offender of below 16 years. In Pakistan the age limit for the juvenile delinquents is 7 years to 16 years. Any offence, committed by persons above this age (7—16years) is a criminal act.

East Pakistan is passing through a transitional period. The country is now heading towards industrialization which is essential to effect an improvement in the standard of living. The process of industrialization is giving impetus to the growth of industrial towns and cities which are attracting our rural population. This has led to the breakdown of old ties and change in the sense of values.

Sometimes, there are conflicts between the old traditional values and the new values, brought about by the process of industrialization in East Pakistan. The increase in crime and the appearance of the problem of juvenile delinquency are the important products of this transitional phase.

NATURE OF CRIME

A common and recurring manifestation of lawlessness in East Pakistan prior to 1947 was the communal riots between the Muslims and the Hindus. With the creation of two independent states of India and Pakistan, the incidence of such rioting gradually disappeared. In 1950 there was a brief reappearance of such violence in Dacca, in

Barisal and in Bogra districts. The total number of riot cases including those of unlawful assembly in the province was 3383[1]. There were communal riots in Dacca and Khulna in 1964.

Another type of riot, occurring in East Pakistan derived from industrial disputes and the deterioration in the discipline of the labour force in the industrial areas of East Pakistan. A different type of criminogenic situation, facing the police developed out of the partition of the subcontinent and has been known as "border troubles". The frontiers of East Pakistan had not been clearly demarcated and this gave rise to a number of border disturbances. There was also a great deal of smuggling of goods in the border regions of East Pakistan. Other crime situations grew out of the intermixture of party politics and socio-economic issues such as labour agitation, industrial strikes, food problems and the like. According to the Annual Police Reports the different types of cognizable offences have been classified as :

(1) Serious offences against the state, public tranquility, safety and justice.

(2) Serious offences against the person.

(3) Serious offences against the person and property or against property only.

(4) Minor offences against the state.

(5) Minor offences against property.

(6) Offences against special and local laws.

There are some other minor crimes such as pick-pocketing, swindling of various kinds, doubling currency notes, impersonation of various kinds etc., in East Pakistan.

CRIME TREND

The study of crime over a number of years, specially in the recent past in any one district of East pakistan will show a downward trend in the crime rate. The study of the crime trends of all the districts and also of the province in general for the last three years will show the same downward trend in crime rate. But before 1960 there was an

---

1. Annual Report on the Police Administration of the Province of East Pakistan, 1950. P. 34. Govt., of East Pakistan, Office of the Inspector General of Police.

upward trend in crime rate. This can be seen in the Annual Police Administration Reports and the Annual Jail Administration Reports of East Pakistan from 1948 to 1959. The statistical figures available from these sources will indicate a sharp rise in Juvenile delinquency and criminality. In 1948 as many as 2513 juvenile delinquents were convicted which represented roughly 21% of the total number of 11924 convicts.

In 1954 as many as 5336 delinquents were convicted. They represented 27% of the total number of 19812 convicts. In 1958 the number of delinquents convicted were 6142, representing 22% of the total of 27041 convicts. The record number of 8046 delinquents who represented 27% of the total of 30089 convicts were found in 1959. But from 1960 to 1962 we find a sharp decline in both crime and juvenile delinquency rates in East Pakistan. The statistical figures available from the Annual Police Reports of the Government of East Pakistan are given below:

Year	Total number of Convicts	Number of Juvenile Delinquents
1960	23680	5327
1961	18738	3445
1962	14287	2691

When East Pakistan is passing through a period of transition and heading towards industialization and urbanization, it would be interesting to find out the reasons for this decline in the crime rate. This will provide a good field of research for the sociologists and criminologists in Pakistan.

PROBLEM OF JUVENILE DELINQUENCY

Juvenile delinquency is an alarming problem specially in urban and industrial areas. It is not yet a serious problem in East Pakistan. After the partition of the sub-continent, urbanization and industrialization are taking place in different parts of the province. With this change, the number of juvenile offences are increasing. But the Criminal Investigation Department does not keep proper statistics of juvenile offences in the province. The increase can be seen from day to day observation. It is difficult to have a correct picture of juvenile delinquency because of the fact that all the cases of delinquency do not come to the court and even in the court many are acquited by the magistrates and judges. Moreover, they have the strong public sympathy in many respects.

As a result, it becomes difficult to prove a case against a juvenile delinquent. Generally, minor offences against property such as pick-pocketing, theft etc., are committed by the delinquents. Disputes with land and property are also found among them.

Social and economic factors are mainly responsible for the growth of juvenile delinquency in East Pakistan. Sex offences, committed by them are increasing everyday. With the urbanization and industrialization of the country the problem of juvenile delinquency is likely to take a serious turn. Though it is not a serious problem in the present East Pakistani society, the government and the people should jointly take steps to stop its spread in our community life.

CAUSES OF CRIME AND DELINQUENCY IN EAST PAKISTAN

Mainly four factors are considered to be the causes of crime and anti-social activities in Pakistan. They are : (i) Physical, (ii) Economic (iii) Social and (iv) Psychological.

As all these factors are interlinked we shall try to show the relative importance of these factors.

1. Physical Factors

(a) **Geography and Topography :** East Pakistan is in the deltoid region, formed mainly by the Padma, the Meghna, the Brahmaputra and their tributaries. Her plain lands are full of streams. These rivers flow with high currents, frequently changing their course of direction. As a result, there is constant change in the formation of lands. Usually in the rainy season these rivers become over-flooded and cause heavy damage to the inhabitants of East Pakistan by damaging their crops. Again due to erosion there is constant disappearance of the existence of old land formation and the appearance of new lands. These newly formed lands are popularly known as "char" land. Previously these lands were regarded as 'No man's land'. So there had been serious competition for the possession of these lands. Consequently rioting among the people of these areas was rampant.

These are highly alluvial lands and too easy to produce more crops with minimum labour and cost. To check these riots and blood-shed Bengal Alluvial Land Act was passed in 1920. But the people cared a little of this Act and went on in the same way as their forefathers did. So the crimes like riot and bloodshed are still going on in the "Char" areas. The absence of boundary line of these lands also fosters such crimes.

The nature of these rivers also moulded the nature of the inhabitants of the adjacent areas. With the changing condition of the rivers the inhabitants are constantly changing their places of shelter and subsistence. Some of them become poor and at the same time ferocious. Even some of the women of these areas have the ferocious nature like their male members and often directly help their men in serious violence.

A large number of rioting and murder cases occurs on property right. A section of the people of these areas, often, becomes professional criminals and indulge in theft, robbery and dacoity. A large part of the gang-cases comes from these areas. During the rainy season crime in water is rampant. In this season the villages are completely isolated from each other by water. The professional criminals get the opportunity to engage themselves in criminal activities. They can not be properly controlled because of communication difficulties. It is quite difficult and often impossible to move police forces in the marshes and rivers.

Land is the main source of livelihood of the people of East Pakistan. As the density of population is high the land with high fertility can not support the people who clash over the possession of one or two decimals of land.

(b) **Change of Season :** Change of season is another important factor of criminality. With the change of season the types of crime also change to some extent. Generally, in summer crime against person increases, while in winter crime against property increases. It is because of the fact that in winter the farmers have some crops in their home and usually in winter night they have sound sleep. The criminals, specially the thiefs take this opportunity to steal the property of others. During the rainy season the villages in the Province appear as islands and the house to house communication becomes difficult. The criminals take this advantage. Besides these when plants like sugar cane, jute etc., grow up the criminals can take shelter into the field to escape detection. During the off season when the cultivators have little work in the field they often take part in village politics and conflicts which lead to various types of crimes. The number of litigation increases in these off seasons.

(c) **Change in the Phases of the Moon :** As the criminals prefer night, specially the dark night for their activities the change in the phases of the moon is to be taken into consideration to analyse the causes of crime. It has been found that there is periodical increase and decrease of criminal activities with the change of the phases of the moon. Generally crime increases during the first and fourth quarter of the month. These are the days, preceding and following the new moon. But the rate of crime decreases with the beginning of the full moon.

2. Economic Factors

Economic factors are the most important causes of crime in East Pakistan. It has got the direct touch with the rise and fall of the crime barometer. It is a common factor of crime in many countries of the world. Whenever any investigator observes the crime situation of a country, he must have to look at the economic background of the country. In case of East Pakistan it can be observed that the criminals are mainly from the poor classes. Agriculture is the basic economy of East Pakistan. Land is fixed and the process of its cultivation is still of primitive nature. So with the increase of population pressure there is no satisfactory increase of products. Though the shifting of population from the villages to the towns and industrial areas is going on, it is too little to cope with the situation. In such a condition the seasonal unemployment causes much for the increase of seasonal crimes in the rural areas of the province. There are a good number of landless agricultural labourers in the villages. This Unemployment generally happens in winter and in rainy season. When the economic distress of the poor villagers knows no bound, crimes like theft, robbery and dacoity increase in the villages. In winter there is little work in the field for the landless labourers and at the same time the store of the land holders is filled up with the harvest. The distressed working people indulge in crime against these stored crops and property. The crime against property is frequent during this time. Again in rainy season, specially in the months of July and August crime rates tend to increase because of the unemployment, caused by heavy rainfall.

The relationship between the economy and crime can be seen in a different way. Though agriculture is the basic economy of our country it depends on the whim of nature. The peasants are not sure about the production of crops. The fearful drought or devastating flood brings about distress to the cultivators by causing serious damage to the crops. In such a situation the people of a particular area may become very poor. It would not be surprising at all to see that they are motivated to criminal activities to satisfy their hunger.

3. Social Factor

Some criminologists hold the opinion that social factors are the fundamental causes of crime in our society. There are reasons behind such an opinion. Almost all the aspects of man's life in the society are influenced by social factors. Man has to pass his normal life with the adjustment of all these social aspects. But there lies immense possibilities of being frustrated in the society. So one may do anti-social activities because of maladjustment with any of these social aspects.

(a) **Family Life :** Like the Western countries the problem of maladjustment is not very serious in East Pakistan. But the number of maladjusted families is increasing with the change of the socio-economic conditions of the people. It has been observed that a large number of criminals come from the maladjusted and unhappy families. Unsatisfactory relationships among the family members such as husband and wife, parents and children etc., lead the children to delinquency. Lack of proper care to the children makes them unbalanced in their very early ages. Moreover, the family is the primary unit for the children to adopt social values, norms, ideals etc. If the family fails to perform these basic functions for the children it would not be very unnatural for the children to become a delinquent and ultimately turn into an expert criminal.

It has been found that in East Pakistan criminals mainly come from the poor and illiterate families. The lack of understanding of children's psychology by their illiterate parents and because of their poverty they often fail to adjust with children's desires and necessities. Sometimes, the unnecessary oppression of the parents on their children makes them notorious. This also helps them in growing ill-feeling and hatred against their family.

(b) Community Environment : Like the family, the community influences are also important in making criminals in our society. There are good, as well as, evil aspects of the social life. An individual may be influenced by the ideals, mentality, morality etc., in the community. But another individual may be influenced by the anti-social elements in the community only to become a criminal.

(c) Education and Recreation : Lack of educational and recreational facilities is of great importance for the crime situation in the province. This problem is more or less same throughout the province. The percentage of literacy is very low in East Pakistan because the majority of the people can not bear the educational expenses of their children who cannot develop a healthy mind. Sometimes the defects of educational system are responsible for the growth of juvenile delinquency. In our system of education the children, from the very beginning of their educational life are over-burdened with the pressure of learning so many languages and subjects. Because of this heavy pressure they divert the attention from the studies and gradually become notorious and indulge in anti-social activities. Some teachers in school are in the habit of punishing the students for their slight faults. There is little attempt to reform them. As a result, the rate of truancy increases in our schools.

Lack of recreational facilities adds much to the educational factor for the growth of crime and delinquency in our society. In most of the academic institutions the recreational arrangements are not sufficient for the students. This situation gives them opportunity to pass their off-time inactively or with harmful activities by mixing with the bad companions.

(d) Play Ground : Man cannot live in isolation. He must have some companions or associations in which he will pass the days of his life.

Bad companionship is responsible for making a man anti-social and criminal. The children and also the teen-agers who are very adoptive in nature may be easily influenced by the misconduct and crime of their bad companionship.

(e) **Customs and Beliefs** : The difference in customs and beliefs of the people, living in the same country, sometimes, causes class hatred in them. This class hatred becomes a factor for mass crime. The conflict between the Hindus and the Muslims is the conflict of customs and beliefs of the two religious groups. During the time of the partition of the Subcontinent this factor took its extreme form and caused a mass crime like communal riot in some parts of Bengal.

(f) **Prostitution** : It is another vital factor for the increase of crime rate in the province. With the growth of urbanization and industrialization in East Pakistan, prostitution is expanding with all its evils. The houses of the prostitutes are the shelters of the criminals. The area of prostitution is the place of criminal environment. Illegal drinking, gambling etc., are frequently done in an easy manner. In many cases the girls and young women are kidnapped by the gang, associated with the prostitutes.

(g) **Legal System** : The legal system of our country has the bad reputation for involving too much time in making any judgment. This causes unnecessary loss of time and money. Considering these two factors often some victims do not dare go to the court.

(h) **Jail** : The jails of our country are not yet up to the mark. There are no proper remedial or correctional measures for the criminals in the jails. They do not have the proper training there for providing themselves in future. Though, at present, some occupational trainings are given to them in the prison, they are not given any fund at the time of returning from the jail. Moreover, all types of criminals are kept in the same place. In this system a first offender has the chance of mixing with hardened criminals and can be influenced by them. There is no necessary protection for the juvenile delinquents to keep them separate from the hardened criminals. There is only one Borstal School in the whole of East Pakistan. It has a very limited accommodation. So the vast number of juvenile delinquents are kept in the ordinary jails with their criminal environment. When a first offender returns from the jail he acquires all the qualities of a hardened criminal.

4. Psychological Factor

Psychological factors are also responsible for some types of crimes. The psychological reaction of an event often leads one to commit crime. Motive for revenge, emotion, mental torture for some causes, hatred etc., become the causes of such crimes. Moreover, maladjustment to some new environment encourages criminal activities. The growing urbanization and industrialization cause the migration of large number of people to the cities and towns. The new life and new environment plus the home sickness create much trouble for their adjustment.

METHODS, DEALING WITH THE CRIMINALS AND DELINQUENTS IN EAST PAKISTAN

Police : The officers of the law are the persons to deal with the criminals. Their chief functions are to preserve the peace and to arrest the offenders and bring them to trial. The task which is imposed on the police is a responsible job. To handle this problem with intelligence he needs much training. He also needs training for his specific field. In our country there are a few police schools. As a result, the police is not adequately trained. This should be modified and more and more training schools for the police should be introduced in the province. He must not only arrest the offenders but also discover evidence on which a trial can be based. He should understand the psychology and behaviour of the criminals. This will help the police to handle the criminals and juvenile delinquents in a better way.

Court : After a man is arrested he is either placed in jail custody to await the trial or is let out on bond. In due time he appears before the court for trial. He pleads either guilty or not guilty. The trial is a legal battle between the prosecutor and the defender. The judge is like an umpire in the game. He conducts the game and hears the evidence to give his verdict in a case. But the decision of the Session Court is not final. The accused may appeal to the High Court and ultimately to the Supreme Court for justice.

Punishment : After the trial is over the criminals are punished or set free by the judges of the court. The following are the various forms of punishment :

(a) Capital Punishment : Capital Punishment is the most ancient and by its nature is the most drastic of all. Abul Hasanat in his book "Crime and Criminal Justice," says that capital punishment must have originated in the primitive societies as a reaction to murder and similar grave offences. Most of the religious codes approve of this punishment. Islam also retained the death penalty. In Pakistan if one commits cold blooded murder he faces this punishment. The argument in favour of retaining capital punishment is to drive away the criminals from our society forever. But there are scholars in Pakistan who advocate the abolition of death penalty. The arguments which Abul Hasanat has forwarded to abolish the capital punishment seem to be logical and sound. He says :

(1) It is an irrevocable penalty. After all we have by no means perfected our machinery of justice so that we may accept the court pronouncements as infallible. Unbalanced persons may often wrongly confess their involvement in a crime and tight evidence, manufactured by over jealous party or agency may secure capital punishment of an innocent person in the present condition.

(2) It gives no chance to the criminals for reformation.

(3) The barbarity of capital punishment has a demoralizing effect upon our society. It violates our humanitarian sentiments.

(b) **Corporal Punishment :** Physical torture is called corporal punishment. It may be whipping. It can not, in a true sense, reduce the number of criminals and delinquents.

(c) **Penal Transportation :** Transportation for life as a modern method of punishment had its origin in England. Life transportation is one of the forms of punishment in Pakistan. From sociological point of view confinement without correction is not good for the society.

(d) **Forfeture of property or imposition of fine :** It is also an ancient type of punishment. It exists in every part of the world. This kind of punishment should be rejected because it may be, to some extent, punishment to the rich but direct suffering to the poor and destitute and his family. This will lead the family of the poor to more corruption and criminal activities which will break the backbone of our society.

Probation : It is another device to mitigate the maladjustment of criminal justice to the needs of the individuals. Probation is sometimes partial. It is carefully used and applied only to those who give promise of doing well at liberty under supervision. If the probation officer is a qualified person and takes active and sympathetic interest in the person committed to his charge, probation becomes most beneficial method for handling the criminals in Pakistan. Probation which puts the offenders under supervision before they are sent to an institution can be socially useful in the treatment of criminals and delinquents. Probation must be improved in the light of the following principles :

(a) Good probation must be based on thorough investigation.

(b) Investigation and treatment should be individualized.

(c) The term of probation should not be fixed in advance.

(d) The home and neighbourhood must be used to rehabilitate those on probation, especially juvenile offenders.

(e) Both diagnosis and treatment must take the account of physical and mental conditions.

(f) Special social organizations and groups may profitably be used as supplementary to the regular probation officers.

(g) The programme should include cooperation with all the agencies of the community which can be of help.

(h) Probation officer should be properly trained and well-paid.

Juvenile and Adult Reformatories : These should be introduced for the correction of criminals and juvenile delinquents in our country.

The Indeterminate Sentences : It is found in the U.S.A. It is not practised in our country. In this case the release of an offender should depend upon the judgment of those who know him. They are qualified to determine when he (offender) is fit to return to society. This may be tried in our country.

Parole : It means that after a man has spent a certain period of time in an institution and has shown the possibility of doing well in the society, he is released under the control of the parole officers. The parole officers should he properly trained to handle the criminals and dilinquents.

Imprisonment : The last penal and correctional institution is the prison. The persons who are found guilty are kept in confinement. In the prison there is no adequate measure to correct the prisoners. As a result, when a criminal after the term of the punishment, comes out of the prison he becomes a hardened criminal. To stop this the prison should be reformed and the measures should be taken to correct the criminals in the prison. They should be sympathetically treated by the prison authority. They should be given some vocational training in the prison which will help them in their future life.

There is no single "Cure-all" for all types of criminals. The criminal laws are social phenomena and they should be based on the results of sociological and anthropological studies. So the punishment should never be isolated from social remedies. The length of imprisonment must depend not only on the moral and material gravity of the offence but also on the results obtained in the treatment in prison. The person, facing the trial should not be judged by the court alone. He should be examined by a physician, a psychologist and a criminologist before the final judgment is given.

Bibliography

Afsaruddin, M. *Sociology and Social Research in Pakistan.* The Pakistan Sociology Association (East Pakistan Unit). Dacca 1963.

Burt, C. *The Young Delinquent.* New York, D. Appleton and Co. 1925.

Clifford R. Shaw and Henry D. Mackay. *Juvenile Delinquency and Urban Areas.* Chicago, University of Chicago Press, 1942.

Gillin, John L. *Criminology and Penology.* New York, D. Appleton and Co., 1945.

Healy, W. and Bronner, A.F. *Delinquents and Criminals : Their making and unmaking.* New York, The Macmillan Co. 1926.

Taft, D.R. *Criminology.* New York, The Macmillan Co. 1942.

Tappan, P.W. *Juvenile Delinquency.* McGraw Hill Book company, New York, 1949.

Annual Report on the Police Administration of the Province of East Pakistan, 1950. Government of East Pakistan, Office of the Inspector General of Police.

Annual Report of East Bengal Police Committee, 1963. Govt., of East Bengal.

British Journal of Criminology. Quadrangle Books, Inc. Chicago.

Dhar, J. *Delinquency is not an isolated problem:* Social welfare Vol. IX No. 6. Coronation Printing Works, Delhi-6. 1962.

Annual Police and Jail Administration Reports, 1948-1959, 1960-1962. Govt., of East Pakistan.

CHAPTER 14
VILLAGE LIFE IN EAST PAKISTAN

East pakistan is a Province of 51 million people (1961 census). Out of these 51 million inhabitants, 9 millions are Hindus and the rest are Muslims. Ninetyfive percent of that population is rural and is dispersed among villages most of which are administrative groupings of dispersed or nucleated homesteads. The homesteads (baris) are usually erected on elevated land to prevent their submersion under water during the rainy season. Each of them comprises one or more of the three types of construction : sleeping house, cooking house and cowshed. Often these homesteads form a chain winding their way through the paddy fields. In many cases, however, they assume the shape of an isolated mound on top of which a few baris are clustered together. In rainy season when the lowland of East Pakistan is covered under several feet of water such villages resemble islands emerging from the middle of a lake.

SOCIAL STRATIFICATION

The Muslims in East Pakistani villages are divided into three main economic classes i.e., (a) The rich, (b) The well-off, and (c) The poor.

Generally the Talukdar and Jotdar belong to the rich class. We can include the Choudhury, Khan, Khandkar, Biswas etc., in the well-off class. The poor class in East Pakistani villages consists of landless labourers i.e., day-labourers, boat-men, chakars (servants) etc.

Socially the Muslims can be divided into two social classes such as (a) 'Bhadralok' (High Muslims) i.e., Syed, Khan, Miah, Khandkar, Choudhury. (b) Other groups (Low Muslims) i.e., Shek, Shikdar, Mandal, Kulu, Jolah, Nikari, Bediya.

Among the Hindus the people are divided along the caste line. In this system one group is enjoying more privileges than the other. There is little scope for social mobility among the Hindus.

Achievements of the people are given little importance to determine their position along the social ladder. The chart given below will give us a general view of the hierachical order of different caste groups in the villages.

CHART
Hierarchy of caste groups among the Hindus

Groups	Castes
A. High Hindus	(1) Brahmin
	(2) Kyastha
B. Low Hindus	(1) Shaha (Trader)
	(2) Kumar (Potter)
	(3) Kamar (Blacksmith)
	(4) Basak (Weaver)
	(5) Namasudra (Cultivator)
	(6) Dhopa (Washer man)
	(7) Sutar (Carpenter)
	(8) Napit (Barber)
	(9) Jalia (Fisher man)
	(10) Teli (Oil Presser)
C. Untouchables	(1) Bagdi
	(2) Chamar
	(3) Chandal

SOCIAL INSTITUTION AND SOCIAL SYSTEM

The family in the village is both single and joint. The single family consists of husband, wife and their children. The joint family is one where husband, wife and their children, husband's parents, as well as, the wives and children of the married sons live under the same roof and share the income and expenditure of the family in common. All the members of the family eat the same food, worship the same God and enjoy the same property. The joint family system is breaking up due to the individualistic tendency of the modern age, the heavy population pressure and the financial difficulties of the people. The system of polygamous marriage is found among the Muslims in the village ; but monogamy is the general pattern of marriage among the villagers. In the village the descent is traced along the male line. The old living male member is usually the head of the family. He administers the family property and commands the obedience of all the members.

The women in the village think that they are the burden on their parents when young and on growing up the burden is shifted to a gentleman, more often unknown to them and when old they are still a burden on her own son or perhaps on her son's wife. In recent times, the status of the women folk of the village has increased. But they are not given equal treatment with men folk. Their status in the society is inferior to that of men. They feel that they are not chattels ; but separate individual entities. They refuse to be a slave of anyone before and after their marriage, even though they have to obey their parents before marriage and husband after marriage.

The children are to obey their parents. The value of the spirit of obedience develops in the congenial atmosphere of the village. The parents direct and guide their children in their day-to-day activities. They also command the children because they have superior knowledge and experience of life. They want their children to be benefited by their advice. The children also develop the spirit of obedience.

The village being traditional in nature, still gives emphasis on caste and heredity as two important determining factors of social status. However, there are changes in the village. Social status is now determined, to some extent, by the education and wealth of the people. Even the landless educated class is gaining its status in the village. The people in this class now occupy good positions in the village and enjoy their full rights. The social status has become, to some extent, horizontal in nature because even a number of Jolah, Kulu, Jalia, Bediya etc., may attain a good position in the society by acquiring education. But this phenomenon is still not very common because the traditional rural society does not allow their members to do so.

The villagers in East Pakistan live in small communities and thus come to know each other more intimately than those in the cities and towns, where even the next door neighbours are often strangers to one another.

The simple recreation and amusement of the village are boat race, horse-cattle race, ha-do-do, riding, kapadi, football, kabigun, jarigun, and jatra (village opera).

SOCIAL CONTROL

The village leadership is still in the hands of the older generation in the village. An educated youngman should, therefore, be very careful not to violate any social norm. With the impact of technological changes on the villages, there are challenges to the old leadership by the younger generation. As a result, the new leadership in rural areas is coming from the young people with some modern out-look.

In the village the family controls the behaviour of its members by discipline, punishment and reward. The children obey their father as the head of the family and carry out his orders. The concept of the conformity to the family norms and values has great influence over its members in various aspects of their social and political life. The children learn about morality and manners from the family. The character and temperament of the children are formed by the influence of their parents, and they help to mould their opinion on socio-political matters.

The other major social control agencies are the following : Village mullahs, Village prodhan, Mosque, Ostracism, Village Panchayat and Union Council. The Mullahs some days back, and to a great extent, even now enjoy the most important right of social control in rural East Pakistan. He is consulted in all sorts of social matters and the punishment is given to the offenders by his orders. The social balance is also maintained by the public opinion of the village community. Today the importance of the Mullahs has decreased and their place has been occupied by the Union Council Chairman. Most of the matters are reported to the Union Council and it takes care of them.

Crime : Different types of crimes are committed in the rural areas in East Pakistan. Usually theft, dacoity, murder, Pick-pocket and sex crime are common in the villages. Besides, there are also some seasonal crimes at the time of harvestings such as the violence over the boundary of lands. These crimes are often dealt with by the nearby police station.

Education : Education is a vital need of the village. The rural people have inherited the educational system, left behind by the British rule in Indo-Pak subcontinent. The education was aimed at getting some literate people to help the British Government to run the administration. This type of education had no ideal of making us good citizens. The schools and colleges grew up to cater the need of the foreigners. But the system of education is undergoing different changes to have a proper system of education which will help to develop good citizenship in the country.

There are primary schools, madrasas and high schools for boys and girls in most of the villages in East Pakistan.

The conditions of the schools and their furniture are generally poor. The benches, tables and chairs are few and mostly broken. So the boys and the girls have to sit, sometimes, on mere planks or mats. The teachers are ill paid. They are always in want and try to secure a subsidiary occupation to maintain their family. In the rainy season certain low lying areas are flooded and it becomes almost impossible for the children to attend their school. Moreover, during the sowing and harvesting season most of the children of the peasants are engaged in the field to help their parents.

This causes the insignificant attendance and many drop-outs of the students in the primary level. The percentage of literacy is very low in our rural areas. About 95% of the rural people are illiterate. But there are many people in the village who can read the holy Quran, sometimes, without understanding the meaning.

The villages near the urban areas get the news-papers daily ; but the interior villages get them very irregularly.

Economy : Agriculture is the main occupation of the village. The villagers are mainly engaged in cultivation. The holdings of land are very small. Even the best methods of improvement of agriculture cannot make the small holdings economical. Only few families in a village have more than five acres of land. There are many landless families in the villages. Disguised unemployment is very common in rural areas. In addition to cultivation different types of cottage industries are found in the villages. Many people such as

'Karikars', potters, gold smiths and black-smiths are associated with cottage industries. They are important pillars of the village economy. These small industries make the villages self-sufficient in many respects even though they are to go to cities and towns and buy things according to their needs.

The prospect of agriculture of the villages entirely depends on the mercy of the monsoons. These villages are mainly agricultural in nature. If there is good yield of crops, the villagers become well off. For three or four months the villagers work hard ; but the produce yields a small return. They do not get sufficient money to maintain the family comfortably through out the year. They are unable to send their children to school for want of money. They hardly get instructions or guidance for improving their own faculties. With the increase of poverty and ignorance of the villagers, the economic condition of the village is deteriorating every day.

The monsoons do not favour all parts of the country equally. There are areas where the amount of rainfall is small. For these areas it is necessary to construct irrigation and drainage system to produce more crops. This will improve the economic condition of the cultivators.

As given above, the general economic condition of the people of the villages is not satisfactory. They can not make both ends meet with the crops which they grow in their fields. They are born in debt, live in debt and die in debt.

The cultivators are unnecessarily extravagant, spending thoughtlessly and lavishly. Lavish expenditure in marriage and other ceremonies to keep up social prestige in the eyes of fellow villagers, compels the cultivators to go to the money-lenders. But today most of the villagers have developed a tendency of minimizing the expenditure. Sometimes this minimization becomes impossible mainly because of the traditional social pressure.

East Pakistan is essentially an agricultural country. For the development of agriculture, attempts were made by the British Government. After independence Pakistan established the Pakistan Industrial Development Corporation and Pakistan Agricultural Development Finance Corporation, popularly Known as P. I. D. C. and P. A. D. F. C. The idea was to set up some big industries and factories in the country and also to help the peasants with money in

order to purchase agricultural implements and seedlings. Formerly
the Village Mahajans used to advance money to the peasants at a high
rate of interest. The peasants could not produce good crops. They
had to hand over the corn or paddy to the money lenders to pay off
the borrowed money. But soon after they had to approach the
money lenders for loans again. The Peasants, as a result, are very
poor.

The P.A.D.F.C. wants to approach the peasants with money to
help them in getting the necessary capital for purchasing tools and
seeds. And the people also welcome this help of the govt., but
when they try to take loan they have to undergo various formalities.
As most of the rural people are illiterate they can not understand
many complicated laws of the Corporation. The P.A.D.F.C. should
advance loans to the cultivators to make the scheme a success.

Religion : The religious life of the villagers is controlled by the
village organization with the help of the Mullahs. In the villages
discretion plays a secondary part and the written laws of the Quran
and the Hadith play a great part. In case of contradiction on
religious points the opinions of Maulavies and Maulanas are often
sought and their verdict is carried out with respect by the villagers.
The social control function of the village, to some extent, centres
around the mosque and the 'Idgah'.

The Muslim mosque is not like the Hindu temple. Friday prayer
is expected to be participated by all the male adult Muslims of the
village. Negligence in such attendanc is questioned by the Mullahs
and the villagers. If there is any violation of the Quranic law (at least
according to the Mullahs) the matter may be brought in the mosque
for trial. In Friday gathering in the mosque questions regarding
social welfare may also be raised. If a section of people is disatisfied
with a particular group of people it might plan to set up a separate
mosque. It is a common phenomenon in almost all the villages. Similar
is the case with the Idgah ; but sometimes the Idgah might unite the
people belonging to more than one mosque. The mutual jealousies
of the villagers as well as of the Mullahs always stand on the way
of larger gatherings in the Idgah. The villagers are expected to invite
the Mullahs to cure certain diseases and also for various mandane
and spiritual purposes. During the 'Ramzan' the Mullahs are

frequently invited to dinner. The dinner of the Mullahs implies a little cash payment.

Health : The health condition in the rural areas is not satisfactory. Cholera, smallpox and diarrhoea, typhoid, kalazar and influenza—all these diseases take a great toll of human life in the village. Malaria was wide spread in large rural areas ; but the villagers are no longer anxious about this disease because of the partially successful malaria eradication project of the Government of East Pakistan. The quinine pill has been found to be a very effective medicine for this disease. To prevent typhoid, cholera and other contagious diseases, the Government has taken initiative and its measures are partially successful.

There are dearth of medical facilities in the villages. There are some charitable and Govt., dispensaries in some of t he villages ; but they are not properly equipped. The doctors, associated with them cannot give attention to all the people in the area. Therefore, the quacks play an important role in the life of villagers to treat their diseases. But the general mass favour the modern medical treatment. The lack of proper medical treatment and facilities is the cause of high death rate in rural East Pakistan.

Recreation : The old people of the village community are very fond of gossips. Sometimes, they sit in a common place and pass their time in gossiping ; but the pass-time of the younger generation is very much influenced by the modern games of adjacent urban areas. The people can have recreation within the village by visiting a community organization existing in almost all the villages. The boys usually like to play football, Ha-do-do, Kapadi etc. There is little facility for the recreation of the female folk except the visiting of relative's house on some occasion. The villagers often organise some cultural shows where music, songs, recitations and comic are included. Sometimes, dance by small girls adds grace to such occasions. In addition to these, jatra (village opera), jari, kabi, boat race etc., are other sources of recreation.

The cultural shows make the villagers understand the higher values of life. They are able to display their finer taste in music or in dances or in dramatic performances.

The cultural shows and functions are not breaking up as the sources of recreation of the villagers, although the radios and transistors

15—

have occupied an important place as the sources of recreation. Due
to the cross contact of the village with the urban areas, some urban
influences can be seen among the villagers. The younger generation likes
the modern way of living. Many young boys and girls take interest
in movies. With modern influences there are changes, affecting the
cultural life of the rural people in East Pakistan.

IMPACT OF BASIC DEMOCRACIES ON OUR RURAL LIFE

Under the Basic Democracies, there is provision for the election of
Basic Democrats (local village member). Three or four villages make an
Union Council. Each village has two or three representatives in the
Union Council. The union councillors are elected by the village
people. The villages are divided into wards. Each ward must have a
councillor. However, the total number of councillors (7 to 15) elect a
chairman from among themselves.

The role of Basic Democrats is most vital in the rural life of Pakistan. By widening the base and opening the representative office to one
in every thousand persons, the system provides a close association of
the people with the management of their day-to-day affairs. It ensures
a proper and well-informed choice of leadership and affords
opportunities of practical training in the conduct of human affairs.

The four higher tiers under this system will enable the functionaries
of various administrative and executive departments and the representatives of the people to work in close co-operation. Jointly they
would ascertain the community's requirements in the socio-economic
sphere and with mutual consultation relate them to the resources available and plan for the solution of the problems.

Pakistan is essentially a nation of villages with a few cities and
towns. If she is to have real democracy, her village folk should have a
say in her political and economic policies. The system of Basic Democracies may give the people a genuine share in the management of Government affairs. Basic Democracies offer them an opportunity to
apply their talents in the management of their affairs. With the introduction of Union Councils, with fairly wide powers and a re-orientation
of attitudes, it can be reasonably expected that a sound, representative
unit at the base will be created upon which it may be possible to build
a workable superstructure of a popularly constituted government.

President Field Marshal Mohammed Ayub Khan promulgated the Basic Democracies system on october 27, 1959. It provides for the constitution of Basic Democracies institutions ranging from the Union Councils to the Provincial Development Advisory Council.

The Union Councils are the most important tier in the scheme of Basic Democracies. They will be responsible for agricultural, industrial and community development in the union. They will have a wide range of functions including promotion and development of co-operative movements, village industries, forests, livestocks and fisheries, adoptation of measures for increased food production, provisions and maintenance of wells, water pumps, tanks, ponds and other works for the supply of water, regulation of offensive and dangerous trades, sanitation and the adoptation of other measures for the cleanliness of the union, provision and maintenance of public roads and public streets, bridges and any other measures likely to promote the welfare, health, safety, comfort or the convenience of inhabitants of the unions.

Now let us discuss the impacts of the introduction of Basic Democracies on our rural people. The functions which are performed by the Union Councils are new in many ways. The present income of each of the Union Councils is about Rs. 10,000 whereas it was only about Rs. 3000 before the introduction of the Basic Democracies. The total income of all the Union Councils of the province is almost 4 crores. They will frame their budgets and have a local fund. They would levy taxes with the permission of the Commissioner.

The Union Councils are engaged in works of different kinds in the province. They have saved many lands from floods by digging canals and constructing dames. They have arranged to sink many tube-wells from where the village people get pure water and are saved from various types of diseases. The government health officers are giving injections and vaccinations to the village people to protect them from epidemics.

The food and agriculture offices are producing and distributing manures to the villagers. Even the farmers are producing manure from water hyacinth. There is a godown in every council from where good seeds are supplied to the villagers. There are some show farms in the province and many more are being established through Basic

Democracies. Here the villagers can learn how more crops are produced and what is the utility of adopting scientific technique in cultivation.

Most of the villagers are illiterate in our country. To educate them some night schools, adult education centres are being established with the initiative of the Basic Democrats. Many new paths have been constructed by the village people with the help of the works programme in Basic Democracies.

The villagers are influenced by the recent Family Planning Programme in which the Basic Democrats have played an important part. They are helping the government in popularizing the practice of Family Planning among the villagers by way of communicating the news of Family Planning to the people. They are telling the people about the benefit of a small family.

Another important effect of the system of Basic Democracies is the emergence of a new class which enjoys more priviledges than other groups in the rural areas. It has got a frustrating effect on the groups who are deprived of these priviledges.

For the publicity of Basic Democracies the redio is playing an important role. The Radio Pakistan is broadcasting a programme called "The Assembly of the Basic Democracies". Various types of topics are discussed here. The main purpose of such an assembly is to educate, to inform and to entertain the village people. The topics discussed are given bellow :

(a) **Aro-chash Baran :** Grow more food.

The purpose of this programme is to encourage our rural people to grow more food with the help of modern and scientific methods.

(b) **Kutir Shilpo :** Handicrafts of East Pakistan.

East Pakistan is making all-out efforts to revive its handicrafts. This programme will deal with various handicrafts of East Pakistan. The aim of these series is to encourage the rural people to devote themselves to such works as will help them in getting an extra income.

(c) **Joar Eseche :** Marching forward.

The aim of this programme is to discuss the development works and to bring home to the rural listeners various development projects, undertaken by the present government.

(d) **Shasya Sangrakkhan :** Plant protection.

The purpose of this programme is to educate our farmers to protect their plants and crops from the attack of insects and pests.

(e) **Shastha-i-Sukher Mul** : Health is wealth.

The purpose of this programme is to educate the villagers about the importance of good health and hygiene so that they can lead a healthy life in the society.

(f) **Sukhi Sangsar** : Planned family is the happy family.

The aim of this programme is to discuss the necessity of family planning and its importance in the spheres of our social, national and economic life. The specialists are brought before the microphone to put forward their views and bring home to the rural listeners the benefits of Family Planning and the danger of successive births.

Bibliography

Afsaruddin, Md. *Rural Life in East Pakistan.* Samakal Mudrayan, Dacca, 1964.

Bernheim, R. *Pakistan in transition.* Swiss Review of World Affairs, 12, July 1962.

Maron S. and others. *Pakistan : Society and Culture.* New Haven, Conn. Human Relations Area Files, 1957.

Ahmad, N. *Economic Geography of East Pakistan.* London, Oxford University Press, 1958.

Ahmad, K.S. *Some aspects of the rural-urban composition of population in East Pakistan.* Pakistan Geographical Review 13 (1), 1958.

Davis, K. *The Population of India and Pakistan.* Princeton University Press, 1951.

Habibullah, M. *Rural Economic Conditions in an East Pakistan district.* Pakistan Economic Journal 8(3) Sep. 1958.

Khan, M. *A note on consumption patterns in the rural areas of East Pakistan.* Pakistan Development Review 3 (3) Autumn 1963.

Karim, A.K.N. *Changing Society in India and Pakistan.* Oxford University Press, Dacca, 1956.

Dube, S.C. *Indian Village.* London, Routledge and Kegan Paul, 1955.

Dar, Iqbal. *Growing up in Pakistan.* International Co-operation Administration, 1957.

Edward, S.M. & Garrat, H.L.O. *Mughal Rule in India.* London, Oxford University Press, 1930.

Goshal, U.N. *The Agrarian System of Ancient India.* Calcutta, Calcutta University, 1930.

Hunter, W.W. *Annals of Bengal.* London 1868.

Kosambi, D.D. *Introduction to the Study of Indian History.* Bombay Popular Book Depot, 1956.

Badenpowell, B.H. *The Indian Village Community.* Longmans & Green. London, 1896.

Sarkar, B.K. *Villages and Towns as Social Patterns.* Chatterjee & Co. Ltd., Calcutta, 1941.

Neheru, S. S. *Caste and Credit in the Rural Area.* Longmans and Green Co. London, 1932.

Blunt, E.A.H. *Social Service in India.* London, H.M. Stationary office, 1946

Spate, O.H.K. *India and Pakistan.* London, Methuen and Co. Ltd., 1954.

CHAPTER 15
TRIBAL LIFE IN EAST PAKISTAN

GEOGRAPHY AND PEOPLE

The high lands of East Pakistan known as the Chittagong Hill Tracts extend over 5,138 square miles from the foot hill of Tripura State of India in the north to Akyab district of Burma in the south and run along the Lushai hill of India and the Arakan hills of Burma in the East and coastal plains of Chittagong district in the west. It is a region of sub-tropical jungle fed by heavy rains, where a dozen of tribal people are inhabiting side by side. The Hill Tracts comprise

three circles (territories) of the three hereditary chiefs roughly coinciding with three subdivisions. These are known as the Chakma circle, the

Bhomang and Mong circles. The Chakma circle is the largest and is inhabited mostly by the Chakma people ; but there are Moghs, Kukis, Murungs, Tanchangyas and Tripuras in it.

It is the most thinly populated district in East Pakistan. The density of population per square mile is only 76. The total population of Chittagong Hill Tracts in 1951 is 2,78,274. After ten years (in 1961 census report) its population is 3,85,079. The rate of increase is 33·9%. It is the highest percentage of increase in East Pakistan during the ten years. Out of the total population of 3,85,079 tribesmen, the Chakmas alone number nearly 1,25,000. The other important tribes are the Moghs, numbering 66,000, the tripuras 37,000 and the Murungs slightly over 16,000. The other primitive tribes are about 8,000, Tanchangyas, and Khumis, Kukis, Riyong, Khyang and Lushais are not more than 15,000 to 2,000 each. The least known are the most primitive people living in highly inaccessible hills and numbering not more than a few hundred each, called the Banjogis and Pankhos. Besides, there are a few thousand Muslims and Hindus, living side by side with the tribal people. All the tribes are ethnically different from the settled population in East Pakistan. They have closer links with the hill people of the region, extending from Tibet down to Thailand. They are white-yellow complexioned, sometimes, fair in colour and have black hair. They are medium in height and physique ; but unlike the other Mongoloid people, their cheek bones are not very prominent and eyes are not so narrow.

HOUSING

The Chakma houses are built entirely of bamboo on a high bamboo platform raised some 6 feet above the ground. The house is divided into compartments according to the number of persons living in the family. A rough wooden ladder, called "Sangu" gives access to the open plat-form which forms the open entrance to the living rooms. Wooden logs are used only as pillars to support the roofs. Each house has a set pattern of rooms, consisting of main hall, the adjoining open courtyard and a few attached rooms-all well-built and ventilated with sliding windows. The hall generally measures between 25 and 40 feet on either side and the attached living rooms are of 15 by 25 feet dimensions. The courtyard is called "Ijar". The courtyard attached to the hall ranges between 20 and 25 feet on either side and protected by a four to five feet high bamboo screen. The courtyard is used for drying paddy and other commodities in the sun and for relaxing in the cool evenings. The corner of the hall is reserved for cooking

ECONOMIC LIFE

The tribesmen are agriculturists. Their traditional method of cultivation is known as "Jhuming" the local name for shifting cultivation.

Apart from Jhuming hill tribes also practise plough cultivation. But this method is not indigenous to the Hill Tracts. It was introduced by the Bengalees who were invited by the tribal "Rajas" to settle on the lower part of the hills where irrigation was possible. From the quantitative point of view, the former is still far more important in the economy of the Hill Tribes.

Agriculture is on the whole the significant source of food for the hill people. Hunting is practically non-existent. Fishing, though practised does not provide much food. It is done with traps or by draining a portion of a stream.

The tribesmen practise other arts which meet the needs of life other than those immediately connected with food. They build their own houses, make their own looms, weave their own cloths, make their baskets, manufacture their household utensils, agricultural implements and so on. Weaving used to be very wide spread and almost every household still has a loom.

The women spin their own cotton threads and weave them into cloths which are used for making their wearing apparel, satchels, bed sheets and wraps.

The essential material in the Hill Tract's economy is bamboo. It grows in the jungle abundantly. With a 'dao' in hand the tribesman has an incredible skill in shaping the objects with a few strokes. Walking sticks, carrying sticks and waterpipes are made on the spot. Houses are entirely made of bamboo. In the subsistence economy of the tribes, the hill people produce to satisfy their own needs.

However, the development of a commercial economy in the area has introduced certain elements of exchange. Trading in cotton, timber

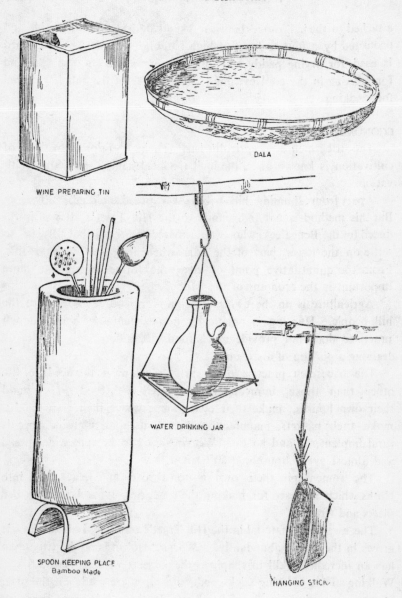

WINE PREPARING TIN

DALA

WATER DRINKING JAR

SPOON KEEPING PLACE
Bamboo Made

HANGING STICK

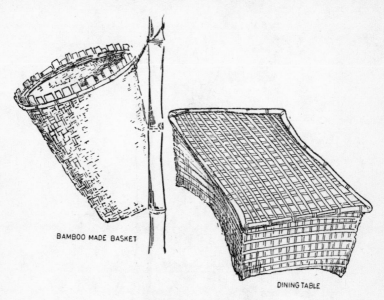

BAMBOO MADE BASKET

DINING TABLE

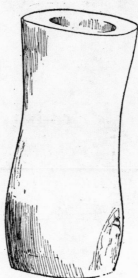

TOBACCO PREPARING BAMBOO JAR

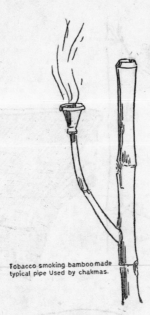

Tobacco smoking bamboo made
typical pipe Used by chakmas.

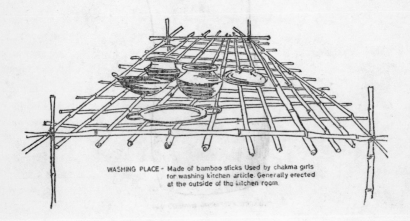

WASHING PLACE - Made of bamboo sticks Used by chakma girls
for washing kitchen article. Generally erected
at the outside of the kitchen room.

and other country products is gradually spreading among the people ; and this is especially the case with the Chakmas who show signs of becoming shrewd traders. With the spread and development of education, others are entering into a professional life and seeking appointment as executive officers, clerks, policemen, hospital assistants, vaccinators, school masters and other employments. Many people are working for the companies for developing new industrial projects along the Karnafully river or for the contractors who recruit them as factory labour. This brings monetary income and exchange into Hill Tribe economy.

DESCRIPTION OF THE CHAKMA TRIBE

The people of the tribe are scattered throughout the Hill Tracts and some of them reside in Chittagong district and in the hill Tippera (India). The chief has his head quarters at Rangamati. The tribe is known as 'Thek' by the Burmese and 'Tni-Thek' by the Kukis. The Chakmas are undoubtedly of Arakanese origin.

A Chakma is a medium stature and thick-set built with fair complexion and cheerful face. Physically, he is a finer specimen of manhood than a Mogh. He possesses none of the hereditary laziness of some other tribes. Although his independence will prevent him from working as a menial for others, yet he works exceedingly hard to further his own interests. He possesses a retentive memory, grasps details quickly and appreciates the advantages that can be secured by industry. As a tribe they are argumentative, and stubborn, but on the whole truthful. Though addicted to drink they do not smoke excessively. The hookah takes the place of the Mogh churoot. Pan is chewed by them.

In dress they resemble the residents of Chittagong district and wear white turban with coat and dhuti. The upper class chakmas wear socks and modern shoes. The higher class Chakma is decidedly a man of thrifty habit. The Customs of Hinduism can be observed amongst the upper class people who secluded their womenfolk. The Chakma women comb their hair back and tie them in a loose knot at the back of the head; the neck and shoulders are bare, and the cloth striped red and blue with a deep red border at the bottom is worn tightly wrapped round the body and reaches almost the ankles. She wears a turban of white home-spun cloth called a "Kabong".

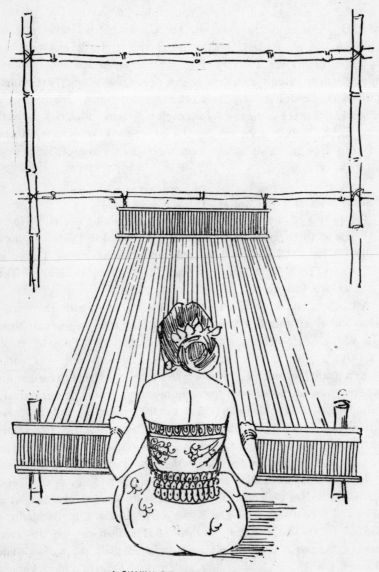

A CHAKMA GIRL WEAVING HER KHADI

Her ornaments consist of silver earrings, necklace, bracelets and anklets. There are three varieties of necklaces—one is of massive make worn close round the neck, the other is a band of biligree in silver reaching below the breasts, the third consists of rupees, sticking to black thread.

SOCIAL STRUCTURE

The Chakmas are divided into different clans. The tribe is generally patriarchal and the descent is traced along the father's line. The head of the family is the most important person in the clan. Many clans are the relics of their previous heroic episodes or their deeds. Each clan consists of some small units which happen to be related to each other. The Chakmas belong to Gentile Society. All the tribal races of Chittagong Hill Tracts are the members of Gentile Society. But only among the Chakmas this practice is most applicable. These clans belong to different tribes. So every body of the clans and tribe are related to each other like the members of the "Phratry". But this system of phratry is not applicable in all respects. Thus, we see the Chakma Society as the confederacy of tribes.

The Chakma Society is constituted of about one hundred and fifty clans, and their only duty is to help each other to confront the dangers. Sir Risley says, "Among the Chakmas, as perhaps among the Greeks and the Romans in the beginnig of their history, the sect is the unit of tribal organization for certain public purposes". So it is evident that brotherly attitudes among the Chakmas are very keen. Like a typical Muslim Society they also think each other as brothers.

The origin of the Chakma tribe is a bit different. The root of their origin lies mainly after the activities of the chief or after the name of the place they live in. For example "Pirra Vanga"—the chief of the clan had broken a 'pirra' in the course of some action, and from that source the name 'pirra vanga' originates.

In Chakma Societies the systems of both endogamy and exogamy are practised regardless of clans and tribes. It is quite relevant to say that although there is no rigid law of preventing marital relations among the clans, but in some cases marital relations are absolutely forbidden in the same tribe. This practice was very strict and was obeyed ; but at present this practice is a bit relaxed.

Now the Chakmas are at the very threshold of modern Society.
Like modern Societies the relation between the husband and wife is
very strong among the Chakmas. The kinship structure is also like that
of modern society. As for example 'Ba' (father or father-in-law); 'Ma'
(mother or mother-in-law); 'Zidhu' (youngest uncle); 'Zedhei' (aunt) ;
'Dada' (eldest brother); 'Bei' (eldest sister); 'Lakhya' (youngest sister);
'Bhuji' (sister-in-law); 'Mujhe' (Aunt); 'Mamu' (uncle); 'Mami' (aunt);
'Akhunda' (grand-father); 'Beiname' (grand-mother); 'Bonoi' (brother-
in-law) etc.

As the Chakma tribes are headed by male members their clans do
not change. But marriage changes the clans of the females or their
origin is traced through their husband's tribe or clan. When a widow
marries for the second time with his previous off-spring, the names of
the previous issues will be called after the name of her previous husband as long as the issues are under the control of their mother.

In Chakma Societies marriage generally is of three types, namely
marriage by elopment, marriage by choice and arranged marriage,
but in some cases the brides are taken to the place of the bridegrooms
and the marriage is performed. These conventions are changing.
The marriage of the royal families or of aristocratic families are termed
as big marriage.

It is not obligatory for a Chakma tribe to marry within the tribe ;
but this refers to men alone. A Chakma woman, marrying outside
her tribe is unknown. The sects or 'Goza' as they are called in the
Chakma language, may intermarry freely.

When a Chakma has reached the marriageable age, his parents and
guardians first of all arrange a homely meeting. This meeting is
known as "Tainmong". When a bride is traced out only then this
'Tainmong' is held. The father of the boy visits the bride's place
with a bottle of wine, betel leaves, betelnuts, and some sweetmeats.
After going there the parents and guardians make the proposal of
marriage; but the way they approach the bride's parents is very interesting. Instead of saying directly they say in a round about manner, "In
your house there is a very beautiful tree. Under the tree's shadow
I want to plant an offshoot". From this the father of the bride assumes
that there must be a proposal of marriage of his daughter. After
this both the parties start obeying some rules. These rules are nothing

but some conventions, commonly respected by them. For instance, if a fox crosses the road from the right side to the left side during the time of journey it is regarded as something good. If a pitcherful of water or a pitcherful of milk is found on the way it is regarded as good omen. But if a vulture, eagle or a crow is found by the left side, it is regarded as a bad omen. The marriage is decided on the result of these good or bad omens.

If the journey time is decided as good, the bridegroom's party visits the house of the bride for the second time with a bottle of wine, betel leaves, betelnuts and cakes. This time both the parties fix a date for a subsequent third visit.

Third visit is also made to the house of the bride. This time a minor girl also accompanies the bridegroom and the final settlement of dowry takes place. The father of the bridegroom gets the right to bless the bride and give her presentations. When the question of marriage is finally settled the father of the bride gets up and publicly says, "Then is it the right moment to prepare right liquor? And now the marriage is fixed."

The day before the marriage a variety show is arranged. Beating of drums is very important in this festival. The first sound or beat of a drum is termed by them as "Kholamanani." According to them the future weal and woe of the bride and bridegroom can be traced by the first beat of the drum.

It is relevant to quote one form of the rule. First of all two boats are made of banana leaves. Then with betel leaves and betelnuts two small packets are put in the boat, completely segregated from each other and are set afloat in a nearby brook. If the boats keep floating side by side it is to be regarded that the life of the husband and wife will be happy. On the other hand, if they do not float side by side it is regarded that there is a possibility of conflicts between them in future.

They arrange a worship-ceremony (chungulang) on the morning of the day the marriage date is settled. The bride must be present at the house of the groom right in this morning. In the bridal party there must always be a minor girl. This time they take 'Pindhan' (wearing material); 'Khadi' (breast-piece-cloth) ; 'Khorlong' (head-piece-cloth) and ornaments with them. The female side receives all these

16—

things for the marriage day. The bride's party arranges a very auspicious ceremonial feast for them.

To supply liquor of very high quality is one of the main features of this feast.

When the time is near to say good-bye to his daughter the father performs some forms of worship for the well being of his daughter. Moreover, in front of the door seven pieces of strings are left hanging. They are called 'sako'. After the mother of the bride tears those pieces of strings it is regarded that the bridal party has got their consent to fetch the bride. From this day all relationships of the bride with their parents is partially cut off. This scene is really very pathetic. The female side sings some songs which are also very pathetic.

The marriage ceremony is performed by a 'voodoo' (ozha). The next very night both the bride and the groom are led to sit in a single bed together. The unmarried girls present there, tie a knot with a brand new cloth around both of them. Behind this practice there lies a very strong superstition. According to the Chakmas the future life of the bride and the bridegroom remains as strong as the knot. After that the bride and bridegroom takes their meal in the same pot. They term this as 'Badagulaya Bhat'. The bride with her right hand and the bridegroom with the help of his left hand feed each other. When this ceremony is over the respectable elders bless the bride and the bridegroom with leaves and water which are kept previously in the 'Mangal Ghot' (a pot for the well-being of the bride and the bridegroom). Then they get the right to pass the night together in the flower bed.

Next morning they both are taken in a nearby river for bathing. During this time one voodoo (Ozha) accompanies them. Before the bath is taken, water and liquor is sprinkled on them. The practice is termed as 'Boorparan'.

They have to get back home long before any one of the house members gets up from bed. On this day a very big variety show and a very big feast are arranged by the bridegroom's family.

The new bridegroom is taken together with his bride to the house of his father-in-law after three, five or seven days of the marriage. This practice is known in the Chakma Society as 'Sooid Bhangan'. It is regarded that if the above ceremony is not done, the living together of the bride and the bridegroom is absolutely forbidden. At the time of 'Sooid Bhangan' new bridegroom receives very cordial behaviour and attendance from his father-in-law.

In case of love-marriage both the boy and the girl become very cautious and as soon as they find the opportunity they flee away. The elopment, generally, happens in the 'Mahamuni' festival. If the girl is kidnapped against her will, the person who kidnaps the girl is liable to pay a fine. This fine is imposed by the headman in presence of the parents of both the husband and the wife. But the eloping practice is found only when both the bride and the bridegroom consent to it. If the parents of either of them are unwilling to the said marriage they flee away for the second time. When they come back there remains no bar or obstruction before them from getting married. For the girls, this practice is not confined only to their circle of clans or tribes. But often they elope with the members of different tribes. In these marriages also 'Chungulang' cult is worshipped and almost all the villagers are invited in the ensuing feast.

The Royal marriages are almost the same as the others, but they have to build three brand new houses,—one house for the bride, one house for the bridegroom and the third house for the newly-wed couples. The third house is called as flower house. At the day of marriage the voodoo priest makes them listen to 'Sizalmogol Tara'.

Divorce system is also found in them. This is done by the head-man and ten other top ranking members of a village. In these cases the guilty party is liable to pay a fine in kind.

If the problem is too complicated it is taken to the king for his decision on the matter

Polygamy is permitted ; but is generally a monopoly of the rich and the wealthy as they alone can afford the luxury of supporting more than one wives.

Although some hill-girls might live a somewhat unrestricted life before marriage, the hill-women in general are very faithful after their marriage.

CUSTOMS

When a Chakma woman has been pregnant for five to seven months, the puja of 'jang sala' is performed. During pregnancy the woman

is allowed to eat anything she fancies and special care is taken to carry
out her wish.

BIRTHS AND DEATHS

When the child is born the husband bring a basketful of earth
and spreads it near the bed and lights a fire on it. This fire is not
allowed to go out for five days. After this, the earth is thrown away
and the mother and child are bathed in water to which some medici-
nal herbs have been added. The woman is impure for the whole month
after child birth and is not allowed to cook during this period. The
children are suckled to a considerable age by their mothers. As is
the practice among the other hill tribes, no woman will suckle another
woman's child, even in the event of the mother being seriously ill.
If a woman dies during pregnancy, her body is cut open and the faetus
removed and buried ; while the body of the woman is burnt. This
practice exists amongst the Moghs and Tiperus. The dead are burnt
on the river bank except in the case of a death from cholera or small
pox. The death rites are as follows : The dead body is washed and
dressed and laid out on a new bamboo bier ; the relatives and villagers
come and visit the body day and night and a drum with a peculiar
note (only used on such occasions) is beaten at intervals. There is no
fixed time for keeping the body. When it is taken to the burning
ghat, it is carried by four men and the afternoon is selected for this
purpose. At the funeral the priest goes through some prayers and
the bier will be lighted first by the priest, then by the nearest relatives.

When the dead body has been reduced to ashes the mourners
go down to the water and after washing themselves return home.

The following morning the burning place is revisited and the
remnants of the body are collected and placed in an earthen pot and
thrown into the river by the nearest blood relative.

Mourning will be observed for six days. During this time no
blood relation will touch fish or meat of any sort. On the seventh
morning the burning place is again visited and a complete meal with
wine is laid out for the departed spirit. The place is enclosed with
a fine bamboo fence, tall bamboos with cloth streamers are hoisted.
If there is a priest prayers are recited. The 'Sraddha' ceremoney
is observed for both sexes and in the case of the wealthy people it is

kept up for some years. The Chakmas are very particular in their observance of it.

DWELLING HOUSE

The hillmen live in villages, very few of which have more than five hundred inhabitants. They have very fine houses. Houses are built entirely of bamboo with a machan (platform) floor raised some six feet above the ground. The house is divided into compartments, and the requirements of the married members of the family are first attended to. In the event of several families living together the rooms are apportioned in due order of seniority. For instance, a family in which three members are married the house will be divided by mat walls into four compartments. The outer one is reserved for the un-married male members or for the use of visitors and called 'pinagidi' ; the next compartment will go to the eldest male representative of the family with his wife ; the third room is given to the second eldest and the fourth one to the youngest married member. In the front of the house is a verandah which is divided into two by a mat partition,— one for the use of the males and the other for the females.

In front of the verandah is a big open space or raised platform, used for various household purposes. Small compartments may be erected on this for the storage of grain, cotton, or household effects ; but as a rule the grain is stored away from the house for safety in case of fire.

A rough step-ladder gives access to this outer space and forms the entrance of the house. This space will generally be enclosed with a bamboo wall, three to four feet high to prevent the small childern from falling down. The back verandah of the house is also used for storage purposes.

RELIGION

Chittagong Hill Tracts is the only distirct in East Pakistan in which Buddhism still survives as the religion of a large proportion of the population. This is due partly to its proximity to the Buddhist country of Burma and partly to its isolation. This isolation has been broken in recent years. In earlier days Chittagong Hill Tracts afforded a shelter to Buddhist refugees from other parts of India. The

Buddhist leaders are striving to shake off the influence of Hinduism and to put a stop to Hindu superstitions and observances which have crept in.

The Buddhist priests are called 'Bhikhus' or more commonly 'Thakurs'. They shave their heads and wear garments, coloured yellow and stitched with ninety pieces of cloth. Their under clothing consists of a piece of cloth, also composed of several patches, which they wear loose. They are prohibited from taking any food or drink in afternoon except water, tea, betelnut and tobacco and from making up their beds in the full moon of 'Asharh' to the full moon of 'Aswin'. Every Barua has to be initiated and to live as a Sramana or novice for at least seven days ; and some of them also take vows to be a member of priestly order for some years after the period following their initiation. When any priest returns to his home after giving up his yellow robe, he can marry and is called a 'Lothak'. The priests do not live in their homes but in the 'Kyaungs' or monasteries which are maintained in almost every Barua village at the cost of the villagers. There, the priest not only performs the daily worship but also teaches the boys of the village and gives them religious instructions.

There are four order of priesthood in this district, viz. (1) Mahathero or Mhatechera (sans. Mahasthavira) (2) Kamethero or Kamechera (sans. Kamathavira), (3) Panygang or Upasainada, and (4) Maisang or samanera (sans. Sramana). The Samanera or novice is the lowest order of priesthood and when he attains the age of twenty and acquires sufficient knowledge of the Buddhist Scriptures, he is elevated to the higher order of Panygang. A Mahathero or a priest of the highest order cannot revert to the position of a house-holder.

The Baruas and Chakmas celebrate four great festivals during the year. 'Baisakhi Purnima' or the full moon in the month of 'Baisakh' is the most sacred day for the Buddhists, as the three most important events in the life of Buddha took place in it, viz., his birth, his attainment of Buddhahood, and his Pari-nirvana. 'Ashari Purnima' or the full moon in 'Ashar' lasts for three months. This period indicates the three months of rainy season. During this period Buddha used to give instructions to his disciples. The Buddhist monks accordingly follow his example and live in a vihara or monastery, giving religious instructions to the people. The third great festival is 'Aswini Purnima'

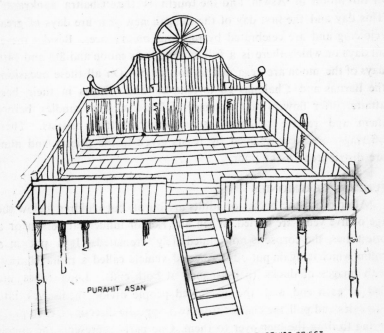

PURAHIT ASAN

PLACE OF WORSHIP SPECIALLY MEANT FOR BUDDHIST PRIEST

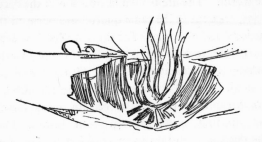

MUD HOLE TYPICAL FIRE PLACE OF CHAKMAS

or full moon of 'Aswin' and the fourth is the 'Chaitra Sankranti'. This day and the first day of the Bengali new year are days of great rejoicing and are celebrated by religious observances. Besides these, all days on which there is a full moon or new moon and 8th and 14th days of the moon are regarded as holy days. On all these occasions the Baruas and Chakmas go to temples and viharas in their best attaire, offer flowers to the image of Buddha, light candles before them, and receive religious instructions from their prisests. These offerings are accompanied by feasts given to the priests and alms are distributed to the poor.

FUNERAL CEREMONIES

After death the bodies of adults are burnt, but children below the age of five years are buried. When any rich or influential person or a priest dies, the corpse is not immediately cremated. It is put in a coffin which is again put on a wheeled vehicle called a ratha (chariot) with images of ducks (hansa-hansi) at both ends. Long ropes are tied at each end and the assembled people divide themselves into two sides and pull the chariot from two opposite directions, each party trying to drag the bier over to them. One party represents the angels of Heaven and the opposite one the Jamadut or guardians of Hell ; and it is arranged that the party of angels must just win. The corpse is then taken and placed on the funeral pyre. Here the assembled people hear Mangal Sutra recited, and themselves recite the Pancha Sila, dictated by the priest who also delivers a sermon about the vanity of the world. The fire is then lit by a son of the deceased.

All persons, resident in the same quarter are burnt in the same spot except the priests and rich men. For them a 'Zedi' is erected. This is a masonry structure, resembling a temple in shape, erected over the place of cremation. A vacant space is left within it, and on an auspicious day a small image of Buddha is placed in the niche. Gold, silver and cloth are put in front of it, after certain sutras have been repeated and the opening is closed up with bricks. The sons and widow of the deceased abstain from taking meat for seven days, and on the 7th day after cremation ; the 'Sraddha or Karma' ceremony of the deceased takes place. On that day the sons are shaved and a bamboo pole with a flag on it, is erected on the cremation ground ; certain Sutras are dictated by the priests, and food, brass utensils and clothes are offered in order to release the deceased from his 'Pretajoni' or spirit life.

'Pindas' or funeral cakes of cooked rice are also offered, and a feast is given to which the priests and neighbours are invited. This ceremony is repeated on the 15th day after cremation, and then every month for one year, and after that annually.

BELIEFS

The Chakmas sometimes believe in spirits and ghosts ; persons who die unnatural deaths are supposed to become ghosts, and for this reason the relations of the deceased offer pindas at Boddha Gaya. They resort to exorcism, especially when anyone is believed to have fallen ill owing to the influence of an evil spirit. The afflicted person is made to sit before the 'ojha' or exorcist holding a 'Jaba' flower in both hands and at this juncture the ojha loudly chants some spells, beating thrice by striking a gong or brass dish. Questions are then put to the afflicted person, enquiring the nature of the evil spirit and the means by which it may be expelled. The process continues for five or six days until the answers to his questions are considered satisfactory or the victim recovers. In cases of a less serious nature, charms are given to the afflicted persons to wear on their body and charms or medicines are sometimes buried around the compound of the haunted place or affixed in the house. In case of epidemic disease the Baruas and Chakmas sing the 'Buddha Sankirtan' and in case of cattle disease Satayapir is worshipped.

CHAKMA SONGS

Lullabies : The lullabies used by the hill mothers to soothe their infants are full of tenderness ; while the love songs convey the pent up emotions in pretty phrases. The similes may appear somewhat crude to our civilised ideas; but it must be remembered that with these people they represent things in daily use and are most essential to the general welfare of the community. To deal properly with this interesting subject would require a separate volume as each tribe has its own store of folk-lore.

(1) A kule kolá gach oi kulé chhara na kánis bábúdhon ghúmjá bhangiba golá.

Oh infant mine ! thy body is smooth and tender as the young plan-tain tree; sleep gently ; do not cry; crying will but hurt the tender throat.

(2)   Sonaro dhulnám ruparo dorina kánis bábudhon ghúmja dhulo not pori.

Your cradle is golden, with net work of silver ; let its beauty delight thee till dazzled thy eyes and in sweet slumber repose.

(3)   Kerénjoo dhulnám keréda chak na khánis lakhá burá ghúmjei thak. Aloo kochoo mileiyé Máthaidi Dogore the Billélye

Your cradle is made of a flowery design and is finely woven; come to make it beautiful and strong. So sleep quietly my darling for if you do not, pussy who is purring near your head will scratch your soft and tender body which is more tender than boiled aloos and Kachoos (yams)

(4)   Aloo páta tháloo ve kúshara pata myong no kánis lakhi bura oil dake dyong.

Your body is softer than the tender leaves of the yams; if pussy whose claws are sharper than the leaves of the sugar cane should scratch you, you will be hurt, my little darling ; so sleep quietly.

(5)   Dáru tuli jariphúl na kánis bábudhon rámgum sarattán ja bábe áni dibe nárekul.

As the physician gathers the "Jariful" for his patients your father will purchase you a coconut from Rangoon ; so do not cry my baby darling, but sleep quietly.

CHAKMA LOVE SONGS

(1)   Másé khálo shilo khei no déle toré moré chikan bei na parong thei.

As the little fishes of the hill stream cannot live without weeds that grow on the stones, I also love you so, my darling, that I cannot live without seeing you.

(2)   Úres pakkhi to chhei yá sarido noparim to méiyá

The birds may cease to fly on high, but you will always possess my heart's deep love.

(3)   Chhorá Chhari beel haba jor hado pán khillik heel habo.

As the fishes are delighted when the streams and pools are full of water, so will my heart dance in joy if I can receive a pan from your dear hands.

(4) Banot dogorér sharing sho jové no délé morimba.

If I do not see you I shall die, my darling as the deer of the forest searches for its mate till it dies.

(5) Dingi kúlémbi to ghatot mor ashal múl paran to hátat.

The bark of my soul is anchored at your ghat; my heart is wholely yours : do with it as you please.

CHAKMA PROVERBS
(1) It is given to the wisest man to make mistakes.
(2) Crow loudly in your own village, but cluck as the hen in the village of another.
(3) Search the bottom of a new boat and beat a new mate.
(4) Tender grass suits aged cows ; aged men seek young wives.
(5) The fat sleep, the lean eat.
(6) A fool will fear death, the wise the here after.

INDEX

17—